THE

Canadian Regime

THE CANADIAN REGIME

Fifth Edition

AN INTRODUCTION TO PARLIAMENTARY GOVERNMENT IN CANADA

Patrick Malcolmson and Richard Myers

UNIVERSITY OF TORONTO PRESS

Library and Archives Canada Cataloguing in Publication

Malcolmson, Patrick N., 1953–
The Canadian regime : an introduction to parliamentary government in Canada / Patrick Malcolmson and Richard Myers.—5th ed.

Includes index.

ISBN 978-1-4426-0590-9

1. Canada—Politics and government—Textbooks.   I. Myers, Richard   II. Title

JL75.M34 2012   320.471   C2012-903069-4

We welcome comments and suggestions regarding any aspect of our publications—please feel free to contact us at news@utphighereducation.com or visit our Internet site at www.utphighereducation.com.

North America
5201 Dufferin Street
North York, Ontario, Canada, M3H 5T8

2250 Military Road
Tonawanda, New York, USA, 14150

ORDERS PHONE: 1–800–565–9523
ORDERS FAX: 1–800–221–9985
ORDERS E-MAIL: utpbooks@utpress.utoronto.ca

UK, Ireland, and continental Europe
NBN International
Estover Road, Plymouth, PL6 7PY, UK
ORDERS PHONE: 44 (0) 1752 202301
ORDERS FAX: 44 (0) 1752 202333
ORDERS E-MAIL: enquiries@nbninternational.com

The University of Toronto Press acknowledges the financial support for its publishing activities of the Government of Canada through the Canada Book Fund.

Printed in Canada

CONTENTS

PREFACE...ix

MAP
PARLIAMENTARY REPRESENTATION
BY PROVINCE..xiv

PART ONE
INTRODUCTION... 1

CHAPTER ONE
CANADA'S REGIME PRINCIPLES.. 3
1.1   Political Regimes 3
1.2   Equality.. 5
1.3   Liberty 8
1.4   The Canadian Regime 11

CHAPTER TWO
THE CONSTITUTION.. 13
2.1   Constitutions and Their Functions................................... 13
2.2   Constitutional Forms... 16
2.3   The Canadian Constitution 22
2.4   Amending Canada's Constitution 27
2.5   Judicial Review of the Constitution 30
2.6   Constitutional Politics Since 1982.................................... 31

PART TWO
BASIC PRINCIPLES OF THE CANADIAN CONSTITUTION ... 35

CHAPTER THREE
RESPONSIBLE GOVERNMENT 37
3.1   The Emergence of Responsible Government 38
3.2   The Conventions of Responsible Government.............. 40
3.3   Responsible Government as "Cabinet Government" 42
3.4   Forming a Government.. 43
3.5   Majority and Minority Government.................................. 47
3.6   Institutional Implications of Responsible Government.............. 49
3.7   Responsible Government and Separation of Powers Compared.............. 54

CHAPTER FOUR
FEDERALISM 58
4.1   What is Federalism? 59
4.2   Why a Federal Union? 60
4.3   The Original Design of the Federal Union 62
4.4   The Historical Development of Federalism in Canada 63
4.5   Financing Government and Federal-Provincial Relations.......... 65
4.6   The Challenge of Canadian Federalism 69
4.7   Current Controversies: The Pressure to Decentralize............... 73

CHAPTER FIVE
THE CANADIAN CHARTER OF RIGHTS AND FREEDOMS ... 77
5.1   What is a Charter of Rights? 77
5.2   How the Charter Works: *Hunter v. Southam* 78
5.3   Remedies 80
5.4   The Adoption of the Charter 81
5.5   Opposition to the Charter 84
5.6   The Notwithstanding Clause 87
5.7   Section 1 89
5.8   The Political Impact of the Charter....................................... 91

PART THREE
INSTITUTIONS 95

CHAPTER SIX
THE CROWN AND ITS SERVANTS 97
6.1   The Crown 98
6.2   The Governor General 99
6.3   The Functions of the Governor General................................. 100
6.4   The Cabinet... 103
6.5   The Cabinet Committee System 106
6.6   The Prime Minister 107
6.7   Prime Ministerial Government? 110
6.8   The Civil Service... 112

CHAPTER SEVEN
PARLIAMENT 116
7.1 The Role of Parliament 117
7.2 The Parliamentary Calendar 119
7.3 The House of Commons: Membership and Officers 120
7.4 The Business of the House of Commons 123
7.5 The Rules of Procedure of the House of Commons 125
7.6 The Backbencher 126
7.7 House of Commons Reform 128
7.8 The Senate 129
7.9 Senate Reform 131

CHAPTER EIGHT
THE JUDICIARY 135
8.1 The Role of the Judiciary 135
8.2 The Fundamental Principles of the Canadian Judiciary 140
8.3 Canada's Courts 145
8.4 The Supreme Court of Canada 150
8.5 The Politics of Judicial Appointments 151
8.6 The "Court Party" Thesis 154

PART FOUR
PARTICIPATION 157

CHAPTER NINE
ELECTIONS 159
9.1 Elections and Representation 159
9.2 Canada's Electoral System 162
9.3 The Effects of SMP 165
9.4 Proportional Representation 168
9.5 Single Transferable Vote 171
9.6 Voting in Canada 172

CHAPTER TEN
POLITICAL PARTIES 176
10.1 Political Parties in the Canadian Regime 176
10.2 The Five Functions of Political Parties 178
10.3 Parties and Ideology 179
10.4 Canada's Major Parties 181
10.5 The Canadian Party System 185
10.6 The Organization of Political Parties 188
10.7 Financing Political Parties 191
10.8 Party Government and Party Politics 192

CHAPTER ELEVEN
INTEREST GROUPS, PUBLIC OPINION, AND DEMOCRATIC CITIZENSHIP 194
11.1 Forms of Political Participation 194
11.2 Interest Groups 195
11.3 Women in Politics 198
11.4 Public Opinion 201
11.5 The Media 203
11.6 The Question of Public Opinion Polls 205
11.7 Civic Education and Democratic Citizenship 207

APPENDIX
THE CONSTITUTION ACTS 1867 AND 1982 211
Constitution Act, 1867 211
Constitution Act, 1982 245

INDEX 261

Preface

Of all regimes, the democratic regime is in greatest need of a politically educated populace. The democratic principle requires the rule of the people. Such rule demands that the people have an education in politics that makes "government by the people" both possible and prudent. If the great body of voting citizens lacks such an education, two consequences follow. First, people become passive and unwitting followers of the opinion leaders of the day. Demagoguery becomes indistinguishable from principled political rhetoric, and the tyranny of the majority—the Achilles' heel of democracy—grows more probable. Second, people come to have entirely unrealistic expectations of politics. Lacking any clear understanding of what is possible, they let their hopes, desires, and dreams govern their political demands.

There is ample evidence to suggest that both of these characteristics are easily observable in Canadian politics today. We believe that this is due, in large part, to the poor condition of civic education in contemporary Canada. This book has been written in the hope of strengthening that Canadian civic education.

Our book is an attempt to explain and describe the most important political institutions of Canada's national government. Its premise is that Canadians—citizens, university students, and even many of our politicians—need a straightforward, explanatory introduction to these institutions. Our aim is to educate Canadians to a more sober and realistic set of expectations about politics by explaining the institutional limitations that structure all political action. The connection between institutions and issues is very clear. How can one intelligently discuss problems concerning the tax structure without some understanding of federalism? Or same-sex marriage without some understanding of the Charter of Rights and Freedoms and the Supreme Court? Or the role of a Member of Parliament (MP) without understanding the nature of parliamentary or responsible government? Yet all too often one finds that people want to discuss current political problems without giving any consideration to how these issues are tied to the structures and institutions of government. Thus, the local MP is criticized for always voting the party line, with little consideration as to how the Canadian form of parliamentary democracy makes it exceedingly difficult for MPs to vote against their party on any crucial political issue. One might liken such discussions to criticizing a chess move without understanding the rules of chess.

Our basic objective is to present the reader with a short and clear account of Canadian government. We have tried to focus on the logic of how our institutions work and how they fit together. For that reason, this book, unlike similar texts, concentrates more on explaining basic principles and less on describing the arcane details of our institutions. We have tried to ensure that our account is written in straightforward language and that all technical terms are clearly explained. We have also tried to write the book so that it presupposes little prior knowledge of the subject matter. It is gratifying to hear from readers of previous editions that its clarity has been appreciated.

While our primary objective has been to provide the reader with a clear account of Canadian government, we have also been guided by a second objective. There is a thread that runs through the entire book, an underlying theme that endows it with unity and purpose. We have used the term "regime" to suggest that a country's political institutions form an organic whole, a kind of complex ecosystem with an inner logic and coherence that holds it together. The Canadian regime is a political ecosystem whose inner logic derives from its unique combination of responsible government and federalism, a combination that explains why our institutions are what they are and why we do things the way we do. By extension, it also explains why we do so many things differently from our neighbours to the south: the American regime is built on a different combination of core principles, namely, separation of powers and federalism. Throughout the book, we try to explain Canadian institutions and practices in terms of the underlying regime principles that govern them. Frequently, one of the best ways to make our point is to contrast Canadian practices with those of the United States, showing how our approach is the logical consequence of responsible government while theirs is the logical consequence of the separation of powers. This direct comparison of regime principles makes it easier for readers on both sides of the border to understand the regime logic of both countries. That, in turn, makes our book particularly useful for political science instructors in the United States who want their students to learn about the parliamentary alternative to separation of powers and find it more appropriate to use their northern neighbours as the test case rather than European countries such as Britain, Italy, or Germany.

Our primary concern, however, is to provide Canadian students with a greater appreciation of, and respect for, their own country's regime. For whatever reasons, it has become fashionable in Canada to advocate the adoption of American political practices in place of our own. In 1982, our Constitution was expanded to include an American-style charter of rights. Now the call is for an American-style Senate, an American-style procedure for screening Supreme Court nominees, American-style primaries for leadership selection, and American-style representation (where MPs vote according to the wishes of their constituents instead of following the "party line"). After the much-hyped debate between Senator Biden and Governor Palin in the 2008 American presidential race, some commentators went so far as to suggest that Canada also needs an American-style vice-presidential debate! Such innovations strike many Canadians as being more "democratic" or more "progressive" than what we have here now, but it is doubtful whether many appreciate the complexities involved in grafting features from one regime onto a very different one.

Years ago, Canadians adopted the American practice of choosing their party leaders at leadership conventions. It was thought that this innovation would further democratize our regime by taking leadership selection out of the hands of a small minority (the caucus) and sharing it with a wider number of Canadians. In practice, however, the introduction of leadership conventions has probably made our institutions *less* democratic. When the leader was chosen by the caucus, the caucus maintained a certain influence over the leader. Because today's party leaders are chosen by several thousand party delegates, they have a "mandate" that allows them to dominate their caucus to an unprecedented degree. It is in this innovation as much as in anything else that we find the roots of "prime ministerial government." Thus an American-inspired innovation which was designed to democratize our party leadership has in the long run made it even more elitist. The point here is not to say that leadership conventions (or primaries or reviewing nominations to the Supreme Court) are bad in some general way. Nor do we argue that it is impossible to adopt practices from the United States. Our point is that features that work well as part of one system of government are likely to cause unanticipated complications when indiscriminately plugged into a very different one. To return to our analogy of the ecosystem, it is certainly possible to introduce American bullfrogs into our lakes and ponds, as was done recently in British Columbia, but biologists in that province are now reporting a host of ecological complications as this new species either displaces or disrupts the lives of the native species.

Canadian political scientists have not always been helpful in terms of defending the integrity of our regime; indeed, they sometimes contribute to the problem. It is surprising to us how many Canadian textbooks discuss our institutions in terms of the legislative and executive "branches" of government. Such a framework makes perfect sense for a book on the government of the United States given that the American Constitution is built around the theory of "separation of powers" into distinct "branches." But the Canadian Constitution is not built on such principles. Our Constitution provides for a "fusion of powers" rather than a "separation of powers." The work done by cabinet ministers is of both a legislative and executive nature. It is therefore misleading and confusing to frame one's discussion of Canadian government in terms of chapters on the legislative and executive "branches." We have no such thing, and pretending we do leads to significant deficiencies in the way Canadian government is described. For instance, because they are composed in light of assumptions about a "separation of powers," many texts are grossly inadequate in their accounts of the principles of responsible government, the principles that create our "fusion of powers." Canadians' general ignorance of those principles became starkly evident during the political crisis of late 2008 when a number of grossly incorrect claims were in circulation as to who should or should not form the government. In this book, by contrast, we attempt to describe the institutions of Canadian government on their own terms. Instead of fitting Canadian institutions into some foreign framework, we try to present them in terms of responsible government, the framework that is appropriate to them.

The underlying objective of our book, then, is to provide Canadians with an account of their regime that permits them to grasp and appreciate its inner logic so as to minimize the appeal of seductive but facile calls for further Americanization. By approaching Canadian institutions on their own terms, we hope to articulate the inner logic and coherence of the regime as a whole. This should make the reader more aware of the problems inherent in borrowing practices from other regimes. More importantly, it should give the reader a deeper appreciation of, and respect for, our own.

We would like to thank Dylan Estey for his work as research assistant, professors Gerald Baier and Tom Bateman for their suggestions for improving the book, Penny Granter, the department assistant at St. Thomas University, and Ashley Rayner, Beate Schwirtlich, Tracey Arndt, and Natalie Fingerhut for their assistance in its production.

Patrick Malcolmson
Professor, Department of Political Science
St. Thomas University
Fredericton, New Brunswick

Richard Myers
President, Algoma University
Sault Ste. Marie, Ontario

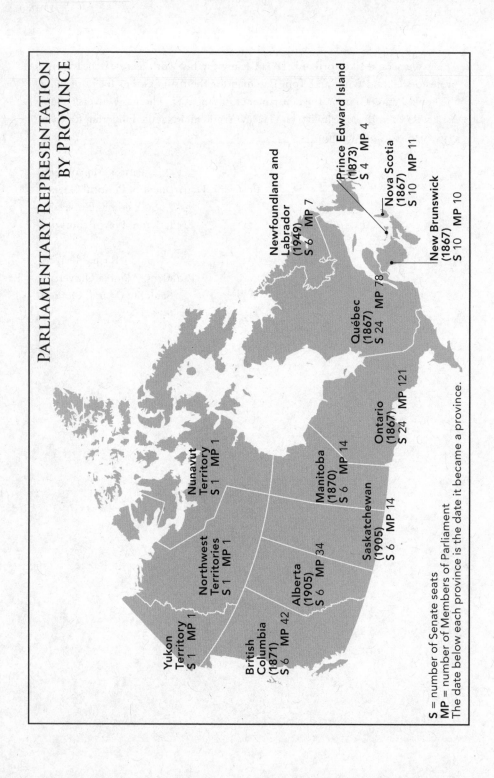

PARLIAMENTARY REPRESENTATION BY PROVINCE

Yukon
Territory
S 1   MP 1

British
Columbia
(1871)
S 6   MP 42

Northwest
Territories
S 1   MP 1

Alberta
(1905)
S 6   MP 34

Nunavut
Territory
S 1   MP 1

Saskatchewan
(1905)
S 6   MP 14

Manitoba
(1870)
S 6   MP 14

Newfoundland and
Labrador
(1949)
S 6   MP 7

Ontario
(1867)
S 24   MP 121

Québec
(1867)
S 24   MP 78

Prince Edward Island
(1873)
S 4   MP 4

Nova Scotia
(1867)
S 10   MP 11

New Brunswick
(1867)
S 10   MP 10

S = number of Senate seats
MP = number of Members of Parliament
The date below each province is the date it became a province.

PART ONE

INTRODUCTION

CHAPTER ONE

CANADA'S REGIME PRINCIPLES

1.1 Political Regimes
1.2 Equality
1.3 Liberty
1.4 The Canadian Regime

1.1 Political Regimes

To the casual observer, it may seem that Canada's political institutions are an arbitrary, perhaps even whimsical, hodgepodge of archaic ideas and quaintly named offices. To the political scientist, however, the political institutions of this, or any other country, have an inner logic that ties them all together into a coherent whole. The term traditionally used by political scientists to describe that whole is **regime**.

The English word regime is derived from the Latin word *regere,* which means to rule. From this Latin root come related words like "regent" (the person who rules on behalf of a monarch who is not yet of age) and "regulate." In common speech, the word regime is sometimes used to refer to a particular group of rulers (we might talk, for example, of "the Castro regime" in Cuba). In political science, however, the term regime has a more precise meaning. It refers to the form of government *and* the underlying political principles that provide the legitimate basis for that form of government. It thus provides the answer to the question:

who rules and why? The question of what sort of political institutions a state has will logically follow from the question of what sort of regime it has. A democracy, for example, will necessarily have political institutions based upon democratic elections. And questions of the efficacy of particular institutions will be settled by assessing how well they fit with the principles of the regime. As we shall see, the question of whether an institution like our current Senate fits with the liberal democratic principles of our regime is one Canadians continue to debate.

The classic discussion of regime types is to be found in Aristotle's *Politics*. His account is not comprehensive enough to provide a complete analysis of contemporary regimes, but it provides an excellent starting point for understanding the differences between them. According to Aristotle, the first question one must ask about any particular political order is how those who rule understand the purpose of political rule. This is the question that each of us would likely ask first if we were being ruled: are the rulers just or unjust? Do they rule in their own interest, or do they look to the common good of the political community? The second question that Aristotle asks is who rules: one person, the few, or the many?

Applying these two considerations, Aristotle generated a typology that included six regimes, three of them just and three of them unjust:

Figure 1.1: To What Purpose Do The Rulers Rule?

Who Rules?	Common Good	Own Interest
One	Kingship	Tyranny
Few	Aristocracy	Oligarchy
Many	Polity	Democracy

When we look back on history, we commonly and quite correctly distinguish between good and bad monarchs. Some kings and queens ruled with the interests of their country and subjects uppermost in mind. Others were concerned primarily with their own benefit. Aristotle calls a monarchy of the first type **kingship** and one of the second type **tyranny**.

The distinction between the common good and self-interest forms the basis of the other regime types. Aristotle calls an elite few ruling for the sake of the common good an **aristocracy**. However, political history does not provide many examples of small elites ruling for the common good. In most cases where political power is in the hands of the few, they use it for their private economic advantage. Aristotle calls this unjust regime **oligarchy**. Today we find oligarchies in many developing countries where rich elites use political power to maintain and increase their wealth.

Aristotle's analysis of rule by the many will come as something of a surprise to the reader. He says that a regime in which the many rule for the sake of the common good could be called **polity**, but he argues that such a regime is non-existent. The reason for this is that in his time political communities were divided into two classes: the many poor—the *demos*—and the few rich. Aristotle had never seen a community in which rule by the demos was anything but an attempt by the poor majority to use its superior force to despoil the rich minority. In other words, ancient Greek democracies had a tendency to degenerate into mob rule. This explains why Aristotle puts **democracy**—rule by the demos—on his list of bad or selfish regimes.

Aristotle's unflattering portrait of majority rule may offend our democratic sensibilities, but his point merits serious consideration. It is undeniable that majority rule can, and too often does, involve unjust treatment of those in the minority. For instance, a majority of voters could elect a government that would forbid members of a non-white minority to own property. Such legislation would be democratic in that it expresses the will of the majority, but it would also be unjust. The fact that something is democratic does not necessarily mean that it is right. In contemporary terms, we would distinguish between a decent democratic regime and **tyranny of the majority**. For us, democracy has come to mean rule by the majority that respects the rights of all individuals, including those who may be in the minority. We use constitutions to provide protection against unrestrained majoritarianism.

It is important to appreciate the danger posed by tyranny of the majority if one is to understand the foundations of the Canadian regime. Canada's regime, as we all know, is a democratic regime. But it has been carefully crafted so as to minimize the dangers of tyranny of the majority. This will become apparent as we examine our most fundamental principles. We call these "regime principles," and there are two of them: **equality** and **liberty**.

1.2 Equality

The fundamental principle of democracy is the principle of equality. In its pure form, democracy grants political power to all citizens equally (excluding children) because democrats believe that no one has any special title to rule. In a democratic regime, there is no special privilege granted to those who come from particular families or to people who own particular lands or businesses. It should be noted that the democratic principle of equality is a political principle, not a social or economic one. Strictly speaking, democracy means that people share equally in political rule; it does not mean that they share equally (or even equitably) in wealth or social status. Still, there are some respects in which political equality is interconnected with questions of social and economic equality. Genuine political equality may be undermined by massive social or economic inequalities. For instance, if those with great wealth are able to use their money to influence the political process in a significant way, that gives them unequal political power. This is why democracies usually enact legislation to regulate donations to political campaigns.

The basic democratic principle of political equality can take different forms. In the democracies observed by Aristotle, the principle was given its fullest expression. The democrats of ancient Greece understood equality to mean that all citizens were equally capable of exercising political power. These were **direct democracies**—regimes in which all of the citizens were directly involved in political decision-making. Moreover, to the extent that special officers were needed, they were to be chosen by lottery on the assumption that all citizens are equally capable of exercising political power. The Fathers of Confederation were democrats, but they did not support such a fully egalitarian form of democracy. Their preference was for **parliamentary democracy**, a regime they thought superior to direct democracy precisely because it was a more limited form of democracy.

Parliamentary democracy must be understood in the first instance as a variety of **representative democracy**. The direct form of democracy practised by the ancient Greeks has been replaced by an indirect form. Instead of managing political matters themselves, the equal citizens of modern democracies delegate the responsibility for public matters to a small group of elected representatives. There are two chief reasons for the emergence of representative democracy. The most obvious is that modern democracies are simply too large to be governed by the people directly: while the direct democracies of ancient Greece may have had only a few thousand citizens, the democracies of the modern world typically have millions. The second justification for representative democracy, though somewhat less obvious, is no less important. We are used to thinking of elections as a democratic exercise, and in one sense they obviously are: all voters get an equal say in the choice of the winner. But elections are also an aristocratic exercise: to attain office, the candidate has to convince the voters that he or she is the *best* person for the job. The founders of modern democracies believed that the introduction of representation would minimize the tendency to mob rule observed in the direct democracies of ancient Greece. The fact that the representatives would be accountable to the people through elections would keep the regime democratic. But at the same time, the exercise of power would be given to a small elite of the best people, an elite that would be less likely than the people as a whole to behave like a mob.

Parliamentary democracy is a regime in which political decisions are made by a representative body called parliament. It is, therefore, like all representative democracies, an indirect and, hence, limited form of democracy. Indeed, it is important to understand that the Fathers of Confederation valued the institutions of parliamentary democracy precisely because it was a more limited form of representative democracy than the alternative.

As we shall see in subsequent chapters, when the Fathers of Confederation created our regime, they borrowed heavily from the United States in some respects. When it came to representative government, however, they emphatically rejected the American congressional/presidential model in favour of the British model of parliamentary government. Their concern was that American-style democracy, though indirect, was nonetheless still too directly linked to the people and thus subject to the dangers of mob rule. One of the problems they noted was that the chief officers of the American regime—the president, the governors, and some of the judges—were chosen directly by the people. The Fathers of Confederation preferred the model of parliamentary government where (as we shall see in Chapter 3) the chief officers of the government are chosen only indirectly: the voters do not directly elect either the prime minister or the ministers of the cabinet; through a complex process called "responsible government," those officers are selected by our elected representatives. Parliamentary democracy is thus in some sense the most indirect of indirect democracies.[1]

The other feature of parliamentary democracy that was important to the Fathers of Confederation was the fact that it gave the Crown a role (albeit a weak one) as a last-chance safety valve. The Constitution of the United States established a **republican** regime, that is, a regime in which full and final authority is placed in the hands of the people's elected representatives and officers. The Fathers of Confederation believed that it would be important to have the monarchy present as a stabilizing influence, one that would prevent democratic politicians from rash action. Today, of course, it would be unthinkable for the Crown to interfere in the normal political process. Still, the anti-republican attitudes of the Fathers of Confederation are worth noting, for it was precisely their desire to avoid the "evils of republicanism" that led them to reject annexation to the United States and to work so hard to create an independent Canada.

While there has been some evolution in our political ideas since the time of the Fathers of Confederation, it is still important to appreciate that the Canadian

---

1   Contemporary thinking on this point has changed somewhat. Canadians now believe that our indirect democracy should provide clear and direct lines of accountability to the electorate. See Chapter 9, section 9.1.

regime is a relatively limited form of democracy. We do not believe that people are so equal that all of us should share equally in the making of political decisions. Nor do we believe that all citizens ought to share equally in the election of all political officers. What makes our regime a fundamentally democratic one is the notion that *the regime belongs to us all equally:* Canadian political equality is an equality of citizenship. This implies two things. The first is that we all have an equal right to run for public office. Second (and more important), whoever is elected or appointed to political office must in some way be accountable (that is, answerable) to the people as a whole for their actions and decisions.

1.3 Liberty

While Canadians view democracy as a key political principle, we do not see it as the only fundamental principle of our regime. Indeed, Canadians believe that democracy can go wrong if it is not tempered by another fundamental principle—the principle of liberty. This explains why our regime is commonly referred to as a **liberal democracy**: it combines the political principles of liberty and democracy.

Liberty is the idea that there is a sphere of human thought and action that is private and that, within that **private sphere**, all individuals have the right to make choices for themselves. According to the political theory of **liberalism**, then, we are free to do whatever we wish provided there is no law prohibiting us from doing so. We have rights, which means that we are free to decide for ourselves whether we will or will not do something. This freedom to decide for ourselves about such matters as which ideas we shall believe and what religion we shall practise is an essential element of the liberal understanding of politics. And from these initial freedoms flow a number of others, notably freedom of expression and freedom of the press.

But what provides the philosophical foundation for the principle of liberty? In contemporary liberal democracies, there are two schools of thought that predominate: **natural rights** and **utilitarianism**. The natural rights school argues that every individual possesses certain rights—for example, the rights to life, liberty, property, or privacy—simply because they are human beings. These rights, now often called human rights, are rights that all human beings possess everywhere and always, whether they are recognized or not. They are "inalienable" rights in that they cannot be given up or taken away. According to the natural rights school, these inalienable or natural rights establish both the purpose and the limits of political power. The purpose of government is to secure these universal and permanent rights, and no government is ever allowed to act in a manner that violates them.

The utilitarian justification for liberty is fundamentally different. For utilitarians, the importance of liberty derives from its usefulness ("utility") as a means of promoting human happiness. Utilitarians do not believe that there are universal and permanently valid "natural" rights. They believe, rather, that rights are created within each regime in response to circumstances. For example, if it is conducive to the general well-being of the citizens to establish a right to separate schools for Roman Catholics, then such a right could be established by law. But utilitarians would deny that such a right exists by nature; they deny, in other words, that the establishment of separate schools is a universal moral imperative binding all governments in all times and places.

It is important to appreciate, however, that utilitarians believe the articulation of rights to be guided by certain fundamental rules. The most important of these rules would be the famous **harm principle** elaborated by John Stuart Mill. According to the harm principle, governments cannot interfere with the actions of individuals so long as those individuals are not harming others. Mill argued that happiness was most likely to be achieved if all individuals were allowed to develop their own individuality as fully as possible. The full development of our individuality requires that we each be left as free as possible to explore our own ideas and to act on the basis of those ideas. Provided we do not harm others, even harming ourselves is, according to Mill, properly within the sphere of individual liberty.

The harm principle means two things for politics. The first point is that the onus of proof is always on the government to show why any law that limits our individual liberty is necessary. The second point is that such a law will be valid only if it is necessary to prevent some direct harm to other human beings. We cannot, for example, pass laws forbidding people to smoke or drink when they are acting in ways that harm only themselves. But when their actions harm others, such as driving while drunk, we are allowed to curtail their liberty for the protection of others' rights.

The best examples of liberal democratic regimes that take their bearings from the natural rights school of liberalism are the United States and France. The leading example of the utilitarian approach to liberty is Britain. Here in Canada, our liberalism was historically of the utilitarian type. The doctrine of natural rights was for many years seen as an abstraction foreign to our traditions. In recent years, however, especially since the adoption of the Charter of Rights and Freedoms, Canadian thinking about rights has shifted dramatically. While our traditional utilitarian approach to rights remains, it is now common for Canadians to think of many of their rights as human rights, just as our American neighbours do. Given that the utilitarian and the natural rights schools are incompatible in important respects, it seems likely that our thinking about rights will be in flux for some time to come.

The list of specific rights enjoyed by citizens of liberal democracies is a long one. It is also a list that varies from one liberal democracy to another. Still, it is possible to summarize the essence of those rights in three general principles:

1. *Protection of the private sphere.* Liberals draw a deep (though not necessarily sharp) distinction between the private sphere and the public sphere. The public sphere includes those areas of human activity where governmental regulation of our conduct is necessary to protect the rights of everyone. The private sphere includes everything else, and liberals insist that governments may not interfere in these areas of our lives. For a liberal, then, government may legitimately tell us how fast we may drive a car or what kind of guns we may own, but it has no right to tell us what religion to believe in or whether we should refrain from engaging in extra-marital sex. Former prime minister Pierre Trudeau once articulated this principle of liberalism in his famous remark that "the government has no place in the bedrooms of the nation."

2. *Respect for minority rights.* A liberal regime will proscribe all discrimination on the basis of race, religion, and other politically irrelevant characteristics. This injunction against discrimination is part of a wider principle, the principle that those in power must assure equal treatment for those in the minority. According to liberals, the fact that 51 per cent of the population can win any vote does not entitle that majority to anything it pleases. For instance, would it not be unjust for a majority of the population to compel an ethnic, religious, or regional minority to pay all of the taxes?

3. *The rule of law.* Liberals believe that the effective protection of the various rights of citizens depends on the principle of the **rule of law**. At a minimum, this principle states that citizens must be able to count on what we often call "law and order," for without the protection of an effective legal order, the rights of everyone would be in jeopardy. But the principle of the rule of law goes far beyond simple law and order. It dictates, first of all, that the government is not itself above the law. Second, it stipulates that the law must be applied equally and impartially. Finally, every action taken by the government must be grounded in some legal authority. The reason for this principle is simple: if those in control of public power were able to treat citizens arbitrarily—that is, however they liked—we would all be at the mercy of the powerful.

Insisting that government act on the basis of established legal authority is a crucial mechanism for guaranteeing our rights. One especially important aspect of the rule of law is the idea of **constitutionalism**, the idea that the regime itself must be ordered in accordance with agreed-upon rules that will be supreme. A dictatorship may be defined as a regime in which those in power rule by force and recognize no limitations on their capacity to act. In a liberal regime, however, we insist on fixing clear limitations to the power of those who rule, and these limitations are to be found in a set of fundamental rules called the constitution.

1.4 The Canadian Regime

Equality and liberty constitute the regime principles of all of the world's liberal democracies. Sweden, Australia, Japan, Israel—all of these countries share the regime principles sketched above. It is important to note, however, that every liberal democracy will apply those principles in its own way.

In Part II of this book (Chapters 3–5), "Basic Principles of the Canadian Constitution," we will explain the way in which the Canadian Constitution adapts and applies the regime principles of liberal democracy to create a uniquely Canadian regime. Chapter 3 discusses the principle of responsible government. We will see in that chapter that the rules of responsible government are the mechanism we use in Canada to apply the principles of democracy in general and parliamentary democracy in particular. In Chapter 4 we examine federalism, the division of political authority between a national government in Ottawa, ten provincial governments, and three territorial governments. As we will see, Canadians adopted a federal regime as the best means of ensuring respect for the rights of regional and linguistic minorities. In Chapter 5, we turn to the Charter of Rights and Freedoms, the constitutional document that serves to protect our liberal rights and freedoms from violation by the governments.

Before turning to Part II, however, we must first complete our introduction to the Canadian regime by describing and explaining Canada's Constitution. We have seen in Section 1.3 above, that liberal democracies are based on constitutionalism, the idea that the rules of the regime must be set down in a constitution. The constitution is thus the skeleton or framework of the regime, and any study of the regime will therefore entail frequent reference to it. For this reason, it is important to begin by familiarizing the reader with Canada's Constitution.

Key Terms

regime	parliamentary democracy
kingship	representative democracy
tyranny	republican
aristocracy	liberal democracy
oligarchy	private sphere
polity	liberalism
democracy	natural rights
tyranny of the majority	utilitarianism
equality	harm principle
liberty	rule of law
direct democracies	constitutionalism

Discussion Questions

1. Developments in information technology have made direct democracy more possible. What are the pros and cons of having a more direct democracy?

2. Can you think of any examples from the past decade or two where the Canadian government has acted as a tyranny of the majority?

CHAPTER TWO

THE CONSTITUTION

2.1 Constitutions and Their Functions

2.2 Constitutional Forms

2.3 The Canadian Constitution

2.4 Amending Canada's Constitution

2.5 Judicial Review of the Constitution

2.6 Constitutional Politics Since 1982

2.1 Constitutions and Their Functions

A constitution may be defined as *a set of rules that authoritatively establishes both the structure and the fundamental principles of the political regime.* We call this set of rules a "constitution" because it is these rules that "constitute" (that is, create or establish) the regime. A constitution will normally do so by performing four major functions.

The *first major function of a constitution* is to establish what person or persons will exercise the various forms of political authority. In modern times, political power is understood to consist of three distinct types. **Legislative power** is the power to make law or policy. For instance, a political community might use its legislative power to pass a law stipulating that no one may drive an automobile when their blood has an alcohol content above .05 per cent. **Executive power** is the power to "execute" or administer that law or policy. This would include the power to establish and maintain a police force to catch impaired drivers. **Judicial power** is the power to settle questions about specific violations of law (is there appropriate evidence to prove the driver's blood-alcohol level exceeded .05 per cent?) and to choose a suitable punishment from among those permitted in the relevant legislation for those found guilty.

Every constitution will, at some point, assign legislative, executive, and judicial powers to some specific persons or bodies of persons. The constitution of a student council, for example, might stipulate that legislative power, the power to set policy, will be exercised by a council consisting of some fixed number of persons who represent specific constituencies of the student population: the senior class, the off-campus students, and so on. It will probably also establish certain fundamental rules to govern the manner in which the council will proceed in its work (for instance, how many members must be present to make a meeting official). The student council's constitution will also specify who is to exercise the executive power. It may, for example, confer this power on a group called "the executive" and stipulate that this executive will have a number of specific members (president, secretary, treasurer), each of whom will have certain specific responsibilities.

The constitution of a political regime will set down similar rules. It will stipulate that legislative power is to be exercised by a "parliament," a "congress," an "assembly," or some other body. It will then dictate the composition of that body (one chamber or two, how many members, how they are to be selected) and probably establish some basic ground rules for its functioning. The constitution will also determine whether executive power will be in the hands of a president, prime minister, cabinet, or perhaps even a queen. Finally, it must establish the broad outlines of a judicial system by stipulating what kind of courts the country will have and by setting down rules for the selection of their judges.

The *second major function of a constitution* is to provide an authoritative division of powers between national and regional governments in federal countries. Countries like Britain or France are said to have "unitary" regimes in the sense that they have only one government for the entire country. Yet, in very large countries (for example, the United States) or countries divided into distinct ethnic or cultural regions (Russia or Germany), it is common to establish two independent levels of government. In these "federal" regimes, a "national" or "federal" government will handle those matters on which it is thought there should be common policy across the country (national defence, for instance). At the same time, however, "state" or "provincial" governments take responsibility for matters on which different parts of the country want distinct policies (education, for example) or which might be more effectively managed by local authorities (the construction and maintenance of roads).

A workable federal system requires a clear division of powers between the two levels of government. If it were left up to each level to decide for itself what its powers were, the result would be chaos. Citizens might find themselves torn between a federal law requiring them to drive on the right-hand side of the road and a state or provincial law requiring them to drive on the left! This is why the constitution in federal countries establishes the powers and responsibilities of each level of government. In theory, this can be done by drawing up two lists, each of which spells out the specific jurisdictions of each level of government. The practical problem, however, is that it is difficult, if not impossible, to make the two lists sufficiently comprehensive. Governments legislate in a wide variety of areas, and new areas emerge on a regular basis (regulating the use of the Internet, for example). It is therefore typical for a constitution in a federal regime to furnish a list of specific jurisdictions reserved for the exclusive attention of one level of government and then to stipulate that everything else (the "**residual power**") be reserved for the other.

The *third major function of a constitution* is to delineate the limits of governmental power. The very existence of a constitution is in some sense a limitation on the power of government. The idea of constitutionalism implies that the constitution is supreme and that government is subordinate to it. Beyond this general limitation, it is not uncommon for constitutions to establish a list of fundamental rights and liberties in some sort of charter or "bill" of rights. Such a charter might specify, for example, that the citizens of a country have a right to freedom of religion. What this means is that no government, national or provincial, has the power to take measures that would violate its citizens' right to religious freedom. Thus, even though a provincial government might under the division of powers have jurisdiction over education, it could not use that jurisdiction to pass legislation requiring schools to indoctrinate their students in some specific religious tradition.

Finally, *the fourth function of a constitution* is to provide for an orderly way to make changes to it. Political regimes do not remain static, and so constitutions must accommodate and structure change. Most constitutions contain clear provisions for amendment. As we shall see, the Constitution of Canada contains a number of provisions for its amendment.

2.2 Constitutional Forms

In saying that a constitution consists of the regime's most fundamental rules, we need to first look at what types of rules these are. A rule is a principle or condition that customarily governs behaviour. Such rules might be written down or unwritten; they might be legally enforced or enforced by public opinion and political custom. Hence some of these rules are likely to be legal rules, while others may be rules that everyone generally understands and follows without any threat of legal sanction. As we shall see, both types of rules can be of fundamental importance.

When it comes to examining the political nature of constitutions, we find that the fundamental rules that make up a regime's constitution are of two basic types: conventions and laws. Conventions are political rules; laws are legal rules. A political rule is typically followed because one fears the political consequences of breaking the rule. A legal rule is a rule enforced by a court and is typically followed because one fears the consequences of legal punishment.[1]

A constitution will thus be a set of fundamental rules, consisting of conventions and laws. *The distinction between conventions and laws is not that the former are unwritten and the latter are written:* the distinction is in how the rule is enforced. Consider the following: statutory law is written down, common law is not. Both are rules enforced by courts. What makes conventions different from laws is that conventions are rules enforced by politics, whereas constitutional laws are rules enforced by courts.

Constitutional laws may in turn be divided into two types: organic statutes and entrenched constitutional laws. Canada's Constitution consists then of a combination of constitutional conventions, entrenched constitutional laws, and organic statutes. It is a complex constitution, and one whose clear understanding often seems to elude many good minds. It poses a challenge to effective democratic citizenship, for a democracy needs to have citizens who are well informed in its most fundamental rules. Let us then turn to look at these different forms of constitutional rules.

1. *Constitutional Convention.* When it comes to understanding the constitution, it is important to understand that in referring to a **constitutional convention**, we are not referring to a big meeting where people get together to talk about the constitution. (Such meetings do take place from time to time, but are unusual

---

1   This discussion relies on the work of A.V. Dicey, whose *Introduction to the Study of Law of the Constitution*, 8th ed. (Indianapolis: Liberty Fund, 1982) remains essential reading for anyone who wishes to understand the British and Canadian constitutions.

events and not generally referred to as conventions.) In constitutional terms, the word "convention" refers to a constitutional rule based on implicit political agreement and enforced in the political arena rather than by the courts. A convention is thus similar to a custom. Think, for example, of the custom of shaking hands when you meet someone. There is no law that says people must shake right hands, but everyone accepts that it is the right hand one offers to another person (except, perhaps, in extraordinary circumstances). Constitutional rules in the form of conventions can operate in much the same way. For instance, traditionally in the British Constitution there has long existed a political rule stipulating that the monarch will not refuse to provide royal assent to legislation that has been passed by both the House of Lords and the House of Commons. This rule takes the form of an unwritten agreement, accepted as binding by everyone, and sanctioned by the force of tradition. But it is not mere tradition that makes a particular practice a convention. The essential point in any convention is its rationale. Today we shake right hands because that just happens to be the custom. Originally, however, people greeted others by extending their right hand for a specific reason: that was the hand in which one would normally hold one's weapon. Extending an empty right hand was thus a way of demonstrating that one's intentions were not hostile. The British convention requiring royal assent is also based on an obvious rationale: as Britain evolved from a monarchy to a democracy, the House of Commons became the primary political power, and withholding royal assent would thus not be viewed as politically legitimate. This convention is now well established, but its legitimacy rests on the perception that there are good reasons for such a rule, not on how constitutionally ingrained it is.

The question, of course, is what happens if someone violates a convention. If politicians break a law, they can be brought before a court, tried, and punished if found guilty. But precisely because the court is a "court of law" and not a "court of conventions" its judges cannot, and will not, enforce constitutional conventions. So who does enforce them? The answer is the voters. In a constitutional system based on conventions, it is assumed that the voters will know what those conventions are and will guard them jealously. Therefore, those holding political office will respect these conventions out of fear of invoking the wrath of the voters. But this is not to say that constitutional conventions are always respected. The great advantage of having constitutional rules in the form of conventions rather than laws is that they can be applied with a certain amount of flexibility. We normally greet other people by shaking their right hand, but if one's right hand is in a cast, it is acceptable to offer the left. This same flexibility is evident in the realm of constitutional convention. The British electorate would never permit a monarch to violate the convention on royal assent, unless there was some obvious necessity for doing so. What might constitute such a necessity is hard to imagine, but the possibility is still there. The public would have to decide whether that specific departure from the rule was well justified. Similarly, in Canada there is no constitutional law stating that the Senate cannot vote against a bill that has been passed by the House of Commons. But there is a constitutional convention that the Senate will ultimately defer to the will of the House of Commons. Occasionally, however, it has refused to do so. In 1988, the Senate refused to pass legislation that would implement a free-trade agreement with the United States. This refusal triggered a national election on the issue. Prime Minister Mulroney's government was returned with a majority and the legislation was ultimately passed. But Canadians did not react negatively to the fact that the Senate had triggered the election, thus proving that a convention can be ignored, but only for the right reason. In both the previous examples, if the convention had been ignored for light and transient reasons, the likely consequence would have been immediate: constitutional reform of the institutions of the monarchy and the Senate.

2. *Organic Statutes.* The second form in which a country may embody its constitutional rules is what we call **organic statutes**. The term "statute" refers to an act of the authoritative legislative body, which is Parliament in Canada. Statutes establishing constitutional rules are called "organic" to distinguish them from statutes dealing with non-constitutional matters—statutes regulating health care, automobile traffic, or unemployment insurance.

The classic example of this form of constitutional rules is, once again, Britain. Because of that country's extensive use of constitutional convention, textbooks will often describe the British Constitution as an "unwritten" one. This is a somewhat misleading description. A good deal of the British Constitution is actually written out in the form of organic statutes, laws passed by the British Parliament to spell out certain constitutional rules in black and white. The *Bill of Rights* of 1689, which placed important new restrictions on the powers of the Crown, is a classic example of such a statute. So too are the *Reform Act* of 1832 and the *Parliament Act* of 1911, both of which dramatically altered the nature and functioning of Britain's legislative institutions.

There are two basic reasons for adopting some constitutional rules as organic statutes rather than conventions. The first is that some rules, especially those which establish and describe institutions, are probably too complex and too detailed to be left to the realm of unwritten agreement. The second is that organic statutes provide a more effective means of introducing substantial innovation to the existing constitutional order. Each of the three statutes cited as examples in the previous paragraph represented a dramatic change in the nature of the British regime. Putting those measures in statute form improved their chances of taking hold because statutes, as opposed to conventions, can be enforced by the courts. For instance, if in 1690 the king had tried to impose new taxes without Parliament's consent (an act prohibited by the *Bill of Rights* of 1689), his subjects could have used the courts to resist the new taxes on the grounds that they were in violation of British law.

3. *Constitutional Laws*. The third form in which a country may express its constitutional rules is what experts refer to as **constitutional laws**. This is a somewhat confusing term since organic statutes are, in effect, laws of a constitutional nature. But a "constitutional law" differs from an "organic statute" in two important respects. The first difference is that constitutional laws tend to be more comprehensive than organic statutes: while organic statutes usually deal with one particular institution or situation, constitutional laws tend to be comprehensive codifications of all (or most) of a country's constitutional rules. The second and more important difference is one of status or authority. The authority of an organic statute derives from the fact that it represents the will of the body that exercises legislative power. This means its authority is always somewhat precarious since any body that has a right to adopt a statute must of necessity have the right to repeal or amend it. The British Parliament that adopted the *Reform Act* of 1832 could have repealed that same bill the day after they adopted it. The authority of a constitutional law is more absolute because constitutional laws are not as easily changed as statutes. In the United States, for example, the Constitution itself proclaims that changes (or "amendments") may be made only if they are supported by two-thirds of the members of each chamber of Congress, and by three-quarters of the states.

The logic of this concept is best explained in the writings of the great British political philosopher, John Locke.[2] Locke's theory of government begins with the argument that since no one has any natural title to rule over anyone else, government can be legitimate only if it is based on the consent of all those who are governed. In saying this Locke does not mean that all political decisions have to be made democratically. He means only that the regime has to meet with the approval of its citizens. Locke suggests that this approval comes in a two-stage process, which he called the "social contract." In the first stage of the contract,

---

2   See Janet Ajzenstat, *The Canadian Founding: John Locke and Parliament* (Montreal: McGill-Queen's University Press, 2007); and Guy Laforest, *Trudeau and the End of a Canadian Dream* (Montreal: McGill-Queen's University Press, 1995).

human beings who are naturally free and equal decide to come together in "civil society" and establish a political regime to govern themselves. In the second stage, they establish the ground rules of the regime by majority vote. They can vote to set up a democratic regime, but they also have the right to institute an aristocracy or even a monarchy. It is not the institutions that have to be democratic for government to be legitimate but the underlying contract that establishes them.

According to Locke, once the people have put the social contract in place, they turn the process of governing over to those who fill the offices established by the contract. But this government is not free to act in any way it pleases. It is always limited by any conditions stipulated in the social contract, because it is on that contract that the legitimacy of the government's very existence depends. If the social contract says that the government may not tax citizens without obtaining the consent of their representatives, then a new tax which has not been approved by the representatives of the people would be in violation of the social contract and hence illegitimate.

In conceptual terms, what we mean by a "constitutional law" is very close to what Locke meant by a "social contract." A constitutional law is a kind of fundamental pact emanating from the will of the people, which provides the foundation for the entire regime. It is therefore of higher status than ordinary laws—statutes adopted by legislative bodies—because those bodies owe their very existence to it. A constitutional law is thus a kind of "super-law," the supreme law of the regime, and this means that any action or statute inconsistent with it can have no validity.

The special authority or status of a constitutional law is the key to understanding a crucial constitutional concept known as **entrenchment**. There are many political principles so fundamental that citizens will want to ensure that their government will never be able to violate them legally. Freedom of religion might be an example of such a principle or the right to use either French or English in the courts. The best way to ensure the inviolability of such principles is to "entrench" them by writing them into the text of a constitutional law. The foundational status of that law will then serve to put those principles safely out of the reach of any institution of government that might seek to violate them.

The classic example of a constitutional law is the Constitution of the United States. Prior to declaring their independence, the American colonists were, of course, British subjects. As such, their constitutional traditions might have led them to opt for a constitution similar in form to the British one, a constitution based on conventions and organic statutes. But for a number of reasons, the Americans opted instead to embody their constitutional rules in a constitutional law. One reason was the fact that the leading figures in colonial

America—people like Jefferson, Franklin, and Madison—were profoundly influenced by the works of John Locke. The so-called "Founding Fathers" insisted that the Constitution of the United States take the form of a fundamental law emanating from the will of the people rather than a set of conventions and organic statutes devised by those politicians who held the legislative power, because this was the approach most consistent with Lockean theory.

But the Americans also had two practical reasons for using a constitutional law instead of conventions and organic statutes. One was the fact that they had decided to establish a federal regime in which responsibilities were to be divided between a "federal" government and a number of "state" governments. It would have been impractical to establish a federal division of powers in the form of a constitutional convention, because a federal division of powers has to be formulated in more precise, detailed, and rigid terms than can be managed in unwritten agreements. It would have been equally impractical to try to embody the division of powers in an organic statute, because that statute would have to be adopted by some particular legislative body. But which one? The state governments would never agree to concede the task to the legislative body of the federal government, for then that body, by virtue of its right to amend its own statutes, would be able at any time to rewrite the division of powers so as to transfer jurisdictions from the state governments to itself. By the same token, leaving the adoption of a division of powers to the state legislatures would put the federal government at the mercy of the state governments. The federal division of powers had to be put in a constitutional form that would be beyond the unilateral reach of either the state or federal governments. This meant it had to take the form of a constitutional law.

The other reason for preferring constitutional law to convention or organic statute was the belief that constitutional law provides the most effective means of guaranteeing citizens' rights and liberties. It should not be forgotten that the 13 colonies broke away from Britain precisely because they believed that the British government was not respecting the American colonists' constitutional rights (for example, the right to "no taxation without representation"). These rights had been guaranteed to all British subjects, including the American colonists, by various conventions and organic statutes. But guarantees offered by conventions and statutes are not iron clad. A government can ignore conventions or repeal statutes if a majority of voters is willing to support it. And in the 1770s the American colonists believed that their constitutional rights were being systematically violated by a government more concerned with the interests of the British majority than the rights of the American minority.

Here, then, was another reason to place the constitutional rules of the new American regime in a constitutional law. Constitutional laws are the preferred constitutional form for rights and liberties because constitutional laws have a higher status than any particular political institution. In a constitutional system based on convention and statute, politicians can adopt the most oppressive of measures as long as they have the support of a majority of voters. But no matter how much public support they have, politicians cannot legally adopt measures that violate a constitutional law.

2.3 The Canadian Constitution

In subsequent chapters, we will see that the Canadian regime is to a large extent a mixture of the British and American forms of government. This is evident in the form of the Canadian Constitution. Like the Americans, we have entrenched many, if not most, of our constitutional rules in constitutional laws: the *Constitution Act, 1867* (*CA 1867*)[3] and the *Constitution Act, 1982* (*CA 1982*). Like the British, however, we rely on constitutional conventions and organic statutes for a substantial number of our constitutional rules. Our entire system of responsible government, for example, is embedded in constitutional convention rather than constitutional law. Specific examples of Canadian constitutional conventions and organic statutes will be discussed later. In this section, we will focus our attention on Canada's two constitutional laws.

It is essential that students of the Canadian regime learn to work with Canada's constitutional documents. In this book, we shall refer to the Constitution on a regular basis, and for that reason we have included a copy of *CA 1867* and *CA 1982* in the Appendix. It will be useful to examine these acts briefly in order to familiarize the reader with their structure and contents.

Figure 2.1: Main Elements of Canada's Constitutional Laws

CA 1867	CA 1982
Executive power	Charter of Rights and Freedoms
Legislative power	Aboriginal Rights
Provincial constitutions	Equalization and Regional Disparities
Federal division of power	Amending Formulas
Judicial power	Definition of the Canadian Constitution

---

3   Canada's first constitutional law was originally called the *British North America Act* (*BNA Act*). Its name was changed to *Constitution Act, 1867* in 1982.

1. *CA 1867* served to create a union of three British colonies into a new political entity called the "Dominion of Canada." The term "dominion" was a new one, invented to describe a regime that was too self-governing to be considered a colony but not entirely independent of the mother country either. Under the terms of Confederation, Canadians were to remain subjects of the British Crown; their foreign policy was to be directed by the British government; the Judicial Committee of the Privy Council, Britain's highest court, would be the final court of appeal for Canadian legal disputes; and Britain would maintain control of Canada's Constitution.

It is this last point that is of particular interest to us here. Constitutional laws normally derive their supreme status from the fact that they emanate from the will of the people, usually as expressed in some kind of popular referendum. Because those creating the new confederation were already subjects of the British Crown, however, their new constitution was not adopted as some kind of Lockean social contract; instead, it was legislated for them, at the request of their colonial legislatures, by the British Parliament. Thus, the status of *CA 1867* as Canada's supreme law depended on the fact that it was an act of our colonial mother country and on the fact that we Canadians, being less than fully independent of her, had no right to disobey her laws.

CA 1867 consists of a **preamble** (an introduction stating the reasons for the act that follows) and 11 "parts." The most noteworthy feature in the preamble is the suggestion that Canada is to have "a Constitution similar in Principle to that of the United Kingdom." This clause is of the greatest importance for understanding the Canadian Constitution. As we have seen, the British Constitution is to a large extent based on conventions. In declaring that Canada's Constitution is to be "similar in Principle to that of the United Kingdom," the preamble serves notice that many of those conventions are to be incorporated into it. This would certainly include those conventions governing the operation of "responsible government," a subject we shall discuss in detail in Chapter 3.

Part I of *CA 1867* deals with relatively unimportant preliminary matters. Part II establishes some basic points about the union of the provinces. Parts III and IV are much more important, for it is here that *CA 1867* sketches the fundamental outlines of executive and legislative power in the federal government. We shall examine the particular sections of Parts III and IV in some detail in Chapter 6 (The Crown and Its Servants) and Chapter 7 (Parliament). Part V deals with "provincial constitutions" and describes some of their distinctive features. For the most part, the constitutions of the provinces are governed by the same principles as that of the federal government.

In Part VI, we find the division of powers between the two levels of government. Of particular importance are the description of the legislative authority of the federal government in Section 91 and the list of provincial jurisdictions in Section 92. Part VII lays down some of the fundamental rules governing judicial power in Canada. Note, however, that nothing is said about the Supreme Court of Canada. Section 101 gives the federal Parliament the right to establish a "General Court of Appeal for Canada," and in 1875, Ottawa used this power to create a supreme court in *The Supreme Court of Canada Act*. Because the Supreme Court of Canada is this country's highest institution of judicial power, the act that establishes it must certainly be considered a constitutional act, even though it is not a constitutional law. Here, then, is a good example of a Canadian "organic statute." Part VIII establishes various provisions governing the financial details of Confederation. Part IX lays down a number of miscellaneous provisions, including Section 133 on the use of the French and English languages.

Part X, which committed the federal government to the immediate construction of the Intercolonial Railway between Québec and Halifax, became obsolete upon the termination of that project and was repealed in 1893. It is a good example of the way in which a constitutional law is sometimes used in Canada to entrench guarantees that have nothing to do with constitutional matters. Part XI establishes two procedures for the admission of new provinces. Existing colonies, such as British Columbia or Prince Edward Island, may be admitted to Canada by an act of the British Parliament if it receives a request to that effect by both the colony and the federal government of Canada. The federal government may pass acts of its own to create new provinces out of "Rupert's Land" and did so when it founded the provinces of Manitoba, Saskatchewan, and Alberta. In either case, the act creating a new province is a constitutional measure and may thus be classified as an "organic statute." This is why in 1994 it was necessary to seek a constitutional amendment in order to clear the way for the construction of a bridge to take the place of ferry service between New Brunswick and Prince Edward Island. The British Parliament's *Prince Edward Island Terms of Union Act, 1871,* passed pursuant to Section 146 of *CA 1867,* had specifically guaranteed that the federal government would provide ferry service to the Island, and Ottawa therefore could not unilaterally cease providing that service.

2. *CA 1982.* For well over 100 years, *CA 1867* and its attendant statutes and conventions formed the core of Canada's constitutional order. Through much of that period, however, there was a sense that this constitutional order was significantly incomplete. From the 1920s right up to the beginning of the 1980s, Canadian

politicians struggled to add another element to our constitution: a constitutional amending formula.

Constitutions need to be amended from time to time when certain of their provisions either become outdated (for example, the section of *CA 1867* dealing with the Intercolonial Railway) or are found to be problematic. Constitutional laws will therefore always (or almost always) contain an amending formula, a rule explaining how the law can be changed. The Constitution of the United States, for example, specifies that it may be amended if the text of a proposed amendment is supported by a two-thirds vote in each of the two houses of Congress and then a majority vote in three-quarters of the state legislatures.

CA 1867 is perhaps the only constitutional law in the history of the world that contained no comprehensive amending formula. Until 1982, Section 92.1 gave each province the right to amend its own internal constitution. And from 1949 to 1982, Section 91.1 gave the federal Parliament the right to make changes to most aspects of its own internal structure. But nowhere in the *Act* is there a formula for the amendment of such crucial matters as the federal-provincial division of powers, the judiciary, or language rights. This, of course, did not mean that the constitutional provisions governing such matters could not be amended. Because *CA 1867* was a statute of the British Parliament, that body retained the right to amend any of its sections. Until 1982, then, Canada could make changes to those parts of *CA 1867* not governed by 91.1 or 92.1 by sending a formal request for amendment to the British Parliament at Westminster. The request took the form of a resolution of the federal Parliament, but a practice emerged according to which Ottawa would not request any amendments that would alter the powers of the provincial governments without first obtaining their consent.

Over time, this arrangement came to be seen as unsatisfactory. As a result of our nation's substantial contributions and sacrifices during World War I, it was agreed by Britain and Canada that the time had come for the Canadian regime to become fully independent. This meant, among other things, that it was time for Canada to take full control of its own constitution. As early as the 1920s, Britain had invited Canada to **patriate** (literally, to "bring to the fatherland") its constitution, but Canada was unable to do so. The problem was that before the British government could hand *CA 1867* over to us, it had to put a comprehensive amending formula into the act. Unfortunately, Canadian politicians were unable to agree what that formula should be. Numerous constitutional conferences were held over the years, but agreement remained elusive.

The problem in these negotiations was not patriation itself: everyone agreed that patriation was a good idea. The catch was that various parties insisted on using the patriation negotiations to pursue other agendas. From the early

1960s on, the government of Québec took the position that it would agree to patriation only if it were accompanied by the transfer of specific legislative jurisdictions from Ottawa to Québec City. In the 1970s, many other provincial governments made similar demands. On the other side of the table, Pierre Trudeau, then prime minister, opposed any such transfer and sought to link patriation of the Constitution to a project of his own: the adoption of an entrenched bill of rights which would, among other things, provide constitutional protection for the bilingual regime of language rights he favoured. His proposal was fiercely resisted by the government of Québec.

In the early 1980s, Trudeau brought the matter to a head by announcing that if Ottawa and the provinces did not soon come to an agreement on patriating the constitution, his government was ready to proceed with a patriation request unilaterally. Two provincial governments supported Trudeau, but the other eight (the "Gang of Eight") opposed him and went to court to challenge the constitutionality of a unilateral initiative.[4] The case was eventually heard by the Supreme Court of Canada, which handed down a complicated split decision: in terms of constitutional law, there was nothing to prevent the federal government from making a unilateral request for patriation, but the court also declared that Trudeau's proposed amendment would diminish the powers of the provincial governments and that it was now a convention that amendments having an impact on the powers of the provinces required the support of a substantial number of the provinces. The effect of this decision was to compel both sides to go back to the negotiating table and show more flexibility. The "Gang of Eight" could not be intransigent knowing that Ottawa had the legal right to proceed unilaterally if no agreement was reached, and Ottawa had a powerful incentive to compromise because it wanted to avoid the stigma that comes from violating constitutional convention.

These negotiations resulted in a compromise agreement that obtained the support of every provincial government except Québec. On the basis of that agreement, the British Parliament passed the *Canada Act, 1982*, which created a second major constitutional law for Canada, the *Constitution Act, 1982*.

CA 1982 is divided into seven parts. Part I is the Canadian Charter of Rights and Freedoms, a document we shall examine in Chapter 5. Part II is a constitutional declaration of the rights of Canada's Aboriginal peoples. Part III entrenches the federal government's practice of making equalization payments to provinces whose revenues are below the national average. This practice will be

---

4   Ontario and New Brunswick sided with the federal government, and the remaining eight provinces were opposed.

explained in Chapter 4. The fourth part committed the governments of Canada, the provinces, and the territories to hold a conference on Aboriginal people's constitutional concerns. The conference was held soon after the adoption of *CA 1982* and resulted in certain amendments to its Section 35. Part V outlines the new procedure for amending the Constitution of Canada, and we shall examine its contents in detail in the next section of this chapter. Part VI makes an amendment to Section 92 of *CA 1867* strengthening the powers of provincial governments in the areas of energy, forestry, and non-renewable resources. This was one of the demands of the "Gang of Eight." Part VII contains a number of miscellaneous provisions. For our purposes, the most noteworthy is Section 52, which gives a legal definition of the Constitution of Canada and proclaims in no uncertain terms its status as Canada's "supreme law."

It should not be forgotten, however, that Section 52 is a clause in an act that is itself a creation of Britain's *Canada Act, 1982*. The supremacy of Canada's constitutional laws is thus still grounded in the fact that they are statutes of our mother-parliament in Westminster. In order to give our constitutional order a more independent foundation, it was proposed that the federal Parliament and the ten provincial legislatures should each pass a resolution adopting *CA 1982*. This, it was suggested, would make our constitution more like a Lockean social contract. The problem with this strategy, however, is that the government of Québec, which has always opposed the agreement now embodied in *CA 1982*, refused—and continues to refuse—to pass such a resolution. Nevertheless, the *Act* is valid in Québec, as well as in the rest of Canada, because the British Parliament has declared it so.

2.4 Amending Canada's Constitution

Part V of *CA 1982* establishes an amending formula for the constitution, or, to speak more precisely, five distinct formulas for five distinct situations. A brief summary is sketched in Figure 2.2.

Section 44 stipulates that amendments to constitutional provisions regarding the executive or legislative offices of the federal government may be made by Parliament[5] on its own. This is essentially the same provision that formerly existed as Section 91.1 of *CA 1867*. In like fashion, Section 45 reproduces the former Section 92.1 of *CA 1867*, stipulating that amendments to the constitution

---

5   In constitutional language, the term "Parliament" refers to the Parliament of Canada. Provincial governments do not have parliaments; the provincial equivalent of Parliament is a "legislature."

Figure 2.2: The Five Amending Formulas

Sections of CA 1982	Subject of Amendment	Amending Formula
General Procedure (secs. 38-40; 42)	• all sections of the Constitution not exempted by secs. 41, 43, 44, 45 • prov. representation in the Senate • Supreme Court reform • principle of proportionate rep. in the House of Commons • the establishment of new provinces • extension of provincial boundaries into the territories	Parliament + seven provinces with 50% of the population
Unanimous Agreement (sec. 41)	• changes to the executive offices (Queen, Gov. Gen., Lt. Gov.) • right of province to have no fewer MPs than Senators • use of French and English languages • composition of the Supreme Court • amendments to sec. 41	Parliament + all provinces
Some Provinces (sec. 43)	• alteration of boundaries between provinces • provisions relating to the use of French and English languages within the province(s)	Parliament + relevant provinces
Parliament (sec. 44)	• laws amending the executive of the Parliament alone • Govt. of Canada or the Senate or the House of Commons (not falling under secs. 41-2)	Parliament
One Province (sec. 45)	• amendments to the Constitution of a provincial govt. alone (not falling under sec. 41)	province

of a province may be made by the legislature of that province. Section 43 contains a third amending formula. It stipulates that amendments that concern some but not all provinces (for example, the alteration of a provincial boundary) or that deal with constitutionally entrenched language rights in a particular province may be made only with the consent of the federal government and the province concerned. The reason for including the second category of amendments is to ensure that a temporary majority in a single province cannot unilaterally diminish or abolish the constitutional language rights of a minority.

The other two formulas are somewhat more complex. Section 41 provides that for five specific matters—the Crown, the right of provinces to a number of MPs not less than the number of its senators, the use of French and English, the composition of the Supreme Court, and the amending procedures themselves—a constitutional amendment must have the support of the federal Parliament and the legislatures of every province. This is an extremely rigid amending formula, but it is argued that the matters in question are so fundamental that they should not be altered without the unanimous consent of Canada's federal and provincial governments.

Any provision of the Constitution not covered by one of these four formulas is to be amended with the "general" formula established in Section 38, which requires the consent of the federal Parliament and the legislatures of two-thirds of the provinces which, taken together, contain at least half of Canada's population. This formula ensures that no single province can **veto** (that is, block) a proposed amendment, but at the same time it ensures that no amendment can be adopted without widespread support, including the support of one of the two largest provinces, Ontario and Québec. Section 38 also establishes that a province may choose to exempt itself from an amendment made under this formula. If, for example, nine provinces were willing to transfer jurisdiction over prisons (a provincial responsibility under *CA 1867*, 92.6) to Ottawa but Québec was not, the amendment could be made, and prisons would thereafter be a federal responsibility in the other nine provinces and a provincial responsibility in Québec. Section 40 adds an interesting twist to this arrangement. This section stipulates that if an amendment involves a transfer of some part of provincial jurisdiction over education or culture, the federal government, which will now take up those responsibilities in all the other provinces, must offer financial compensation to the province that is retaining them. This is because it would be unfair for the taxpayers of a particular province to have to pay a share of the cost of those responsibilities in the other nine provinces through their federal taxes as well as the total cost of those responsibilities in their own province.

2.5 Judicial Review of the Constitution

Our overview of the Constitution would be incomplete if we did not say a word about judicial review.

By their very nature, constitutions have to regulate every single aspect and activity of a political regime. This means that constitutional rules must be applicable to an almost infinite number of possible situations. But the number of constitutional rules cannot itself be infinite. For this reason, constitutional laws are of necessity written in language that is highly general and seemingly vague. A constitutional division of powers cannot list every possible object of legislative activity: the regulation of automobile engine emissions, the regulation of industrial effluents, the regulation of garbage disposal, and so on. It will therefore collect all of these matters under a general heading like "protection of the environment." By the same token, the Charter of Rights and Freedoms cannot specify all the types of police searches that are acceptable and all those that are not. It therefore defines our rights in general terms: the right to be secure against "unreasonable" searches.

The problem, however, is that it is often difficult to know how to apply general rules in specific cases. Let us take as a hypothetical example a constitution that stipulates that "protection of the environment" is a jurisdiction of the federal government and that "management of natural resources" is a provincial jurisdiction. Which level of government has the authority to regulate the clear-cutting of forests? The answer is not self-evident, and it is likely that each of them would insist that it had exclusive jurisdiction over the matter. Obviously, then, someone has to be in a position to offer an authoritative interpretation of what the Constitution means in these circumstances.

This is a task that normally falls to the judiciary. Judicial review of the Constitution refers to the judiciary's task of defining and applying its terms. The courts will decide, for example, whether the Constitution says that a particular legislative matter is of federal or provincial jurisdiction. To do so, they will determine the concrete meaning of abstract phrases such as "the Peace, Order, and good Government of Canada," "subject only to such reasonable limits prescribed by law as can be demonstrably justified in a free and democratic society," or "the right to be secure against unreasonable search or seizure." It is therefore essential that students of Canadian politics pay close attention to judicial review, for to understand our regime one has to understand the Constitution, and to understand the Constitution, one must understand how the courts have interpreted and applied it.

2.6 Constitutional Politics Since 1982

Canada's constitutional struggles did not end with the adoption of *CA 1982*. The government of the province of Québec was resolutely opposed to the agreement made by Ottawa and the other nine provinces in 1982. This led Prime Minister Mulroney to initiate negotiations between Ottawa and the ten provincial premiers aimed at producing a new package of constitutional amendments designed to meet Québec's concerns. The result of those negotiations was the Meech Lake Accord. Among other things, this Accord would have declared Québec to be a "distinct society" and would have given Québec and all the other provinces a veto over constitutional amendments affecting the matters listed in Section 42, matters which in *CA 1982* are governed by the two-thirds/50-per-cent formula in Section 38.

Because the Accord proposed a change to the amending formula—one of the subjects mentioned in Section 41 of *CA 1982*—its adoption required the consent of all the provincial legislatures. This proved to be a problem. Although all the premiers who participated in the Meech Lake negotiations personally endorsed the final package, a number of them were defeated in provincial elections before they were able to get the necessary resolution of approval passed in their legislatures. In the face of mounting public opposition to the Accord, the new governments that replaced them were reluctant to proceed. A series of complex federal-provincial negotiations ensued in a last-ditch effort to save it. Finally, in 1990, with the three-year window for approval fast closing, Elijah Harper, an Aboriginal member of the Manitoba Legislature, effectively killed the Accord by opposing a crucial procedural motion that required unanimous consent.

Two years later, Prime Minister Mulroney initiated a new round of negotiations. One of the reasons for the defeat of the Meech Lake Accord was that it focused almost exclusively on the constitutional concerns of the government of Québec. Aboriginal Canadians, women's groups, and Western Canadians, among others, were unwilling to endorse a constitutional package that did not address their constitutional concerns. The 1992 negotiations produced a new proposal, the Charlottetown Accord, which was designed to address the concerns of not only Québec but other constituencies as well. The Charlottetown Accord retained the essential elements of Meech Lake: a "distinct society" clause, the Meech Lake amending formula, and limitations on new federal spending in provincial jurisdictions. It added to that formula a constitutional commitment to Aboriginal self-government, a new Senate designed to meet the demands of Westerners (as well, perhaps, of women) for better representation in Ottawa, and a "Canada Clause" that was meant to encapsulate the fundamental political principles of the regime.

Once the Charlottetown Accord was drafted, the federal government announced that it would not be willing to support a parliamentary resolution adopting it unless a majority of voters in each province gave it their approval in a national referendum, because there had been many complaints that the process that produced the Meech Lake Accord had been "undemocratic." Although CA 1982 places the responsibility for amending the Constitution in the hands of Parliament and the ten legislatures, many Canadians thought they should have been directly consulted on the matter. Confident that the "something-for-every-one" approach of Charlottetown would prove popular, Prime Minister Mulroney gave in to those who advocated putting the Accord to a referendum. To the surprise of many, however, a majority of voters in six provinces voted against it. The "something-for-everybody" approach turned out also to be a "something-to-offend-everybody" approach.

Ottawa's recourse to a referendum leaves us with an interesting constitutional question: do proposed amendments to the Constitution now have to be submitted to the people for a popular vote of approval? If we look at the relevant constitutional law, Part V of CA 1982, in which there is no mention of the term "referendum," the answer appears to be no. Nevertheless, it is difficult to believe that Canadian voters would not insist on the right to have a direct voice in future decisions about the Constitution now that they have had that opportunity in the Charlottetown process. If this is so, then perhaps we are witnessing the emergence of a new constitutional convention.

The most significant constitutional development since the rejection of the Charlottetown Accord was the Supreme Court of Canada's decision in the 1998 Reference re Secession of Québec. After separatist forces had come within a whisker of winning a referendum on Québec sovereignty in 1995, the Chrétien government asked the Supreme Court of Canada to clarify whether unilateral secession was permitted under the Canadian Constitution. The court held unanimously that the Constitution does not permit unilateral declarations of independence but went on to say that if a "clear majority" of Quebeckers voted in favour of a clear proposal for secession, that would confer on the rest of Canada an obligation to enter into negotiations for separation. The court also stipulated that it would be up to political leaders to determine what constitutes "a clear majority on a clear question." Acting upon the judges' invitation, Parliament adopted in 2000 the **Clarity Act**, under which the right to determine whether a "question" and a "majority" are "clear" is reserved to Parliament itself. Predictably, the adoption of the Clarity Act was denounced by a wide range of Quebeckers as an intrusion on what they took to be their province's right to decide its future on its own. Yet if Ottawa's strategy was to deflate the separatist cause by making separation appear even more complicated and risky, it seems to have been quite successful. In the years since the adoption of the *Act,* support in Québec for separation has declined significantly. Moreover, studies tabled by the separatist Parti Québécois government in March of 2002 now recognize that there would be major obstacles to any attempt to negotiate independence.

Canada has been through 30 years of what can be called "constitutional politics"—the major political issues being of a constitutional nature. In recent years, the fires of constitutional politics no longer burn as hot, and the country has returned to a more normal politics focusing primarily on issues of public and foreign policy. The fall from power of the Parti Québécois, and the seven years of national minority governments that ended in 2011, probably effected this change. Constitutional discussions are currently focused on the perennial issue of Senate reform, and it remains to be seen whether the Harper majority government can be successful where so many others have failed.

Key Terms

legislative power	entrenchment
executive power	preamble
judicial power	patriate
residual power	veto
constitutional convention	judicial review
organic statute	Clarity Act
constitutional laws	

Discussion Questions

1. Since Canada is a democracy based on majority rule, why should a minority of provinces be able to block constitutional amendments?

2. If you had to choose between a constitution based on law and a constitution based on convention, which would you prefer?

PART TWO

BASIC PRINCIPLES OF THE CANADIAN CONSTITUTION

CHAPTER THREE

RESPONSIBLE GOVERNMENT

3.1 The Emergence of Responsible Government

3.2 The Conventions of Responsible Government

3.3 Responsible Government as "Cabinet Government"

3.4 Forming a Government

3.5 Majority and Minority Government

3.6 Institutional Implications of Responsible Government

3.7 Responsible Government and Separation of Powers Compared

We have seen that one of the chief functions of a constitution is to determine who will exercise legislative, executive, and judicial power. It is therefore not surprising that this should be one of the very first topics addressed in *CA 1867*. In the preamble to that act, it is stipulated that Canada is to have "a Constitution similar in Principle to that of the United Kingdom." Above all else, this phrase means that legislative and executive power are to be organized in accordance with a set of principles that may be summarized by the term responsible government. The purpose of this chapter is to explain the meaning, the application, and the rationale of those principles.

3.1 The Emergence of Responsible Government

The British regime is one that has evolved through a number of different forms. In its earliest stage, which may roughly be described as absolute monarchy, the Crown wielded both legislative and executive power. In other words, the king or queen both made the laws and administered them. But the possession of so much power by unelected (and hence unaccountable) monarchs inevitably led to abuses of that power. In reaction to such abuses, the English nobles and commoners were gradually able to compel the Crown to turn legislative power over to their assembly, which they called Parliament.

By the mid-eighteenth century, the political philosopher Montesquieu could cite the British regime as an example of the principle of **the separation of powers**. Following an argument first made by John Locke, Montesquieu claimed that the best way to protect freedom and to prevent the abuse of political power is to ensure that legislative and executive powers are assigned to separate people or bodies. Since any tyrannical act would ultimately require the application of both legislative and executive power, placing those powers in different hands would minimize the chances that such acts could be taken. Because it assigned executive power to the Crown and legislative power to Parliament, the British Constitution of his day was held by Montesquieu to be the very model of a free political order.

The principle of the separation of powers also became one of the cornerstones of the American regime. The American Founding Fathers were well versed in the ideas of Montesquieu and Locke, and their experience with British "tyranny" made them keenly concerned about the control of political power. They therefore opted for a constitution that placed legislative power in the hands of an assembly known as Congress and executive power in the hands of a president. Indeed, the Americans extended Montesquieu's principle. Not only did they place legislative and executive power in separate hands, but because both the president and the Congress were elected democratically, each would to some extent be in competition with the other for public favour. It was thought that this competition or rivalry would reduce further still the chances of tyrannical collusion between the two branches of government.

In the early years of British rule, the colonies of what would later become Canada were ruled by imperial governors appointed by the British Crown. As early as 1748, the subjects of Nova Scotia gained the right to elect legislative assemblies with authority to legislate on most internal matters. The subjects of Upper Canada (Ontario) and Lower Canada (Québec) received the same right late in the eighteenth century. Yet, since executive power remained in the hands of the governors and their advisers, our colonial constitutions were based on a kind of separation of powers, such as that set out in the American Constitution. The difference, of course, was that we had a separation of powers for imperial reasons (that is, to ensure British control) rather than for the liberal reasons advanced by Montesquieu and Locke. These colonial constitutions were unworkable precisely because of the separation between legislative and executive powers. When those powers are placed in different hands, friction between the two branches of government is inevitable. Such friction is tolerable when each of the branches is elected, as is the case in the United States. But when only the legislative branch is elected, as was the case in our colonial constitutions, conflict between the two branches comes to be seen in terms of democratic rights.

The experience of Upper Canada provides a good illustration of the problem. In the early nineteenth century, political life in Upper Canada centred on the attempts of "reformers" to break the power of the so-called "Family Compact," a small clique of wealthy citizens who controlled much of the colony's political and economic life. Even when the reformers won control of the Legislative Assembly, they found the governors unwilling to cooperate in the implementation of the reform program, because they had appointed as their advisers an executive council composed almost exclusively of members of the Family Compact. For Upper Canada's reformers, the separation of legislative and executive powers amounted to a constitutional subversion of democratic self-rule. Discontent with this constitutional order led to armed rebellions in both Upper and Lower Canada in 1837. These were easily crushed by British troops, but they showed the British government that some kind of reform was necessary. The government therefore dispatched to the Canadas one of the leading political figures of the day, Lord Durham, asking him to investigate the situation and to recommend appropriate measures. The central recommendation of Durham's famous *Report* was that the colonial constitutions be amended so as to replace the principle of separation of powers by the principle of **responsible government**. The fundamental feature of responsible government is that it makes the executive responsible for its actions to a democratically elected legislative body. Instead of choosing as his advisers anyone he liked, the governor would have to choose them from among those who had been democratically elected to the Legislative Assembly. This principle had recently been incorporated into the ever-evolving British regime, and the Canadian rebels of 1837 had demanded that the same step be taken in the colonies. The British government hesitated at first but agreed in 1848 to introduce responsible government first in Nova Scotia and then in the other colonies. By the time of Confederation, then, responsible government was well established as a fundamental principle of Canadian political life.

3.2 The Conventions of Responsible Government

In the British and Canadian regimes, responsible government makes the executive accountable to the House of Commons. This accountability implies firstly that the executive is required to defend its actions in the House. But accountability is meaningless if the House before which the executive defends its actions is unable to do anything about executive actions it finds unacceptable. The principle of responsible government therefore demands of those exercising executive power that they obtain the approval of the House for their use of that power. In this way, responsible government allows for meaningful democratic control of executive power.

The achievement of responsible government requires the adoption of a number of rules, which take the form of constitutional conventions. The **five conventions of responsible government** may be summarized as follows.

1. The *first convention* is that the Crown, which still has formal title to executive power, will act only "on the advice of" its ministers. In other words, it is the ministers themselves who exercise executive power; their "advice" to the Crown is really a command, and the Crown is thus a mere figurehead when it comes to the use of executive power.

2. The *second convention* is that the Crown normally appoints as ministers or advisers only persons who are Members of Parliament (MPs). This rule is intended to facilitate executive accountability: putting the Crown's ministers in the House itself makes them more accessible to other MPs who wish to question or criticize them. A certain amount of flexibility is always shown in the application of this rule. It is generally acceptable to appoint one or two senators as ministers. It is also possible to appoint people who are neither senators nor MPs, as happened in 1996 when Université de Montréal political scientist Stéphane Dion was named Minister of Intergovernmental Affairs. In such cases, however, the persons appointed must take the first possible opportunity to run for a seat in the House of Commons; if they lose that election, they must immediately resign their position as minister.

3. The *third convention* is that the ministers will act together as a team or "ministry," led by a prime minister (or "first" minister), with each minister sharing in the responsibility for all policy decisions made by any member of the ministry. This third rule is known as the convention of **collective responsibility**.

4. The *fourth convention* is that the Crown will appoint and maintain as ministers only people who "have the **confidence** of" (that is, the support of a majority of members of) the House of Commons. Without this rule, responsible government would not necessarily be democratic, for the Crown could appoint a ministry consisting only of MPs from some minor party whose views were representative of only a small minority of the electorate.

5. If the House of Commons expresses a lack of confidence in a ministry (either by adopting an explicit motion of non-confidence or by voting down a proposal that the ministry deems a matter of confidence), responsible government has in a sense broken down, because the executive is no longer acting in a manner that reflects the wishes of a majority of the people's representatives. In order to keep responsible government going, then, either the ministry or the House must be replaced. Therefore the *fifth convention* of responsible government is that when the ministry loses the confidence of the House, the prime minister must either resign (which entails the resignation of the entire ministry) or request new elections. The first of these options clears the way for the formation of a new ministry, one in which the House will have confidence. The second option (elections) will resolve the problem by producing one of two possible results. One is that the voters will take the side of the ministry and return a new contingent of MPs who will be more favourably disposed toward it. (This is what happened in the 2011 election. The Harper ministry had lost a vote of confidence in the House, but in the subsequent election, the voters elected a majority of MPs who supported that ministry. Mr. Harper therefore remained in office.) The other possibility is that the voters will take the side of the House and elect a majority of MPs who do not support the existing ministry. (This is what happened in the election of 1980, when voters elected a House with a strong majority of Liberal members who would not support the Progressive Conservative ministry headed by Prime Minister Joe Clark. Clark, seeing that he would not have the confidence of the House, promptly resigned.)

Taken together, these five conventions create a political order that makes those who exercise executive power fully accountable to the elected representatives of the people and, thus, indirectly accountable to the people themselves. (This relationship is expressed schematically in Figure 3.1.) By law, executive power is invested in the Crown. But the conventions described above modify the law of the Constitution dramatically. Under the principle of responsible government, the Crown must in effect delegate its executive power to a ministry composed of MPs. This ministry (or "cabinet" as it is usually called) must have the confidence (that is, the support of a majority of the members) of the House of

Commons and must resign or face an election if it loses that confidence. In sum, these arrangements provide the kind of democratic accountability sought by the reformers of 1837.

Figure 3.1: Responsible Government

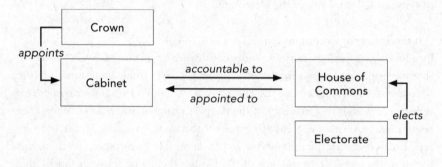

3.3   Responsible Government as "Cabinet Government"

From the description of the principle of responsible government given above, one would likely conclude that the introduction of that principle substantially weakened the cabinet by subordinating it to the control of the House of Commons. This is why responsible government is often referred to as **parliamentary government**. In theory, responsible government makes the House of Commons (the dominant chamber of Parliament) the ultimate authority for both legislative and executive action. In reality, however, the introduction of responsible government actually strengthened the power of the cabinet. It is therefore more accurate to think of responsible government as **cabinet government**.

To understand why, it is essential to grasp that the introduction of responsible government entails a transfer of effective legislative power from the House to the cabinet. We have noted that the cabinet must be composed of MPs who have the confidence of a majority of the members of the House. The cabinet and its supporters in the House are thus by definition in a position to control the legislative activity of that body.

This control becomes especially tight if the members of the House have formed themselves into highly disciplined parties, as has been the case in Canada since the late nineteenth century. For reasons we shall discuss below, modern Canadian parties are able to ensure that almost every member elected to the House will vote as his or her party wishes. In such a situation, the cabinet can count on virtually automatic support from a majority in the House for any measure it proposes. It is thus a natural result of the introduction of responsible government that the cabinet comes to dominate the legislative agenda of the House that supervises it.

In a regime based on responsible government, then, the cabinet becomes the dominant political institution. Under the law of the constitution, it possesses no power of its own, but constitutional convention gives it control of both executive and legislative power. Although constitutional law places legislative and executive powers in separate hands, responsible government leads in practice to a **fusion of powers** in the hands of the cabinet. Indeed, one may say that responsible government is best defined as *a regime in which legislative and executive power are fused together in a cabinet that is accountable to an assembly of the people's elected representatives.*

3.4 Forming a Government

To say that Canada is governed by a cabinet is to imply something very surprising about our regime: we do not elect our government—at least, not directly. Canadians often talk about having "elected" the "Harper government" or the "Chrétien government," but in this they are mistaken. In a regime based on the principle of responsible government, the people's role in the selection of their government is an indirect one.

This is no accident. The principle of responsible government is inconsistent with the notion of a directly elected executive. We have seen that at the core of responsible government is the idea that the government must be accountable to the House of Commons. Having the people elect the government directly would necessarily make the government accountable to the people as well. As the old proverb teaches, however, no one can serve two masters because the two masters may demand contradictory things. What if the voters were to elect a Conservative government pledged to free trade and a House of Commons dominated by Liberal and New Democratic Party (NDP) members who were opposed to it? The government would either have to drop its free trade policy (thereby repudiating its accountability to the voters) or it would have to introduce free trade by executive decree (thereby repudiating responsible government).

In responsible government, then, we do not directly elect our government. It is more accurate to speak of the "formation" of a government. This is a complex process in which the Crown, the prime minister, and the House of Commons work together to provide Canadians with a government that has the confidence of the elected representatives of the people. One may summarize this process in **four conventions for the formation of a government**, some of which overlap with those described in 3.2 above.

1. The first convention is that the ultimate responsibility for choosing the government must rest with the Crown. In practice, this means that the Crown will select a prime minister, who will in turn nominate the other members of the government. There are good reasons for this rule. To begin, the Crown is uniquely suited for choosing the government. For obvious reasons, the government cannot choose itself: in that case, every member of Parliament might proclaim himself or herself the head of a new government. It would be workable (though perhaps cumbersome) to leave the choice of government in the hands of the House of Commons, but this would be inconsistent with certain aspects of our regime. It will be recalled that, formally speaking, the ministers who compose the government are merely advising the Crown on the use of the Crown's powers. The Crown must, therefore, have a formal role in the appointment of its own advisers.

2. The second convention for forming a government is that in appointing a prime minister, the Crown must choose the person who is most likely to have the confidence of the House of Commons. This rule is obviously necessary for the functioning of responsible government, the regime in which the executive is accountable to the legislature. It also brings a democratic element into the process by ensuring that the person who heads the government and chooses its other members has the support of a majority of the elected representatives of the people.

3. The third convention for forming a government is that the government remains in power until the prime minister resigns on its behalf.

4. The fourth convention is that the prime minister must resign if his or her government has lost the confidence of the House of Commons and has no prospect of winning the confidence of a newly elected House. These rules may seem complicated, but working through a couple of historical examples will make them easier to understand.

At the beginning of 1993, Brian Mulroney was Canada's prime minister. He was the leader of the Progressive Conservative Party (the PCs), which held a substantial majority of the seats in the House of Commons. Mulroney decided to retire from politics. The PCs called a leadership convention at which Kim Campbell was chosen to succeed him as party leader. The Governor General, Ramon Hnatyshyn, then had no difficulty deciding whom to appoint as the new prime minister. The PCs still controlled a majority of the seats in the House of Commons, Campbell was their leader, and therefore Campbell would obviously be able to form a government that would command the confidence of the House.

In October 1993, a parliamentary election was held. In that election, Campbell was defeated in her own constituency, and her party lost all its seats but two. Technically, she was still the prime minister, because governments remain in office until the prime minister resigns. Yet it was obvious to Campbell that when the new House convened, it would not have confidence in her government. It was equally obvious that Liberal leader Jean Chrétien would be able to command the confidence of the House of Commons. Consequently, within a few days of the election, Campbell resigned.

It is important to appreciate that this was a resignation, not a firing. As the elections of 1957 and 1972 illustrate, it is the prime minister, and not the voters, who decides the future of his or her government. As a result of the 1957 election, Louis St. Laurent's Liberals no longer had a majority of seats in the House of Commons and actually had seven fewer seats than the PCs. St. Laurent might have tried to govern by cultivating the support of one or more of the other parties, but he interpreted the results of the election to mean that the voters were not happy with his government and suspected that he would not have the confidence of the House. He therefore resigned. The Governor General then invited John Diefenbaker, the PC leader, to form a new government. From 1968 to 1972, Pierre Trudeau's Liberal Party held well over half of the seats in the House of Commons. In the election of 1972, the Liberals won fewer than half the seats, only two more than their main rivals, the PCs. Trudeau suspected that the not insignificant block of members elected for the NDP would prefer his government to the PC alternative, and he knew that this would give him enough votes to command the confidence of the House. He therefore chose not to resign. It is important to note that Trudeau could have made exactly the same decision had he won two fewer seats than the Conservatives instead of two more. The crucial question is not which party leader has the most seats but which party leader has the confidence of the House of Commons.

What these examples demonstrate is that the process of forming a government is more complex than it appears. Canadians like to think that they elected a Chrétien government or a Harper government; in fact, however, they elect members of the House of Commons. Because no ministry may govern without the confidence of the House, the choices made by the voters have an important, and usually decisive, influence on the formation of government. Yet that influence is not always decisive. After the 1993 election, it was obvious that Kim Campbell would have to step down, and it was equally obvious that the new prime minister would have to be Jean Chrétien. As the elections of 1957 and 1972 demonstrate, however, when the voters give no party a clear-cut majority in the House, the prime minister may have the decisive first move in determining who will form the government. Alternatively, if several opposition parties with a majority of seats between them publicly agree to a **coalition**—a formal sharing of the cabinet—the Governor General would have to appoint as prime minister the person they had designated as the leader of the coalition. In this case—which is essentially what happened in the Ontario election of 1985[1]—the decisive role was played by the opposition parties, not by the prime minister. Finally, should Canadians ever elect a House in which three or four parties have roughly equal strength, the choice of the new prime minister (should the incumbent resign) might well require the exercise of some discretion by the Governor General. Such a situation has not yet occurred, but it becomes a more realistic possibility in periods like the past decade: none of the major national parties could gain a majority, and a major regional party (the Bloc Québécois) had a large number of seats.

Canadians' understanding of how governments are formed was put to the test in late 2008. Six weeks after the 2008 election, the minority Conservative government delivered a "fiscal update" to Parliament that was unacceptable to the three opposition parties. The Liberal leader Stéphane Dion, the NDP leader Jack Layton, and the Bloc leader Gilles Duceppe announced that they intended to defeat the government in the House by passing a motion of non-confidence. They also announced that the Liberals and the NDP had agreed to then replace the Conservatives with a coalition government. In this case, the Liberals and the NDP had agreed that Mr. Dion would serve as the prime minister of the proposed coalition and that the Liberals and the NDP would share the seats in cabinet based on the number of seats each of them had in the House. The Bloc would not participate in the government but Mr. Duceppe pledged to support it for at least 18 months provided that his party was consulted on all matters affecting the interests of Québec. (The Bloc's support was critical because the Liberals and NDP did not have enough seats between them to command a majority of votes in the House.) Mr. Harper denounced the proposed coalition as a *"coup d'état,"* insisting that he had won the election because he had the most seats and that the coalition could not legitimately take power until it had won a mandate from the people in an election. While a large majority of Canadians were opposed to the proposed coalition, Mr. Harper was surely wrong to claim that Canadians had elected him prime minister and that the coalition had no right to take office. Strictly speaking, the only Canadians who voted for Mr. Harper were the people in Calgary Southwest, who elected him as their MP. Moreover, winning the most seats in the House does not give a party a mandate to form the

---

1   In that election, the ruling PC party won the most seats, but not a majority. The NDP formally supported the Liberal Party, and the Liberals subsequently formed the new government.

government and does not make its leader prime minister. The only legitimate prime minister in our regime is the person who commands the confidence of the House of Commons.

3.5 Majority and Minority Government

In a political order based on the principle of responsible government, the ministry which takes office is said to have either a **majority government** or a **minority government**. The term "majority government" refers to a situation in which the party that forms the government possesses over half the seats in the House of Commons. Because party organizations are able to exercise a high degree of control over the way their members vote, a cabinet backed by a parliamentary majority is almost guaranteed the automatic confidence of the House. This does not mean that such a ministry can do whatever it likes: the cabinet will back away from any measure that is resolutely opposed by its parliamentary "caucus" (the group of MPs who are members of that party) whose votes are essential for sustaining the House's confidence in the government. But a majority government that has the support of its caucus can govern as it sees fit.

The term "minority government" refers to a situation in which no single party possesses a majority of the seats in the House of Commons. In such a situation, the government must be formed by some party that controls less than half the seats. In the 1963 election, for example, 265 members were elected: 129 of these were members of the Liberal Party, 95 were PCs, 17 were members of the NDP, and 24 were members of the Social Credit Party. Obviously, no party had a majority of seats. The PC prime minister, John Diefenbaker, did not expect that his government would maintain the confidence of the House, and he therefore resigned. The Governor General called on the leader of the Liberals, Lester Pearson, to form a government. Pearson's party did not have enough seats to control the House of Commons. Under the rules of responsible government, however, it is sufficient if a government is able to command the confidence of the House. Pearson knew that he would be able to win and maintain that confidence as long as he adopted policies that would either find favour with, or not be opposed by, the members of one of the two smaller parties. In this, he was quite successful: his Liberal government remained in office for two terms totalling five years, despite the fact that it never had a majority of seats in the House. More recently, Prime Minister Harper duplicated this feat before winning a majority in 2011.

In Canada, it has been more common to have majority rather than minority governments, but minority governments are not rare: since 1867, there have been 12 of them, including the minority Conservative government that emerged from the general election in 2008. Not all of these governments have been as stable as Pearson's or Harper's. Arthur Meighen's minority government lasted a mere three months in 1921 before the House declared a lack of confidence in it. In 1979, Joe Clark formed a minority government for the PCs, yet announced that he would govern as if he had a majority. By this he meant that, unlike Pearson, he would not attempt to tailor his policies to maintain the confidence of the House. This rather bold stance cost Clark dearly: his government lost the confidence of the House after eight months in office, and a new election was held. In that election the Liberals won a majority of seats in the House, and Clark was therefore compelled to resign.

It is worth noting, however, that Clark's government fell only because both the PCs and the Liberals believed that a new election would be in their interest. The PCs thought they had momentum on their side. The Liberals, on the other hand, thought that the electorate had merely wanted to give them a spanking in 1979 and would now prefer to have them back. As both parties hoped to improve their fortunes through a new general election, Clark's government was unlikely to last very long. Often, however, the situation is just the reverse. Minority governments draw a certain amount of strength from the fact that it is rarely in the interests of everyone to fight another election campaign. For one thing, campaigns are quite expensive. Moreover, individual MPs who have just been elected are in many cases nervous about going back to the polls: why risk the seat they have just worked so hard to win? Most importantly, though, the defeat of a minority government requires the collaboration of at least two opposition parties who can combine for a majority of votes in the House. Are there likely to be two opposition parties with good reason to believe that they will come out of fresh elections with more seats than they currently have? Not often. After the election of 2006, Stephen Harper led a Conservative minority government that for a time operated with the self-confidence of a majority government. Mr. Harper realized that the Liberals were at that time afraid of an election due to a lack of money and an unpopular leader. He was therefore certain that the Liberals would not join the other opposition parties in voting against the government and forcing new elections. Consequently, Mr. Harper brought forward a number of pieces of legislation that the Liberals did not like but could not afford to oppose, and their failure to vote against those measures simply added to the general perception that they were weak and indecisive.

In reality, minority government creates a fascinating game of political cat-and-mouse. A government that wishes to stay in power has to try to keep the opposition divided. It typically does so by introducing measures that it hopes at least one of the major opposition parties cannot possibly disagree with. For instance, after the Liberals, the NDP, and the Bloc made it clear that they were ready to vote the Conservative government out and replace it with a coalition in the late fall of 2008, Mr. Harper suddenly reversed his aggressive tactics; the budget introduced in January 2009 was designed to look as much as possible like a Liberal budget so as to ensure that the Liberal Party would support it and leave Mr. Harper in office. On the other hand, when a minority government feels that public support is swinging behind it, it may try to introduce legislation that the opposition parties cannot possibly agree with. Why? This way, the government not only gets the election it would like, but it can blame the opposition for "forcing" the country to go through an election the government will surely present as wasteful, bothersome, and unnecessary!

There is a general (though not universal) opinion in Canada that majority government is better than minority government. The superiority of majority government is said to rest on its greater stability, longevity, and vigour. But this opinion is open to debate; certainly, many Canadians welcomed a return to minority government in 2004 after 24 years of majority government. Moreover, as the examples cited above suggest, minority government is not necessarily unstable and short-lived. In the right circumstances, and with appropriate leadership, minority governments can last as long as majority governments. Concerning the relative vigour of minority and majority governments, one should consider the arguments made by the distinguished constitutional specialist Eugene Forsey. Forsey notes that sometimes a government backed by an absolute majority of seats may vigorously ride off in the wrong direction. Conversely, minority governments are often compelled by their need for support from outside their own party to govern in a more moderate and less arrogant fashion.[2] In sum, it is probably wrong-headed to ask which form is superior, minority or majority. It is more sensible to recognize that each has potential advantages and disadvantages, and that circumstances and personalities will do much to determine which form is more desirable in a given situation.

3.6 Institutional Implications of Responsible Government

As was mentioned in the first chapter of this book, we have chosen the term "regime" to emphasize the extent to which political rules and institutions form a complex web with an internal logic of its own. Nowhere is this more evident than when one considers the principle of responsible government. For the most

---

2   Eugene Forsey, "The Problem of 'Minority' Government in Canada," *The Canadian Journal of Economics and Political Science* 30, 1 (February 1964): 1–11.

part, our arrangements with respect to legislative and executive power are highly complex—certainly much more complex than the relatively straightforward arrangements to be found in the Constitution of the United States. Canadians often wonder why we don't jettison some of our quaint practices and institutions and adopt American alternatives instead. The difficulty, of course, is that the logic of responsible government will not easily permit it.

It is essential to appreciate that these two quite different constitutional principles—responsible government and separation of powers—each has its own internal logic, a logic that will then determine many of the regime's institutional features. The decision to adopt responsible government as a fundamental principle will, by the internal logic of the principle, necessitate certain institutional arrangements and rule out others. The same would be true if one opted for the principle of the separation of powers. To demonstrate this point, let us explore a few of the key institutional differences between Canada's regime and that of the United States: elections, cabinet appointments, head of state, and party discipline.

1. *The timing of elections.* In the United States, the principle of separation of powers implies that each "branch" of government is elected separately. Congress is chosen by the people in one set of elections; the president is chosen by the people in a separate election. Each branch thus has its own mandate, and neither depends on the confidence of the other for its legitimacy; even if the Congress believes the president is doing a terrible job, the president will remain in office for four full years because the presidential election gives him a four-year mandate. Because the term of office is fixed by the Constitution (two years for the House of Representatives, four years for the presidency, and six years for the Senate), elections in the United States are held at fixed, predictable intervals. President Barack Obama was elected on the first Tuesday of November in 2008. We know that the next American presidential elections will be held on the Tuesday after the first Monday of November in 2012, 2016, 2020, and so on.

In a regime based on the principle of responsible government, the fundamental logic of the regime makes such an orderly predictable schedule difficult, to say the least. In Canada, the timing of parliamentary elections is normally decided by the prime minister. Strictly speaking, it is the Crown (that is, the Governor General) that dissolves Parliament and calls elections, but the decision to do so is made on the basis of "advice" tendered by the prime minister, advice that is almost always followed. There is one fixed rule governing the prime minister's choice of election date: Section 4(1) of *CA 1982* specifies that the interval between elections may not exceed five years. In the Canadian tradition of responsible government, the prime minister traditionally looks to call new elections after four years.

Of course, leaving the timing of the elections to the prime minister gives him or her a significant partisan advantage over the opposition. The prime minister will typically call elections when the polls are most favourable for his or her own party, or perhaps when the main opposition party is in disarray. Jean Chrétien twice called elections (1997 and 2000) after less than three and a half years in office, primarily because opinion polls indicated that early elections would work to his advantage. Each time, Chrétien's decision led to (somewhat predictable) calls to change Canada's electoral practice in this respect and to adopt the American practice of holding elections at fixed intervals. There is little doubt that moving to fixed election dates would be more equitable. The problem, however, is that the practice of fixed election dates is not fully compatible with the principle of responsible government. Under responsible government, the prime minister and cabinet are not directly elected by the people (as is the American president) and therefore have no direct mandate of their own. Their democratic legitimacy thus depends entirely on their capacity to maintain the confidence of the House of Commons. Because a ministry can, in principle, lose that confidence at any time (especially if no party commands a majority in the House), it is essential to be able to hold elections at any time; as we have seen, holding new elections is sometimes the only way to resolve the impasse that results when the House and the ministry are in disagreement. The existence of a floating or non-fixed election date is thus an inescapable consequence of the logic of responsible government.[3]

The problem with fixed election dates was beautifully illustrated in 2008. Mr. Harper's government passed legislation stipulating that elections were to be held in the third week of October of every fourth year. However, the legislation had to make allowance for the need to call elections at other times should a minority government lose the confidence of the House. Mr. Harper exploited this loophole late in the summer of 2008. Sensing that his party would find it advantageous to hold a general election that year (though one was not scheduled until October of 2009), Mr. Harper tried to manoeuvre the opposition into defeating him. When the opposition would not take the bait, Mr. Harper simply declared that he thought Parliament had become "dysfunctional" and therefore asked the

---

3   The problems of setting fixed election dates with a parliamentary system based on the confidence convention were articulated in an essay by Canada's great constitutionalist Eugene Forsey in 1966: "Fixed Dates for Election?," reprinted in *Freedom and Order: Collected Essays* (Toronto: McClelland and Stewart, 1974). The interesting question is why Canadians feel compelled to legislate fixed election dates. There is nothing that prevents any particular government from committing itself to setting an election date, whether in the press or in a throne speech.

Governor General to dissolve Parliament and call an election. Some commentators called on the Governor General to refuse this request, but she was surely right to grant it: the request was perfectly legal. Yet Mr. Harper's action was just as surely a violation of the spirit of his own law insofar as the rationale for the law was to prevent prime ministers from setting election dates based on partisan advantage.

2. *Cabinet appointments.* A second important institutional difference between Canada and the United States is the selection of cabinet ministers (or cabinet secretaries, as they are called in the United States). Here the practice in one country is almost the exact opposite of what is done across the border. An American president may choose for his cabinet virtually any citizen of the United States; the only restriction is that if he selects a member of Congress, that person must resign his or her congressional seat. This flexibility allows presidents to seek out the most talented people in the nation to run the government. John F. Kennedy, for instance, plucked Robert McNamara from the presidency of the Ford Motor Company to be his Secretary of Defense. Richard Nixon reached out to Harvard University to bring to Washington the famous international relations expert, Dr. Henry Kissinger, as his Secretary of State. More recently, George W. Bush, during his first term, chose retired General Colin Powell to be his Secretary of State, and Barack Obama chose Timothy Geithner, president of the Federal Reserve Bank of New York, as his Treasury Secretary. In Canada, on the other hand, a prime minister looking for cabinet material is essentially restricted to the membership of the House of Commons; other Canadians might be appointed to cabinet temporarily but may not stay unless they are able to get themselves elected quickly to a vacant seat in the House. A Canadian prime minister's choice of cabinet ministers is thus restricted to a very small group of people, few of whom have meaningful technical expertise in the area for which they will be responsible.

Here, too, the difference between the two regimes is a direct consequence of the difference between the principles of separation of powers and responsible government. The Constitution of the United States bars members of Congress from holding cabinet posts precisely because its underlying objective is to have the two branches of government "check and balance" each other as a means of protecting liberty. In Canada, on the other hand, it is the logic of responsible government that requires us to restrict a prime minister's choice of cabinet ministers to members of the House of Commons. Because the prime minister and cabinet are not directly elected to their positions by the people, their democratic legitimacy depends on their capacity to maintain the confidence of the House of Commons. If the prime minister and cabinet were not themselves members of the House, it is hard to imagine how the House would be in a position to hold them accountable for their actions and to determine whether they deserve its continued confidence.

3. *Head of government and head of state.* Another noteworthy difference between the two regimes is that the Canadian regime draws a distinction between the "**head of government**" (the prime minister) and the "formal **head of state**" (the Queen). No such distinction exists in the United States, where the president fulfills both roles. Why this difference? Once again, the crucial point is the difference between the logic of responsible government and the logic of separation of powers. In a regime based on the principle of responsible government, democratic legitimacy depends on our capacity to maintain agreement between the House and the government to ensure that we always have a government that commands the confidence of the House of Commons. Yet such agreement does not arise on its own; someone must actively intervene to ensure that a ministry that has lost the confidence of the House steps down and that a new ministry more likely to have the confidence of the House will take its place. In the Canadian version of responsible government, that official is the Governor General (who represents the Queen). As the official whose job it is to keep the system of responsible government running, the Governor General is, in effect, responsible for the regime; and that is why, logically, the prime minister cannot serve as Canada's formal head of state. In the United States, on the other hand, there is no office corresponding to our Governor General because, in a regime based on separation of powers, democratic legitimacy is maintained automatically by the system itself. Each branch of government is elected by the people for a fixed period of time and thus has its own democratic mandate. No one is required to oversee the system or to intervene to ensure that one branch has confidence in the other.

4. *Party discipline.* One final illustration of our general point is the matter of **party discipline**. Party discipline in Canada is quite strong—so strong that it is common for Canadians to complain that their MPs, who almost always vote the party line in the House of Commons, are "little better than trained seals." In the United States, by contrast, members of both the Senate and the House of Representatives are freer to vote as they wish, and it is not unusual for them to vote against the position favoured by their own party. This is a practice many Canadians would like to see adopted in this country.

The difficulty, however, is that here, too, the different approach of the two countries is to a large extent determined by the basic difference in their fundamental principles. The United States can afford to have weaker party discipline because under separation of powers the president's mandate does not depend on the support of Congress. The president has a direct mandate from the people and can legitimately remain in office even if Congress consistently votes against his program. There is thus no pressing reason for members of Congress to follow their party line. In Canada, on the other hand, the internal logic of responsible government makes necessary a relatively strict form of party discipline. Because the prime minister and cabinet are not directly elected by the people, their democratic legitimacy depends entirely on the continued confidence of the House of Commons. If members of the party in power do not stick together in support of the ministry, the ministry will not have the confidence of the House, thereby losing its only title to rule. Unless Canadians are willing to see their governments change on a semi-annual basis, they have to accept that responsible government will of necessity require a high level of party discipline.

As these examples illustrate, when contemplating reforms to our political institutions and practices, it is essential to consider very carefully whether specific proposals for change are consistent with the internal logic of responsible government. The fact that certain practices work well in the United States does not mean that they will work here. A political regime is somewhat like an ecosystem. Species from one ecosystem may not be able to adapt to another. Or they may be able to adapt, provided certain adjustments are made. Of course, the introduction of a new plant or animal species to a particular ecosystem may have unintended (and undesirable) side effects as well. Our point, then, is not that change is undesirable or impossible; rather, it is that advocates of reform need to reflect very carefully on whether—and to what extent—practices imported from other regimes are consistent with the internal logic of responsible government.

3.7 Responsible Government and Separation of Powers Compared

The principle of responsible government is of British origin, but it now forms the cornerstone of many, if not most, liberal democratic regimes. In one way or another, all the nations of Western Europe, as well as most members of the British Commonwealth, subscribe to the principle that the executive must be responsible for its actions to a legislative body consisting of the elected representatives of the people. In almost all of the world's other liberal democratic regimes, the most influential constitutional model has been the United States rather than Britain. (This is especially true in Latin America.) One may thus think of responsible government and separation of powers as the two great alternative principles for the formation of a liberal democratic regime.

As we have noted, the political objective that inspires the principle of separation of powers is liberty. Montesquieu and Locke argued for a separation of powers on the grounds that placing legislative and executive power in different hands would minimize the chances of the government becoming tyrannical. What they argued for in theory seems to be validated by the experience of the United States. In that country, even when the legislative and executive branches of government are held by members of the same political party, the relationship between them is often one of rivalry rather than collusion. It is thus very difficult to imagine the two branches cooperating for anti-democratic purposes. Indeed, the rivalry between the two is so strong that it typically becomes a problem. In 1993, for example, the government of the United States came to a standstill when the president and the Congress (both in the hands of the Democratic Party) could not agree on a budget. A series of similar crises occurred in 2011. One may thus say that the price of liberty in regimes based on the separation of powers is a substantial inefficiency in government.

In contrast, regimes based on the principle of responsible government are remarkable for their efficiency, particularly during majority governments. Because of the fusion of powers, the same small group exercises both legislative and executive power. In such regimes, standstills of the sort seen in the United States simply do not take place. Once a cabinet backed by a parliamentary majority decides what it wants to do, there is almost nothing to stand in its way. When the Pearson cabinet decided to introduce universal medical insurance in Canada, the adoption and implementation of the policy followed quickly and smoothly. This is in striking contrast to the United States. Though most Americans agree that action is needed to extend coverage of medical insurance, former President Clinton's initiatives on that issue were stalled and then blocked by Congress, which favoured different policies. President Obama reintroduced the issue and has had more success in getting the legislation through, although many are still opposed to his reforms.

Yet, some people would argue that the efficiency of responsible government is purchased at the price of a certain loss of political liberty. Because it is difficult to stop a cabinet that has a solid majority supporting it in the House of Commons, it is sometimes said that responsible government amounts to a four-year elected dictatorship. Critics of our regime will point to the introduction of the highly unpopular Goods and Services Tax (GST) as an example of the way in which Canadian governments can introduce and impose policies that lack public support. It is probably safe to speculate that the separation of powers in the Constitution of the United States would make it far more difficult for politicians to introduce a similar tax in that country.

Nevertheless, it would be an exaggeration to suggest that responsible government equals an elected dictatorship. In the first place, it should not be forgotten that all governments seek re-election. Since no government will be re-elected if it consistently or conspicuously ignores public opinion, those in power will have great incentives to behave democratically. Secondly, one must keep in mind that the activity of the government is subject to the authority of the constitution, especially the Charter of Rights and Freedoms. Finally, in responsible government, there is an important political check on the power of the cabinet: the presence of an institutionalized parliamentary opposition. As we shall see in Chapter 7, the House of Commons, to which the cabinet is responsible, affords those who oppose government policy a wide range of opportunities to question and attack the government, opportunities that do not exist in a regime like that of the United States. One can thus plausibly argue that the cabinet's accountability to the House of Commons makes responsible government as favourable to liberty as does a regime based on the separation of powers.

There is, of course, a more general issue of accountability to be considered, and that is accountability to the voters. In certain respects, democratic accountability appears to be stronger under separation of powers. The leading executive and legislative officers are directly elected by the people under separation of powers, while only the legislative officers are directly elected in responsible government. Moreover, under separation of powers, legislative officers can respond more directly to the wishes of their constituents since they are not restricted by party discipline. In responsible government, when MPs have to choose between voting in support of their party and voting in response to the wishes of their constituents, they will almost always take the side of their party.

On the other hand, responsible government offers substantially greater accountability in that it is much easier for the voters to judge the performance of their elected servants. Under separation of powers, it is often difficult to know who is responsible for the state of the nation's affairs. When the economy is doing well, for example, both the president and the Congress will take credit for it. On the other hand, when the economy is doing poorly (or when there is a crisis over the budget, Medicare, or some other issue), the president and the Congress will each insist that everything is the fault of the other branch. The voter has a difficult time evaluating office-holders because it is frequently difficult to know who was responsible for what. In responsible government one always knows exactly who deserves praise or blame for the state of things. Because responsible government fuses legislative and executive power in the hands of the prime minister and cabinet, there is no debate over who to praise or blame for specific situations. American President Harry Truman was famous for having a sign on his desk that said "The Buck Stops Here." Such a sign would be far more appropriate on the desk of a prime minister, since a president has relatively little control over the nation's legislative activity while a prime minister controls it almost completely.

Accountability to the voters is in this sense much greater in regimes based on responsible government than in regimes based on separation of powers.

In a simple, abstract comparison, then, a strong case can be made that responsible government is a superior choice to separation of powers. This case is especially compelling in the twenty-first century, when people are generally less inclined to worry about government tyranny than were the American Founding Fathers and more inclined to expect government to intervene effectively in economic and social life. This probably explains why one regularly sees influential figures in the United States advocating reforms that would move the American regime in the direction of responsible government. Yet, politics does not take place in a vacuum, and abstractions that do not take proper account of context can be very dangerous. The attractions of responsible government may not be equally compelling in all situations. One variable that has a considerable impact on the debate over the relative merits of responsible government and separation of powers is federalism. As we shall see in the next chapter, responsible government is substantially inferior to separation of powers with respect to the capacity to manage the tensions that arise in countries that decided to embrace the principle of federalism.

Key Terms

separation of powers	four conventions for the formation of a government
responsible government	coalition
five conventions of responsible government	majority government
collective responsibility	minority government
confidence	head of government
parliamentary government	head of state
cabinet government	party discipline
fusion of powers	

Discussion Questions

1. Since 1993, Canada has had four majority governments and three minority governments. Which of the two do you think provides better government?

2. Which system of government is more democratic: responsible government or separation of powers?

4.1   What is Federalism?

4.2   Why a Federal Union?

4.3   The Original Design of the Federal Union

4.4   The Historical Development of Federalism in Canada

4.5   Financing Government and Federal-Provincial Relations

4.6   The Challenge of Canadian Federalism

4.7   Current Controversies: The Pressure to Decentralize

The preamble to *CA 1867* indicates that the Dominion of Canada is to have "a Constitution similar in Principle to that of the United Kingdom." We have seen, in Chapter 3, that this phrase is primarily a reference to Canada's adoption of the British tradition of responsible government. Yet the British constitution was not the only model for the Fathers of Confederation. Their new dominion was to be a *federal* union, although the principle of federalism was utterly foreign to the British constitution. In developing the federal aspect of the Canadian regime, then, the Fathers of Confederation had to look south of the border to see what could be learned from the Constitution of the United States, the blueprint of the first great modern federal regime. It is thus through federalism that American constitutional practice first enters the Canadian regime.

4.1 What is Federalism?

In order to understand what federalism is, we must first understand the distinction between **unitary** and **federal** systems of government. As the name suggests, a unitary system of government is a system in which all sovereign authority of that nation-state resides in one governing body—the national government. That national government may delegate some of its authority to lower levels of government, such as the governments of counties, towns, cities, or administrative districts. But the national government decides how much power it will delegate— it gives the power, and it can always take that power away. In a unitary system, there may be other governments besides the national government, but they will always be simply the servants of the national government. The country has one sovereign government.

Modern federalism is a relatively recent phenomenon, invented by the American founders in 1787 when they designed the Constitution of the United States. Canada, Australia, India, Switzerland, and Germany are examples of countries that have used some version of the federal principle to organize their governments. They stand in contrast to countries such as the United Kingdom, France, the Republic of Ireland, Sweden, and Japan—all of which have unitary systems of government.

In a federal system of government, authority is constitutionally divided between two levels of government. This means that neither level of government can be understood to have sovereign authority. Each receives its authority from the constitution and is thus subordinate to it. The constitution gives legal jurisdiction over matters of national concern to the national government and legal jurisdiction over matters of local or regional concern to the provincial or state governments. In some instances, the two levels of government may share jurisdiction. The point of fundamental importance is that in a federal system, the provincial or state governments are not beholden to the national government in the way that local governments are beholden in a unitary system. In a unitary system, authority flows from the centre out; in a federal system, authority is constitutionally divided.

In Canada, we commonly speak of **three levels of government**: national, provincial, and municipal. The national government is also referred to as the federal government because it is the government of the whole federal union. Each level of government has jurisdiction over legally specified matters and hence carries on the business of government concerning different, albeit often related, matters. It is important to understand that the relationship between the federal and provincial governments is not the same as that between the provincial and municipal governments. Municipal governments fall within the jurisdiction of the provincial governments, which can alter, reorganize, or abolish them.[1] They are subordinate to their respective provincial government. But the provincial governments are not subordinates of the federal government any more than the federal government is subordinate to the provinces. Both are equally subordinate to the Constitution.

This equal subordination is made clear in the Constitution itself. *CA 1982* contains a complex amending formula, which works on the basic principle that the provinces and the federal government must agree on changes to the federal division of powers. In this respect, federalism can be understood as a contract between two levels of government. Neither party can change the terms of the contract on its own.

4.2 Why a Federal Union?

In order to understand why the Fathers of Confederation opted for a federal union, we must consider the political situation that confronted the founders of the country in the 1860s. British North America consisted of six colonies—British Columbia, New Brunswick, Nova Scotia, Prince Edward Island, Newfoundland, and the Province of Canada (now Ontario and Québec). It also included a vast expanse of territory under the charter of the Hudson's Bay Company. Each of the six colonies had its own colonial government. The government of the Province of Canada was a massive failure, as the divisions that existed between the French and English colonists made it unworkable. Politicians from the Province of Canada were thus eager, if not desperate, to reform the system of government.

The scheme that seemed most logical was to unite the British colonies within North America under one government. This would have numerous advantages. First, the new government would break the deadlock that existed between the French and English in Canada by tilting the balance of power in favour of the English-speaking colonists. Second, the new Dominion government could provide for a coordinated plan of economic development of railways, canals, and roads. Third, it could provide greater security for the small colonies, who were concerned about American imperial designs on the unsettled parts of North America. Fourth, it would help to relieve the burden on Britain of providing

---

[1]   A parallel relationship exists between the federal government and the three "territorial" governments in Canada's north. In those parts of Canada not under control of a province, the federal government has a free hand to establish territorial boundaries and territorial governments as it wishes.

troops and personnel to administer the colonies; furthermore, the British believed that the time had come for Canada to begin to stand on its own. Finally, it would make expansion into the western part of North America easier. The intention to include British Columbia in Confederation was there from the start. Linking the western colony with the rest of Canada would ensure that the United States would not be able to expand northward.

Those seeking union faced immense political obstacles. The English-speaking colonists in central Canada were enthusiastically in favour of a "legislative union" (a unitary system) rather than a federal union. But a legislative union was not a realistic political option. The French-speaking colonists in Lower Canada would never have agreed to a unitary system in which they would be a minority. They had to have their own provincial government, which would have jurisdiction over those matters relating to their preservation as a people. And the Maritime colonies were similarly ill-disposed toward a legislative union. They were among the oldest British colonies, and their governments were long established. They were not inclined to see their interests submerged as they became a small minority in a large Dominion dominated by central Canada. Thus, from the very beginning, Canada was confronted with two serious political divisions: the split between French and English; and a division between the centre and the periphery.

The obvious solution to the objections of the French Canadians and the Maritimers was the creation of a federal union. Yet, for a number of good reasons, Canadians were reluctant to organize the government on the federal principle. First, federalism was perceived to have failed in the United States. That country had just emerged from one of the worst civil wars in human history, a war fought in order to preserve the United States as one country without slavery. The Southern states had argued that every state had the right to decide for itself whether it should be a slave state or a free state. Federalism and the doctrine of states' rights were thus associated with war and slavery. Moreover, it was often argued that federalism had created a divided system of government and that the weakness of the national government in Washington was one of the main causes of the war. Given the obvious problems that plagued our federal neighbour to the south, it is easy to see why Canadians would have been less than enthusiastic about federalism.

The second objection to federalism was that it would create two levels of government and hence be more costly than unitary government. The colonies in British North America could not easily afford one level of government, let alone two. Moreover, it was suggested that federalism would be a weaker regime. Who would speak for Canadians? Under a unitary system, the people of the country could speak with one voice. But federalism would mean that each Canadian would be the citizen of both a country and a province, and it was easy to foresee that this would create divided loyalties. The challenge for the Fathers of Confederation, then, was to find a form of federalism that would minimize the perceived defects of federal unions and yet meet the objections of those colonists who opposed a unitary system.

4.3   The Original Design of the Federal Union

The Fathers of Confederation believed that the federal arrangements agreed to at the Québec Conference of 1864 constituted a workable solution to their problem. The key was the creation of a federal system in which the federal government would have a clear preponderance of power. A brief examination of some of the essential sections of *CA 1867* will make that preponderance obvious.

The first point to notice is those sections of the Constitution that outline the division of powers between the two levels of government. Sir John A. Macdonald argued that the Fathers of Confederation had given "all the great subjects of legislation" to the federal Parliament. A comparison of **Section 91** (which establishes the exclusive legislative jurisdictions of the federal government) and **Section 92** (which establishes those of the provinces) shows that Macdonald was indeed correct.

Unlike the Constitution of the United States, which restricted Washington to the regulation of international and inter-state commerce (as well as commerce with the "Indians"), Section 91.2 grants to the federal Parliament exclusive jurisdiction over trade and commerce. This was intended to provide a constitutional basis for putting the general management of the economy in Ottawa's hands. Section 91.27 gives the federal government exclusive control over the important matter of criminal law, a jurisdiction that had been reserved for the individual states in the American Constitution. Section 91.3 makes Ottawa the financial powerhouse of Confederation, granting it the right to any form of taxation. Finally, Section 91 appears to place the **residual power** in the hands of the federal government; anything not specifically reserved for the provinces is to be part of a general federal power to legislate for the "peace, order, and good government of Canada."

In comparison, the powers of the provincial governments appear paltry. The legislatures of the provinces are to have jurisdiction over "all matters of a strictly local or private nature in the province" (92.16). This includes such mundane items as hospitals and charities (92.7), local works (92.10), property and civil rights (92.13), and municipal institutions (92.8). Significantly, the provinces' powers to raise revenue are limited to two modest sources: "direct taxation" (92.3), which was relatively unimportant in 1867, and "shop, saloon, tavern, auctioneer and other licenses" (92.9).

The pre-eminence of the federal government was evident in a number of other provisions of *CA 1867*. Section 58 provides that the representative of the Crown for each of the provincial governments—the lieutenant-governor—is to be appointed by Ottawa. The lieutenant-governors are given the right to reserve provincial legislation, that is, to withhold royal assent, so as to give the federal government a chance to examine it. Under Section 56, Ottawa is granted the power of **disallowance,** by which means the federal government can annul provincial legislation of which it disapproves. These powers of **reservation** and disallowance actually make the provincial governments subordinate to the federal government in a certain sense. Since true federalism rests on the principle that the two levels of government are equally sovereign in their own jurisdictions, it has been said that *CA 1867* establishes not a federal system, but a quasi-federal system, in which the federal government is the dominant partner.[2]

4.4 The Historical Development of Federalism in Canada

Although the Fathers of Confederation intended to create a highly **centralized** federal union—one in which the federal government would dominate—Canada now has one of the most **decentralized** federal unions in the world. This may sound confusing, but one must remember that federal systems, like the constitutions that describe them, are not rigid; they evolve over time in response to a number of factors.

We saw in Chapter 2 that the meaning of a constitution will depend on judicial review—how the courts interpret it. Constitutional provisions that appear to establish a highly centralized form of federalism may be given a decentralized interpretation, thus changing the nature of the federal system. Moreover, jurisdictions that were unimportant in the nineteenth century have become extremely important in the twenty-first. Because medical science was relatively crude in 1867, it seemed to the Fathers of Confederation that jurisdiction over hospitals (and by extension, health) was not a major item. Today, however, health care is one of the largest areas of public expenditure. The fact that it is a provincial jurisdiction makes provincial governments more important than they were in

---

2   The powers of reservation and disallowance have not been used for decades and there is widespread agreement that they should not be used. It would be fair to argue that it has become a constitutional convention that the federal government not exercise these powers.

1867. The same is true of provincial taxing powers. *CA 1867* restricts provincial governments to "direct taxation." Before the invention of personal and corporate income taxes, direct taxation was not very lucrative. The introduction of such taxes by provincial governments has given those governments revenue sources that would have made the premiers of 1867 green with envy.

Perhaps the most influential factor shaping the relative strength of the two levels of government is public favour. There are a number of decentralizing forces that sometimes lead the public to favour a greater role for provincial governments, including the regional pattern of economic development in Canada, the lack of a strong Canadian identity and the corresponding strength of local attachments, and the demands of Québécois nationalists for a strong *état du Québec*. On the other hand, a number of forces can push the public to favour a strong central government, including the desire for national standards in both social services and human rights and the desire to protect our economy and our culture from American domination. The balance between these forces at a given point in time will determine whether the public favours greater centralization, greater decentralization, or the status quo.

Over the years, the interplay of these various factors has left us with remarkably different federal systems at different points in our history. Without undue simplification, one can divide the historical development of Canadian federalism into four basic periods.

1. **Quasi-federalism** (1867–1896). The era of John A. Macdonald's long tenure as prime minister and the ascendancy of the Conservative Party was one in which the national government proved much stronger than the provincial governments. For most of this era, the relationship between the national and provincial governments was analogous to the colonial relationship between Britain and Canada. Provincial legislation was frequently reserved or disallowed, and most of the great initiatives were undertaken by Ottawa, not the provinces.

2. **Classical federalism** (1896–1914). Beginning with the election of Wilfrid Laurier and the rise of the Liberal Party to national pre-eminence, the balance of power clearly shifted to a more equal relationship between the provinces and Ottawa. The Liberal Party had championed provincial rights in Ontario, and a French-Canadian prime minister was naturally more sensitive to such rights for Québec. During this period, the courts handed down a series of important constitutional decisions, each of which contributed to a steady erosion of important federal powers (notably the "peace, order, and good government" clause, and Section 91.2, trade and commerce) while at the same time expanding the scope of provincial jurisdictions such as 92.13, property and civil rights. Of particular

note was the *Maritime Bank* case of 1892, in which our highest court explicitly repudiated the notion that provincial governments are subordinates of the federal government. The court declared that the Constitution would henceforth be interpreted in light of the principles of classical federalism, according to which each level of government is sovereign in the jurisdictions assigned to it.

3. *Emergency federalism* (1914–1960). In this era, the balance of power swung back toward the federal government. The two world wars required strong and decisive leadership that could be given only by a national government. Moreover, the period between the wars was marked by the economic collapse of the Western democracies and the massive depression that ensued. The Great Depression fostered increased centralization because it led to the idea that the purpose of government should be expanded to include ensuring the welfare of the people; since the Depression had virtually bankrupted most of the provincial governments, it was evident that only Ottawa would be able to afford the costs involved in this new responsibility.

4. *"Cooperative" federalism* (1960–present). In the postwar era, the economies of the Western democracies have steadily grown. Canada's provincial governments now have a much greater ability to raise revenues and exercise power over their respective jurisdictions. Moreover, as the public level of expectations continue to rise and people demand ever more services from the government, the jurisdictions of the provincial government continue to grow in importance. With both levels of government often supplying services in each other's jurisdictions, federalism has become a system of federal-provincial "cooperation," meaning that the two levels of government must constantly bargain and coordinate their actions. Increasingly over the past four decades, this process of federal-provincial negotiations has involved regular meetings of first ministers and of cabinet ministers with common responsibilities. It is not unusual, for example, for there to be yearly meetings of the 11 ministers of health to discuss Canada's health system. Because of the proliferation of such meetings between federal and provincial executive officers, this era is sometimes referred to as the age of **executive federalism**.

4.5 Financing Government and Federal-Provincial Relations

One of the major problems associated with federalism is the need to balance a government's responsibilities with its ability to finance its role. A federal system will not work well if this balance is not attained, for it does little good to give a level of government the responsibility for providing a service if it cannot afford to provide it. The jurisdictional rights and responsibilities of government are mere legal niceties if the government lacks the will or the means to act.

This problem of balancing revenues with jurisdiction has plagued the Canadian federal system from the outset. In one sense, our federal system was designed to create an imbalance so that the provinces would always be subordinated to the federal government. But as the provinces grew more powerful, their inability to finance themselves also grew, which in turn has put enormous stress on the federal system. In response to that stress, federal and provincial politicians have developed an elaborate web of financial relations that usually goes by the name of **fiscal federalism**. This fiscal federalism may be divided into three distinct branches: taxation, federal spending power, and equalization payments.

1. *Taxation.* If we go back and examine *CA 1867,* we find that the federal government was given both a much greater ability to raise revenues and the ability to spend money within provincial jurisdiction. It was clear from the outset that the provincial governments were to be the poor cousins of the federal government and that the federal government would be able to play a major role in areas of provincial jurisdiction because they would have the superior financial resources.

In the area of jurisdiction over taxation, the federal government can raise money "by any mode or system of taxation" (Section 91.3), whereas the provincial government has only the more specific jurisdiction over "direct taxation within the province" (Section 92.2). At the time the Constitution was written, government financing was done largely through systems of indirect, as opposed to direct, taxation. A **direct tax** is one in which the taxpayer is taxed directly by the government. A good example is the income tax. An **indirect tax** is one in which the tax is not collected directly from the taxpayer. Examples of such taxes are custom duties, excise taxes, and the HST. The merchant pays the tax but then passes it on in the price paid by the individual buyer, or collects the tax from the customer. The buyer ultimately pays the tax indirectly, through the merchant.

Jurisdiction over taxation was thus divided between the federal and provincial governments so as to favour the former. And up until the early part of the twentieth century, the provincial governments were heavily dependent on federal subsidies. As the field of government responsibilities expanded, governments sought new areas of finance. In the early part of the twentieth century, both the federal and the provincial governments introduced income taxes. Both levels of government have resorted to sales taxes.[3] What is important to note is that the

---

3   It was thought, in 1867, that a sales tax was a form of indirect tax and hence not within the jurisdiction of the provinces. In the 1943 case of *Atlantic Smoke Shops vs. Conlon,* however, the courts

federal government has historically been ahead of the provincial government in occupying and thus dominating these fields. It is politically difficult for the provincial government to raise provincial income tax when the federal tax is already widely perceived as burdensome enough. Taxation is thus one of the major areas of conflict between federal and provincial governments. Joint occupancy of what are now the major fields of taxation requires constant negotiation between the two levels of government over "**tax room.**" Rather than simply transfer its own revenues to the provinces in support of provincial programs, Ottawa can relinquish some of its tax room and allow the provinces to take over the vacated "tax points."

2. *Federal spending power.* The federal division of powers divides the areas of jurisdiction in a fairly precise fashion. Nonetheless, today we find the federal government involved in many important areas of provincial jurisdiction. One reason is that the federal government has the financial resources, which it uses to aid the provinces in areas such as education and health care. Although health care is a matter of provincial jurisdiction, that need not prevent the federal government from establishing and financing programs in that area. The **federal spending power** (Ottawa's power to spend its money as it pleases) has been a major factor in determining how the federal system operates.

The most important aspect of this spending power is the way it has allowed the federal government to wield massive political power in areas that legally belong to the provinces. The federal government will supply monies for programs in health care, education, or transportation, for example, but will also attach conditions as to how that money can be spent. Thus, while the federal government is not exercising direct legal control over an area of provincial jurisdiction, it can nonetheless establish substantial political influence. Perhaps the best-known example is in the area of health care. The federal government transfers billions of dollars to the provinces so that they may run their provincial health care programs. In exchange for this money, however, the federal government demands that provinces respect certain principles (such as the prohibition of user fees). While it is constitutionally within a province's power to allow for medical user fees, it is difficult for a province to do so if that means losing millions of dollars in federal monies.

This type of federal spending was traditionally known as a **conditional grant.** In response to political pressure from the provinces, particularly Québec, the federal government has in recent decades moved more in the direction of

declared that a sales tax could be seen as a direct tax if one considered the merchant as a government tax collector. This decision opened the door to provincial sales taxes.

unconditional grants. These involve a transfer of a large block of funds to each province, which allows for greater provincial discretion in how the monies are spent. Programs must still meet some broad national standards set by the federal government. Most federal funding to the provinces is used to finance health care, post-secondary education, welfare, and social services. This funding is now accomplished mainly through the Canada Health Transfer (CHT) and the Canada Social Transfer (CST). For 2010, the total transfer to the provinces and territories through these grants was approximately $37 billion.

3. *Equalization payments*. The federal government is also responsible for providing monies to provinces that fall below the national average economically. The precedent for such responsibility was established by *CA 1867*, which required the federal government to provide subsidies to the provinces for the expense of their governments. This responsibility has developed into a responsibility to ensure that social and economic conditions across the country remain roughly equal and that regional disparities do not become too great.

Attempts by the federal government to ameliorate regional disparities were once made mainly by means of shared-cost programs and federal grants. But today the more well-known means for doing this are the unconditional **equalization payments**. This type of financing was established in the 1950s and was entrenched in the Constitution in Section 36 of *CA 1982*. Equalization payments are an attempt to redistribute money from the wealthier to the poorer regions in order to ensure that Canadian citizens have roughly the same level of government services and taxation. While the principle of equalization is entrenched in *CA 1982*, the implementation of it is governed by federal regulations. In essence, a formula is used to determine the average fiscal capacity of provincial governments, assuming average tax rates. (Fiscal capacity is the amount of revenue a government can raise through taxation. A province such as Ontario, with a strong concentration of corporate head offices, will normally raise much more in corporate income taxes per capita than will a province such as New Brunswick. Ontario thus has a substantially stronger fiscal capacity.) Provinces with a fiscal capacity below the national average receive a transfer of funds from Ottawa sufficient to bring them to 97 per cent of the national average. These transfers are unconditional, meaning the provincial government that receives them may spend the money on any area within its jurisdiction. Currently, the total amount of equalization payments is approximately $14 billion per year. In 2011, six provinces will receive equalization payments. Ontario has recently fallen below the national average and has therefore become a recipient of equalization. For many provinces, these payments are extremely important. In New Brunswick and Prince Edward Island, for instance, equalization payments alone account for at least 20 per cent of the provincial governments' revenues.

In 2004, an interesting controversy over equalization arose between Ottawa and the province of Newfoundland and Labrador. The development of oil resources off the coast of that province has substantially improved its fiscal capacity. Under the equalization formula, that improvement would automatically lead to lower equalization payments from Ottawa to that provincial government. Danny Williams, the former premier of Newfoundland and Labrador, demanded that the payments remain at their current level. Williams's position was that have-not provinces will lose any incentive to improve their situation if the benefits of any economic progress they make are automatically clawed back through a cut in equalization transfers. On the other hand, Ottawa (and many people in other provinces) wonder why a province that now has fiscal resources greater than most other provinces (and above the national average) should still be receiving money from the equalization fund. Mr. Williams's anger over this issue prompted him to orchestrate an anti-Harper campaign in the 2008 election (despite the fact that both men are Conservatives) and to demand that all MPs from his province vote against the 2009 budget.

4.6 The Challenge of Canadian Federalism

The Fathers of Confederation imported the federal element of the Canadian regime from the constitutional design of the United States. To be sure, significant modifications were made to the American model of federalism. For instance, our Constitution lays out (at least on paper) a more centralized division of powers than is to be found south of the border. Still, the basic principle of federalism is the same in the Canadian and the American regimes—two levels of government, each supreme in its own areas of jurisdiction, and both subordinate to a constitutional law.

Given this fundamental similarity, it is at first somewhat surprising to see how strikingly different our experience with federalism has been from the experience of our southern neighbours. To put the matter simply, federalism is not as important an issue in American political life. The Constitution of the United States established a relatively decentralized form of federalism. Over time, the American regime has evolved into a much more centralized federation in which Washington plays the dominant political role, and the governments of the states are clearly less important. The current pre-eminence of the American federal government is relatively uncontroversial, and there is no interest in undertaking significant reform of the status quo.

In Canada, on the other hand, just the opposite is true. Almost from the beginning, Canadian political life has been dominated by quarrels over the nature of our federal arrangements. The point should be obvious if one considers for a minute only a few of the semi-permanent issues that plague our political agenda, all of which are problems of federalism: Québec separatism, Western alienation, responsibility for funding health care and other services, regional economic development, and constitutional reform. Canada is probably the only country in the world where issues of federalism are the national political obsession.[4] The "Québec question" has always been, at bottom, a dispute over the division of jurisdiction between the government of Québec and the federal government. Rightly or wrongly, a majority of Québeckers believes that the current division of powers does not give the "state of Québec" (as Québeckers like to call their government) sufficient control over those matters that are essential to the protection and development of the Québec "people." Over the past 40 years, this dispute has been at the centre of six major constitutional conferences, as well as the 1980 referendum on sovereignty association, *CA 1982,* the Meech Lake Accord, the Charlottetown Accord referendum, and a referendum on Québec sovereignty in 1995. The underlying issue throughout this process has been whether Québec can acquire the powers it believes are necessary to govern itself within the bounds of some federal form of political union, or whether that objective can be achieved only by becoming a sovereign state. Sovereignty or "renewed federalism"—for most Québeckers, these are the only serious options; the status quo is generally considered to be simply unacceptable.

There can be little doubt that Québec's presence in Confederation is a large part of the reason why federalism has been so much more of a problem or question in Canada than it has in the United States. Yet the role of Québec does

---

4   The validity of this observation is confirmed by the oft-repeated joke about the elephant, which runs something like this: a Frenchman, a German, and a Canadian were asked to give a speech on the subject "the elephant." The German began with a learned discourse on how the elephant's strength could be used in industry. The Frenchman followed with a talk about the love life of the elephant. When the Canadian was called upon to speak, he announced that his theme would be "The Elephant: federal or provincial responsibility?" Another illustration of the point may be found in comparing television panels in Canada and the United States. In Canada, it seems almost mandatory that every political panel on television must have members from the four main regions of the country (or at least three of them). In the United States, it would be incomprehensible to suggest that a panel must include "representation" from the Northeast, the South, the Mid-West, and the West. Americans are much more likely to see gender, race, or political ideology as the politically relevant categories.

not fully account for this. Even if Québec had never been a part of Canada (or alternatively, if Québec were to someday secede from Canada), federalism would still be more controversial here than it is in the United States.[5] The reason for this is that, in one key respect, federalism does not work as well with responsible government as it does with separation of powers. The crux of the issue is representation within the national government.

The citizens of a federal regime will by definition have dual loyalties, feeling themselves to be both citizens of a province or state and citizens of the country as a whole. By extension, they will also, of necessity, have a dual view of the union itself: on the one hand, it will be seen as a union of individual Americans, Canadians, or Australians; on the other hand, it will be seen as a union of states or provinces. To the extent that we are democrats and respect the principle of equality, this duality leads to a dilemma: should political representation within the national government be based on the principle of the equality of all individual citizens or on the principle of the equality of all the states or provinces?

The Founding Fathers of the United States resolved this dilemma by adopting **bicameralism**. In a bicameral legislative body, power is shared by two separate chambers so that neither can act without the agreement of the other. The Founding Fathers created a legislature (Congress) in which representation in one chamber was based on the principle of the equality of all individual citizens (the House of Representatives) and representation in the other was based on the principle of the equality of the states (the Senate). In the House of Representatives, states with larger populations have more seats, and states with smaller populations have fewer seats. In the Senate, however, all states have the same number of seats—two—regardless of population. The American Congress thus gives equal voice to the two visions of union—the United States as a union of individual Americans (in which all Americans are equal) and the United States as a union of states (in which all states are equal). This bicameral solution was essential to the adoption of the Constitution of the United States. If legislative power had been assigned only to a chamber based on equality of the states, the small states would have dominated the national government—something the large states would never have accepted. If legislative power had been assigned only to a chamber based on equality of individual citizens, the large states would have dominated the national government—something the small states would never have agreed

---

5   In his separatist manifesto, *An Option For Québec,* René Lévesque claimed that separatism would be good for English Canada because once Québec had left, the rest of the country would no longer have any disputes about federalism. On this point, at least, Lévesque certainly misunderstood political life in English Canada.

to. Bicameralism allowed the Founding Fathers to give fair weight to both claims, so that neither the small states nor the large states would dominate.

The Fathers of Confederation learned from the experience of the United States that bicameralism would be essential to Confederation. This is the main reason why Canada's Parliament includes both a House of Commons and a Senate. Representation in the House of Commons is based on the principle of the equality of all Canadians, so that provinces with larger populations have a larger number of seats. Representation in the Senate, on the other hand, is based on the principle of the equality of the regions, with each of the four main regions of the country receiving about the same number of seats. The problem in the Canadian case, however, is that responsible government makes it difficult, if not impossible, for the two chambers to be equal in power. The House of Commons is not merely a legislative body, it is also the chamber from which the executive is drawn and to which the executive must be responsible. To the extent that this role cannot be shared with the Senate, the House will of necessity dominate Parliament, and the Senate will always have a peripheral role. This means, however, that the principle of representation embedded in the Senate—the equality of the regions—is not really given meaningful expression within our national government. The chamber with real power is one where the two largest provinces possess nearly 60 per cent of the seats. Not surprisingly, this leads citizens in the other eight provinces to believe they have little control over their national government. (This feeling is dangerously prevalent in the four Western provinces.) Accordingly, the eight smaller provinces must look to their provincial governments to champion their causes, and these provincial governments typically court public favour by "running against Ottawa"—by blaming the federal government for all their province's woes. Instead of being dealt with *within* the federal government, regional concerns are thus funnelled through the federal-provincial division of powers, which has the effect of making federalism our country's main battleground. Canadians can confidently expect each year to see a **First Ministers' Conference** at which the premiers and the federal prime minister wrangle over financial and jurisdictional questions. Since 2003, the premiers have had their own **Council of the Federation** which for the most part serves as a vehicle for promoting the view that Ottawa should give provincial governments more money and more freedom to spend the money they receive as they wish. This political dynamic does not prevail in the United States, for the Senate ensures that the interests of the small states are well protected *within* Washington.

4.7 Current Controversies: The Pressure to Decentralize

Through much of the twentieth century, Ottawa has used its spending power to ameliorate regional disparities and to influence public policy in areas of provincial jurisdiction. For most political leaders in Québec, these federal "intrusions" are unacceptable since they effectively transfer decision-making authority in some areas from the *Assemblée nationale* in Québec City to the English-Canadian dominated government in Ottawa. Nationalist politicians in Québec believe that the division of powers developed in 1867 is already too centralist; for Ottawa to "invade" jurisdictions that are supposed to belong exclusively to the provinces is intolerable.

Yet there are powerful reasons why many Canadians steadfastly oppose the call for a more decentralized federal system. It is often argued that a strong federal presence in key provincial jurisdictions is essential for the defence of national standards of service in health care, welfare, and education. Many Canadians fear that if Ottawa retreats from these areas, Canadians will end up with dramatically different levels of services in the different provinces. Those who live in rich provinces would receive first-class health care, for example, while those in the less prosperous provinces would have to settle for something substantially worse. According to opponents of decentralization, then, a federal retreat from provincial jurisdictions would make Canada less of a country and something more akin to a patchwork quilt.

One way to "square the circle"—to combine centralization and decentralization—would be to engage in **asymmetrical federalism**, an approach to federalism in which different provinces may have somewhat different powers. We might then allow Québec to take greater control of its own affairs while maintaining a more centralized form of federalism in the rest of the country. Baier and Boothe[6] point out that Canadian federalism is already asymmetrical in a number of respects: the Constitution provides special guarantees for a number of provinces in the House and the Senate; our constitutional amending formulas treat different provinces differently; and many federal-provincial agreements typically involve only the nine provinces outside of Québec, as Ottawa and Québec negotiate separate agreements of their own. On a more symbolic level, Canada's Parliament recently adopted a significant asymmetry in recognizing the "people of Québec" as a "nation" within Canada.

---

6   Gerald Baier and Katherine Boothe, "What is Asymmetrical Federalism and Why Should Canadians Care?," in Thomas Bateman, ed., *Braving the New World: Readings in Contemporary Politics*, 4th ed. (Toronto: Thomson-Nelson, 2008) 206–16.

Yet asymmetrical federalism is unlikely to provide a solution to the problem of Canadian federalism. To begin with, the institutionalization of special rights, special deals, or special status is offensive to the egalitarian sensibilities of most Canadians. It is therefore unlikely that the idea of asymmetry could be pushed very far without sparking a backlash. Moreover, it is not clear that a more decentralized arrangement for Québec would not lead to similar demands from Canada's wealthier provinces. In Alberta and British Columbia, the intrusions of the federal government into areas of exclusive provincial jurisdiction (and the concomitant transfer of tax dollars from West to East) have also become unpopular. These two provinces are now dominated by an ideology of "alienation" and a view of provincial rights that suggests that their dissatisfaction with Canadian federalism is only slightly less than that of Quebeckers.[7] Their sense of grievance against Central Canada is expressed in terms of demands that Ottawa remove itself from areas of provincial jurisdiction and that federalism take a more decentralized form in the future. In other words, Alberta and British Columbia have a perspective on Canadian federalism that is in some ways not all that different from the perspective of Québec nationalists.

The opponents of decentralization were able to carry the day in their fight against the Meech Lake and Charlottetown Accords. Those Accords would have placed restrictions on new federal initiatives in areas of provincial jurisdiction and, in the case of Charlottetown, would have seen the federal government withdraw entirely from a number of the less important provincial jurisdictions. Oddly enough, however, today's federal system is perhaps becoming far more decentralized than anything contemplated in either of the Accords. One of the catalysts for this transformation was the near victory of the separatist side in the 1995 referendum on sovereignty in Québec. That close call with disaster has led our national politicians to take more seriously the traditional Québec demands for limits to Ottawa's use of the spending power. Under the 1999 **Social Union Framework**, for example, Ottawa agreed not to introduce any new shared-cost programs in provincial jurisdictions without first obtaining the approval of seven provinces that, taken together, have 50 per cent of the total Canadian population. Ottawa also agreed that any province that chooses not to participate in such a program will be provided with equivalent federal dollars to run a program of its own.

A second (and perhaps even more important) catalyst of decentralization has been the federal debt and deficit. By the early 1990s, it was evident that the federal debt was getting out of control and that continuing deficits each year were

---

7   See Doug Owram, "Reluctant Hinterland," in R.S. Blair and J.T. McLeod, eds., *The Canadian Political Tradition: Basic Readings*, 2nd ed. (Scarborough: Nelson Canada, 1993) 153–68.

seriously threatening the long-term fiscal health of the nation. A large part of Ottawa's response was to scale back its spending in areas of provincial jurisdiction such as health care and post-secondary education—in effect, to offload its fiscal problems on provincial governments. The decline in federal financial contributions in these areas naturally led to a decline in the federal government's influence on provincial policies and standards. For instance, provincial politicians now ask why they should be forced to make their health care policies conform to the *Canada Health Act* when federal contributions to health care have slipped from historic highs of 50 per cent to somewhere in the 20–25 per cent range.

Will this new trend to decentralization be sufficient to satisfy the politicians and voters in Québec, Alberta, and British Columbia? On the other hand, will it be so strong that it unravels the fabric of Canadian nationhood? These sorts of questions reveal how Canada's future will, in large part, be tied to the development of our federal system. When we consider whether the present federal system works, how it might be reformed, and whether Canadians can ever agree on the constitutional changes required for such reforms, the fundamental issue of federalism comes to light: to what extent do Canadians believe there should be a powerful national government that rules them from the centre of the country and is controlled by a national majority, and to what extent do Canadians believe that Canada should become more of a confederation of ten largely independent provinces for whom the federal government is merely a coordinator, not a leader? Federalism is a system of divided loyalties: each of us is a citizen of both a province and a country, ruled by two different governments. Canadians are being forced to confront the question of which government they believe to be the most important and why.

Key Terms

unitary	executive federalism
federal	fiscal federalism
three levels of government	direct tax
Section 91	indirect tax
Section 92	tax room
residual power	federal spending power
disallowance	conditional grant
reservation	unconditional grant
centralized	equalization payments
decentralized	bicameralism
quasi-federalism	First Ministers' Conference

classical federalism

Council of the Federation

emergency federalism

asymmetrical federalism

cooperative federalism

Social Union Framework

Discussion Questions

1. Should Canadian federalism be more centralized or more decentralized? Or is the current balance pretty much right?

2. Should the areas of provincial jurisdiction be identical for every province, or should some provinces have control over some jurisdictions that other provinces do not—for instance, immigration, agriculture, or broadcasting?

Chapter Five

The Canadian Charter of Rights and Freedoms

5.1   What is a Charter of Rights?

5.2   How the Charter Works: *Hunter v. Southam*

5.3   Remedies

5.4   The Adoption of the Charter

5.5   Opposition to the Charter

5.6   The Notwithstanding Clause

5.7   Section 1

5.8   The Political Impact of the Charter

5.1   What is a Charter of Rights?

With the adoption of *CA 1982,* Canada acquired a constitutionally entrenched charter of rights. For reasons that will become evident later in this chapter, the introduction of the Charter marked a profound transformation of the Canadian regime. But there are many other questions that must be addressed before we can discuss its impact. The first of these is the most obvious: what is a charter of rights?

The basic idea behind a charter of rights is best understood by thinking back to our discussion of Canada's regime principles in Chapter 1. Because Canada is a democracy, one of our regime's central principles is majority rule. Yet, because Canada is not just a democracy, but a *liberal* democracy, we may also say that our regime is devoted to the protection of fundamental rights. The great problem in liberal democracy is that these two fundamental principles—majority rule and fundamental rights—are not always in harmony. A majority of the people's elected representatives might decide to pass a law that violates the rights of some minority. For instance, since the vast majority of Canadians and their MPs are at least nominally connected to the Christian faith, Parliament might find it reasonable to declare Sunday a day sacred to the Lord and to prohibit shop-owners from doing business on that day. Yet a law that did so might be seen by non-Christians as an attempt to force them to follow Christian rules. In other words, it could be seen as a violation of their right to freedom of religion.

The purpose of a charter of rights is to prevent democratic majorities from using political power[1] to violate rights, especially the rights of minorities. A charter does so by entrenching those rights in the text of the constitution. You will recall from Chapter 2 that *CA 1867* and *CA 1982* are the supreme laws of the regime. It therefore follows that any statute that is inconsistent with the Constitution can have no force or effect. Thus, a constitutional charter of rights will put rights beyond the reach of the majority and its elected representatives by incorporating them into the supreme law of the regime.

5.2 How the Charter Works: *Hunter v. Southam*

To see how the Charter works, it is useful to work through an example. One of the Supreme Court's first Charter decisions was the case of *Lawson Hunter v. Southam* (1984). This case involved a federal statute called the *Combines Investigation Act*. Combines are a form of monopoly, and the government normally regulates or even prohibits monopolistic practices because they often lead to exploitation of the consumer. The *Combines Investigation Act* established certain rules to govern investigations by the Department of Justice of monopolistic practices. Among other things, this legislation provided that agents of that department might search any premises (and seize any materials therefrom) that they suspected

---

[1]　It is important not to confuse constitutional charters of rights with statutory **human rights codes**. A human rights code is a statute that protects rights in the private sphere. A human rights code provision prohibiting racial discrimination would thus prevent one private individual (a landlord) from discriminating against another private individual (a tenant) on the basis of race. A constitutional charter of rights, on the other hand, is meant to protect rights from violations in the public sphere, that is, violations by the government. A charter provision prohibiting racial discrimination would thus prevent a government from passing a law that was itself racially discriminatory (for example, not providing welfare for Asians) or permitting others to behave in a discriminatory fashion.

might contain evidence relevant to one of their investigations. The only limitation on this provision was that the agents conducting the search had to obtain a kind of warrant beforehand from a member of the Restrictive Trade Practices Commission.

In the early 1980s, the Combines Investigation branch of the Department of Justice was looking into the activities of the Thomson and Southam newspaper chains because it suspected that they had made a secret deal so that one chain would have a monopoly on the Winnipeg market while the other would have a monopoly on the Ottawa market. Pursuant to this investigation, an official of the Combines Investigation unit, Lawson Hunter, sent four of his agents to search the offices of the *Edmonton Journal*, a Southam paper, and to seize a number of the paper's files. In conformity with the law, the agents had obtained an authorization for the search from Dr. Frank Roseman of the Restrictive Trade Practices Commission before carrying out their mission.

Southam Press was unhappy about this search and decided to take the Department of Justice to court. There was nothing illegal in the activities of Hunter and his agents; their search had been carried out in perfect conformity with the *Combines Investigation Act*. What Southam argued was not that the law had been broken but that the law was itself unconstitutional. Section 8 of the Charter stipulates that "Everyone has the right to be free against unreasonable search or seizure." The allegation made by Southam was that the search and seizure provisions of the *Combines Investigation Act*, which provided the legal authorization for Hunter's search of the *Edmonton Journal*, were "unreasonable." If Southam was right about this, the *Combines Investigation Act* would be in violation of a part of the Constitution—the supreme law—and would thus be of no force or effect. Consequently, there would be no legal authority for the search that had taken place, and the items seized in that search would have to be returned to Southam.

But was Southam's allegation correct? When the Supreme Court heard this case, its task obviously was to decide how to define "reasonable" and "unreasonable" search and seizure laws. To do so, it began by suggesting that the purpose of the right entrenched in Section 8 is to ensure a sensible balance between the government's need to conduct searches and seizures for the prosecution of criminal cases and the public's right to privacy. The court went on to suggest that to ensure that such a balance be maintained, any legislation establishing search and seizure procedures must make those procedures conform to three conditions: the searchers must obtain prior authorization for their search, the official who grants that authorization must be impartial (that is, not a member of the organization conducting the search), and the probability that the search would in fact uncover important evidence must be high (in other words, no "fishing expeditions"). Applying these standards to the case at hand, the court ruled that the *Combines Investigation Act* was in violation of Section 8. The *Act* did meet the first condition—it required the agents of the Department of Justice to seek prior authorization for their search. But, because the official from whom they were to seek authorization for the search was himself an official of the Department of Justice, the *Act* did not meet the second condition; the official granting the authorization for the search was not sufficiently impartial. The court therefore concluded that the *Combines Investigation Act* was in violation of Section 8 of the Charter.

5.3 Remedies

What happens if courts declare a law to be in violation of a constitutional right, as happened in *Hunter v. Southam*? What are the possible "remedies"? Section 24(1) of the Charter addresses this matter as follows:

> Anyone whose rights or freedoms, as guaranteed by this Charter, have been infringed or denied may apply to a court of competent jurisdiction to obtain *such remedy as the court considers appropriate and just in the circumstances* (emphasis added).

In most cases where the courts find a law in violation of the Charter, they employ what is called a **Section 52 remedy**. Section 52 (1) of *CA 1982* states that any law that is "inconsistent" with the Constitution is "of no force or effect." In a S.52 remedy, the legislation (or more often, the specific sections of the legislation at issue) is declared to be "of no force or effect," which means that the government no longer has the authority to act in the way the law provided. In the case of *Hunter v. Southam*, for example, the Court's S.52 remedy meant that the Department of Justice had to return Southam's files since the law under which the files were seized was not valid. Moreover, the Court's decision also meant that the Department of Justice would not have the authority to conduct *any* criminal investigations of suspected monopolistic practices until Parliament passed new legislation that met all three of the Court's criteria for "reasonable" searches. In a S.52 remedy, then, the judiciary restricts itself to determining whether the law in question is consistent with the Charter, but it is up to Parliament (or the relevant provincial legislature) to decide if and how to amend the legislation so as to make it consistent with the Charter as interpreted by the courts.

In some countries, the judiciary is explicitly restricted to declaratory remedies such as our S.52 remedy.[2] Notice, however, that the wording of Section 24(1) gives Canada's courts leeway to determine for themselves what remedies are available to them when they find legislation in violation of the Charter.

The Supreme Court of Canada first tackled the question of remedies in a 1992 case called *Schachter v. Canada*. The Schachters were adoptive parents. The *Unemployment Insurance Act* created certain parental leave benefits but restricted those benefits to natural parents. The Schachters argued that the *Act* was discriminatory and the Court agreed. But the Court was reluctant to use a S.52 remedy because to strike down the relevant portions of the *Act* would mean that no parents—adoptive or natural—would receive any benefits until new legislation was adopted. The Court considered a remedy known as **reading in**, that is, reading the law the way the Court thought it *should have been worded* (to include adoptive parents) rather than the way *it actually was worded* (excluding adoptive parents). To do so, of course, would have been tantamount to having the Court rewrite Parliament's law—something it declared itself reluctant to do in this case. Instead, the Court declared the law unconstitutional, using the S.52 remedy, but put a one-year delay on the implementation of its decision so as to provide Parliament with sufficient time to fix the legislation itself. In subsequent cases, however, the Supreme Court has made use of the reading-in technique from time to time. The most prominent example is the 1998 case of *Vriend vs. Alberta* in which the Supreme Court read the words "sexual orientation" into the text of the non-discrimination clause of Section 15 of the Charter.

5.4 The Adoption of the Charter

It is sometimes suggested that the adoption of the Charter in 1982 marked the introduction or creation of a new set of rights. This suggestion is misleading. Although a number of the rights set down in it might be thought of as new, the Charter was primarily a new mechanism for the protection of rights that were already well established in the Canadian political tradition.

To see that the protection of rights does not necessarily depend on the existence of a charter of rights, it suffices to look at the example of Britain. Britain has never had a constitutionally entrenched charter of rights, but certain fundamental rights and freedoms have long been as well respected there as they are in

---

2   In 2000, when Britain signed a treaty obligating it to recognize the European *Charter of Fundamental Rights*, it stipulated that British courts applying the Charter would be restricted to declaratory remedies.

regimes that have constitutional charters. In some cases, those rights have been codified in organic statutes, but for the most part they exist merely as traditions (or in some cases, as constitutional conventions). The British Parliament is legally entitled to pass legislation that violates those rights, but the inescapable necessity of keeping the support of the voters, coupled with the presence of an official opposition in the House of Commons, makes it difficult for any government to go very far in terms of violating rights.

For most of its life, the Canadian regime took the British approach to the protection of rights. Rights such as freedom of religion and freedom of speech were seen to be part of the liberal democratic tradition we inherited from Britain,[3] and Canadians generally thought it possible and desirable to trust our parliamentarians not to violate those rights.

On the whole, this approach worked reasonably well. Compared with most countries, Canada had an excellent human rights record. Yet there were important exceptions to this general trend. Provincial governments were sometimes not as careful about respecting rights as they should have been. In the 1930s, the Aberhart government in Alberta enacted legislation that clearly violated the right to freedom of speech. In the 1950s, the Duplessis government in Québec passed a number of measures that were inconsistent with freedom of speech and freedom of religion.[4] In all of these cases, the offending measures were struck down by the Supreme Court, but only because the legislation in question was *ultra vires:* the court held that under the division of powers, only the federal government could regulate speech and religion so as to limit the right to free speech or religious freedom. But it was not clear that the federal government was entirely trustworthy on this matter either. During World War II, Ottawa had confined Canadians of Japanese origin in detention camps, alleging that their Japanese ancestry made them potential security threats. Though the government had widespread public support for this policy at the time, it was later recognized to have been a clear violation of the right to liberty and the right not to be arbitrarily detained or

---

3   Some members of the Supreme Court of Canada flirted with the thesis that the reference to a constitution "similar in principle to that of the United Kingdom" in the preamble to *CA 1867* contained an "implied bill of rights" granting constitutional protection to all those rights that formed part of British constitutional traditions. See, for example, *Switzman v. Elbling* (1957). This thesis was never endorsed by a majority of the court.

4   The Aberhart government in Alberta passed a law requiring that province's newspapers to print government responses to all articles critical of the government. The Duplessis government in Québec enacted legislation designed to suppress communist ideas and to curtail the activities of Jehovah's Witnesses.

imprisoned. Finally, the records of both levels of government in observing and protecting the rights of Canada's Aboriginal peoples are poor.

By the end of the 1950s, then, many Canadians came to be dissatisfied with our traditional approach to the protection of rights and freedoms. At that same time, the Supreme Court of the United States was just beginning to use that country's Bill of Rights to take bold steps in the fight for racial equality, striking down discriminatory legislation as unconstitutional. Rights activists in Canada began to argue that Canada should abandon its traditional British approach to the protection of rights and embrace the American idea of a constitutionally en-trenched bill or charter of rights. The ground for such an innovation was already well prepared by our experience with federal judicial review; as a result of our interminable litigation over the division of powers, Canadians were quite used to the idea that courts might tell parliaments and legislatures what they were permitted to do and what they were not.

In 1960, the Diefenbaker government moved to address the human rights issue by adopting the Canadian **Bill of Rights**. This document recognized and declared the existence of a number of "human rights and fundamental freedoms" including freedom of religion, freedom of speech, freedom of assembly and as-sociation, the right to the enjoyment of property, and a number of procedural legal rights, such as the right to retain legal counsel upon arrest. But there was a fundamental flaw in this document: it was merely an organic statute. This cre-ated two problems. The first was that this Bill of Rights, as a *federal* statute, did not apply to acts of the provincial governments and legislatures. Moreover, it was not even clear that it could be used to annul federal legislation. Courts are able to strike down one type of law only by applying or appealing to some higher law. Since the Canadian Bill of Rights was itself merely a statute, however, there was no logical reason to give it precedence over any other statute. Thus, the Canadian Bill of Rights presented the courts with a constitutional dilemma, one they were never able to resolve. In the case of *The Queen v. Drybones*, a divided Supreme Court did use the Bill of Rights to invalidate a federal law that discriminated against Aboriginal Canadians. But in the other cases it heard involving the Bill of Rights, the Supreme Court always found some reason for upholding whatever legislation was being challenged.

By the 1970s then, human rights activists came to argue that what Canada needed was a constitutionally entrenched charter of rights—a charter that would apply to all levels of government and that would be manifestly superior in sta-tus to ordinary legislation. These activists found a keen ally in Prime Minister Trudeau, who saw a constitutional charter as an excellent device for entrench-ing his particular vision of a bilingual Canada. At Trudeau's insistence, the constitutional accord worked out in Victoria in 1971 contained a basic charter which provided for the entrenchment of bilingual language rights, as well as a number of fundamental civil liberties.

Although the Victoria proposal was never adopted, it did set the agenda for future constitutional development. Within a decade, Trudeau was able to succeed in sponsoring the adoption of a much broader document, the Canadian Charter of Rights and Freedoms. From the point of view of its development, the Charter may be said to have three elements. First, it entrenches, in expanded form, most of the basic rights that were included in the Canadian Bill of Rights.[5] It guarantees fundamental freedoms such as freedom of speech and freedom of religion (Section 2), basic democratic rights including the right to vote (Sections 3–5), basic legal rights like the right not to be subjected to any cruel or unusual punishments (Sections 7–14), and the right to non-discriminatory treatment under the law (Section 15). Second, the Charter includes a number of language rights which serve to entrench the Trudeau vision of a bilingual Canada (Sections 16–23). Beyond these first two elements, the Charter includes various specific provisions for which there was no precedent in the Canadian Bill of Rights. Section 6 creates a regime of "mobility rights," including the right to enter, remain in, and leave Canada, and the right to pursue the gaining of a livelihood in any province. Section 27 provides an explicit recognition of the "multicultural heritage" of Canadians. Sections 1 and 33 (each of which will be discussed in detail below) establish principles and mechanisms for limiting the application of the rights enumerated in the Charter.

5.5 Opposition to the Charter

From the day the Charter was adopted, an overwhelming majority of Canadian citizens has supported it enthusiastically. Indeed, many Canadians see it as the fullest and clearest expression of the moral foundations of our regime. Yet there has always been a powerful undercurrent of opposition to it. During the negotiations that ultimately produced *CA 1982*, Manitoba's Premier Stirling Lyon attacked the idea of an entrenched charter of rights as an unacceptable departure from the principle of parliamentary sovereignty. Lyon argued that in a parliamentary regime, the final responsibility for public policy should rest with the democratically elected representatives of the people in Parliament. This, he feared, would no longer be true once the Charter gave the judiciary the power

---

5   One exception is the right to the "enjoyment of property," which is protected in Section 1a of the Bill of Rights but is not mentioned in the Charter.

to invalidate federal and provincial legislation.[6] Though Lyon's criticisms did not derail the adoption of the Charter, they have been taken up by some of Canada's leading constitutional experts, and skepticism about the Charter remains strong in some academic circles.

At the heart of the matter is the question of democracy. Charter skeptics argue that the adoption of an entrenched charter has effectively transferred a great deal of political power to the judiciary (especially the Supreme Court of Canada). This transfer is said to be a profoundly undemocratic development since it means that an unelected and unaccountable judiciary can use the Charter to impose its own policies on the rest of the country in a host of areas, including matters such as abortion, Sunday shopping, euthanasia, capital punishment, and the use of marijuana.

Those who defend the Charter do not deny that it has certain undemocratic effects. Indeed, they retort, that is precisely the point of having an entrenched Charter of Rights. Canada is not simply a democracy, it is a *liberal* democracy. And this means that the democratic principle of majority rule must always be tempered by a respect for the rights of the minority. However, as the example of our treatment of Japanese-Canadians during World War II shows, the rights of the minority are sometimes subject to flagrant violation by Canada's democratically elected leaders. It is therefore not only reasonable but necessary to empower a judicial elite to correct the illiberal excesses of the democratic majority.

On its face, this rebuttal appears impressive, yet Charter skeptics claim that it loses its force when one looks at how the Charter is actually used by the courts in practice. Charter cases rarely, if ever, involve a blatant violation of clear-cut rights comparable to what happened in the case of the Japanese-Canadians.[7]

---

6   Lyon may, in some respects, have been trying to lock the barn door after the cows had left. The noted nineteenth-century British constitutionalist A.V. Dicey once wryly remarked that the drafters of the *BNA Act* should have said in its preamble that Canada was to have a constitution similar in principle to that of the United States, not the United Kingdom. His point was that Canada's federal system, modelled on that of the United States, required a division of powers established in constitutional law. The adoption of a constitutional law logically meant that Canada's Parliament was not supreme, for the courts would have to possess the authority to determine whether a particular matter was *intra vires* or *ultra vires*. To the extent that the courts have been placing limits on the scope of Parliament's actions since Confederation, parliamentary supremacy has always been something of a misnomer, and the step from judicial review on the basis of federalism to judicial review on the basis of a charter was not, conceptually, a difficult one.

7   And even when they do, it is not clear that a charter will make much difference. Charter skeptics often point out that the American Bill of Rights did not prevent the government of the

The typical Charter case will focus instead on what Peter Russell has called the "periphery" of the rights it guarantees, the grey area where the precise meaning of the right is in doubt and where there can be reasonable differences of opinion as to what does or does not constitute a violation of the right.[8] Canadians agree, for example, that the right "not to be subjected to any cruel or unusual treatment or punishment" (Section 12) includes, at its core, the principle that punishment must be proportionate to the crime. We would therefore find it reasonable for a judicial minority to use Section 12 to overturn an act of a parliamentary majority imposing a minimum prison sentence of ten years on jaywalkers. But would a law permitting capital punishment for serial killers be a violation of Section 12? On a question like this there would be profound disagreement among Canadians, and it is not evident why the nine judges of the Supreme Court should have the final say on the matter. Their legal training provides them with no special expertise for deciding a moral-political question about capital punishment. Why, then, should they, a very tiny minority, have the right to impose their moral or political views on the democratic majority? Critics of Charter review point to a recent decision concerning the operation of a provincial government-sanctioned and -financed safe drug-injection facility in Vancouver. Producing, trafficking and possessing narcotics such as heroin and cocaine are prohibited under the terms of the federal government's *Controlled Drugs and Substances Act* (CDSA). A provision of that *Act* gives the federal Minister of Health the discretion to exempt certain persons from the application of the *Act* if "in the opinion of the Minister, the exemption is necessary for a medical or scientific purpose or is otherwise in the public interest." Acting on the assumption that drug addiction is an illness requiring medical intervention and that illicit drug use creates several collateral diseases such as HIV and hepatitis, community groups, with the support of provincial health authorities and a five-year exemption from the terms of the CDSA, opened the Insite safe injection facility in 2003. When the federal government in 2008 signalled its unwillingness to renew the exemption, the courts were asked to order the federal Minister to issue another exemption.

The Supreme Court's 2011 decision hinges mainly on an assessment of social fact evidence that drug addiction is an illness to which medical intervention is the most appropriate response, that Insite's operations have reduced collateral health effects of drug addiction in downtown Vancouver, and that they have had

---

United States from taking the same action against Japanese-Americans that our government took against Japanese-Canadians.

8   Peter Russell, *et al., The Court and the Constitution: Leading Cases* (Toronto: Emond Montgomery, 2008).

no discernible effect on increased drug abuse or crime. As the Court pithily put it in its unanimous decision, "Insite saves lives."[9] It gave short shrift to arguments that legitimate criminal law objectives in the control of illicit drug abuse are impaired by the operation of such facilities, and that the use and abuse of drugs are decisions for which users are properly held criminally responsible. (The Court did not consider an implication of its ruling, that the potential ill-health effects of contraband drugs imply a government role in regulating the strength and quality of illicit drugs that users consume.) More importantly, it considered that such determinations are not properly the subject of normal democratic debate, creating the impression that reasonable people reading the Charter could not but conclude that a ministerial refusal to authorize the operation of the injection facility violates users' rights to "security of the person" under S.7 of the Charter. Charter critics contend that such policy issues are precisely the sorts of matters on which reasonable people can and do disagree, and should be left to the cut and thrust of democratic electoral debate rather than to the decisions of nine jurists.[10]

5.6 The Notwithstanding Clause

Though Lyon's objection to the Charter did not block the adoption of that document, it was not without impact. A number of the premiers supported his position, and Prime Minister Trudeau was able to get the Charter passed only by agreeing to an important concession: the inclusion of Section 33, the **notwithstanding clause**.

Section 33 provides that Parliament or a provincial legislature may pass a law and declare it to be valid "notwithstanding" (that is, in spite of) the guarantees offered by Sections 2 and 7–15 of the Charter. Such a declaration renders the legislation immune to judicial review under those sections for a period of five years. At the end of that period, the declaration may be renewed for another five years, and Parliament or a legislature may renew such a declaration as many times as they wish.

The notwithstanding clause has vigorous partisans and equally vigorous detractors. For those who share Stirling Lyon's reservations about the Charter, Section 33 is a flexible instrument that allows us to combine judicial review with parliamentary supremacy: the courts may use the Charter to invalidate legislation, but in cases where Parliament or a legislature think the judges' decision is wrong,

---

9   *Canada (Attorney General) v. PHS Community Services Society.* 2011 SCC 44, para 133.

10   Our thanks to Dr. Thomas Bateman for sharing his analysis of this decision and its importance with the authors.

they may use Section 33 to reserve the final word for themselves. From the point of view of those who oppose the notwithstanding clause, however, Section 33 is a regrettable measure because it seriously compromises the efficacy of the Charter and thus weakens the protection of human rights in Canada. Brian Mulroney once expressed this view in its extreme form when he claimed that Section 33 meant that "the Charter is not worth the paper it's printed on."

Mulroney's claim is certainly an exaggeration. The historical record suggests that the notwithstanding clause has had little impact on the effectiveness of the Charter. Section 33 has been invoked only three times. In 1982, the Parti Québécois government of René Lévesque applied it to all Québec legislation as a means of showing its disapproval of *CA 1982,* an act that Québec has still not endorsed. Several years later, the government of Saskatchewan applied the notwithstanding clause to a piece of labour legislation. Then in 1988, after the Supreme Court declared the French-only sign provisions of Québec's Bill 101 unconstitutional, the government of that province passed a new version of that legislation, Bill 178, and shielded it from judicial review by invoking Section 33.

The use of the notwithstanding clause in this third case met with hearty approval among francophone Quebeckers, but many anglophone Canadians thought it scandalous that the Québec government could use Section 33 to do something the Supreme Court had declared a violation of rights. Though English Canadians had been almost completely indifferent about the notwithstanding clause when it had been used by the government of Saskatchewan, they now came to see it as a serious defect in the Constitution. As a result, it is now extremely difficult for a government to use Section 33 because Canadians (especially English Canadians) tend to interpret such an act not as an assertion of parliamentary supremacy but as an attack on their beloved Charter. In 2005, for instance, opponents of same-sex marriages called on politicians to use Section 33 to prevent the judiciary from using the Charter to legalize such marriages. While most members of the Conservative Party opposed same-sex marriage, party leader Stephen Harper was careful to rule out support of the use of the notwithstanding clause. While not personally opposed to the principle of Section 33, Mr. Harper recognized that a stated willingness to use it would, rightly or wrongly, allow his political rivals to paint the Conservatives as enemies of the Charter—a portrait that might be disastrous for his party. For better or for worse, then, it appears that Canadians are unlikely to see federal parliamentarians use the notwithstanding clause, at least in the foreseeable future.

5.7 Section 1

Canadians who are concerned about preserving the sanctity and integrity of Charter rights have relatively little to worry about in Section 33. A much more significant source of concern is **Section 1:**

> The *Canadian Charter of Rights and Freedoms* guarantees the rights and freedoms set out in it subject only to such reasonable limits prescribed by law as can be demonstrably justified in a free and democratic society.

Section 1 appears to be at odds with itself. It begins by "guaranteeing" the rights set down in the rest of the Charter, but it then concedes that the enjoyment of those rights shall be subject to such limitations as are "demonstrably justified in a free and democratic society." That concession has the effect of enabling the courts to permit exceptions to the rights supposedly guaranteed by the Charter, and experience has shown that the courts are willing to do this on a regular basis. One might therefore characterize Section 1 as a giant constitutional "loophole."

It may seem surprising that our Charter should have this kind of loophole in it, but the framers of that document had reasons for writing Section 1 the way they did. It is generally accepted that no right is absolute. Rights conflict, and decisions must be made about their order of value. Moreover, in any political order, rights must sometimes be limited for the sake of the common good. For instance, though we believe we have a right to freedom of speech, we recognize that in a free and democratic society it is perfectly reasonable to pass laws prohibiting speech of a libellous or slanderous character. We would therefore not want our Charter of Rights to entrench a freedom of speech so general or absolute as to make libel and slander laws unconstitutional. Section 1 was included in the Charter to resolve this type of problem for us.

Section 1 effectively turns most Charter cases into a two-stage process. In the first stage, the courts must decide whether the legislation in question violates one of the rights guaranteed by the Charter. If it does, the courts must then ask whether that violation might not be a reasonable limitation of the right in question under the terms of Section 1. If the Section 1 question is answered in the negative, then the legislation is deemed unconstitutional. If it is answered in the affirmative, however, the legislation is "saved" by Section 1, despite the fact that it violates a Charter right.

In the 1986 case of *Queen v. Oakes*, the Supreme Court of Canada developed a systematic procedure for adjudicating Section 1 questions. A brief examination of *Oakes* will provide an excellent introduction to the meaning and significance of Section 1.

David Edwin Oakes was arrested by police officers who found eight one-gram vials of hashish oil in his possession. Section 8 of the *Narcotic Control Act* stipulated that once a court has determined that an individual was in possession of illegal narcotics, the burden of proof would then be on that individual to demonstrate that he or she was not in possession of them for the purpose of trafficking. Thus, if Oakes could not prove that he had no plans to sell the narcotics found in his possession, he would have been found guilty not merely of possession but of the far more serious offence of drug trafficking. Oakes protested that it should have been up to the Crown to prove him guilty and not up to him to prove his innocence. To make his case, he argued that Section 8 of the *Narcotic Control Act* was unconstitutional because it violated Section 11(d) of the Charter, which guarantees the right to be "presumed innocent until proven guilty." The court had little trouble in concluding that Section 8 of the *Act* was in violation of Section 11(d) of the Charter, but it was then obliged to consider whether the *Act* might not be "saved" as a reasonable limitation of Section 11(d) by virtue of Section 1.

In order to tackle this question rationally, the court began by establishing a general procedure for Section 1 questions. The court argued that a law in violation of some Charter right could be saved under Section 1 only if it met two tests. The first concerned the purpose or objective of the law: a law must be a response to a "pressing and substantial" problem in order to justify overriding a Charter right. The second concerned "proportionality," that is, the suitability of the means used to pursue the law's objective. The court said it would use three criteria when applying that test. First, are the means rational and non-arbitrary? Second, do the means impair the right in question as little as possible? Might there be other ways of achieving the same objective without limiting Charter rights? Third, is the good that will be achieved by these means sufficient to outweigh the deleterious effects they will have on those individuals or groups whose rights are being set aside?

With this framework in place, the court was able to consider Oakes's claim in a reasonable and systematic fashion. The judges easily concluded that Section 8 of the *Narcotic Control Act* met the first test. The purpose of the provision was to allow the government to suppress the drug trade, and the court accepted that this was a "substantial and pressing" concern, one of "sufficient importance to warrant overriding a constitutionally protected right."[11] When it came to the second

---

11   *Queen v. Oakes* (1986) in Peter Russell, ed., *Federalism and the Charter* (Ottawa: Carleton University Press, 1989) 458.

test, however, they were not as indulgent. Writing for the majority, Chief Justice Brian Dickson argued that the means for fighting the drug trade contemplated in Section 8 of the *Narcotic Control Act* could not meet the first criterion of being rational and non-arbitrary. Innocent people who had no intention of trafficking might not be able to prove that fact. This could lead to erroneous convictions, with severe consequences for the accused. The court therefore concluded that Section 8 of the *Act* could not be saved under Section 1, and they declared it to be unconstitutional. Oakes was thus innocent of the charge of drug trafficking.

Although in *Oakes* the Supreme Court decided that Section 1 could not be used to save Section 8 of the *Narcotic Control Act*, the interpretive framework developed in that case has been applied in many others with the opposite result. A number of laws that violate some Charter right have been able to pass the **Oakes test** and have thus been upheld under Section 1 as "reasonable limitations" of the Charter. In the 2001 case *R. v Sharpe*, for example, the Supreme Court held that although criminal code restrictions on the distribution of child pornography constitute a limitation of freedom of expression (Section 2b), most of the law could be upheld as a reasonable limitation on that section. Using the Oakes test, the court ruled that it is important to protect children from exploitation and that the measures in the law restricting distribution of child pornography were a suitable means for achieving that end.

5.8 The Political Impact of the Charter

The adoption of a constitutionally entrenched charter of rights has substantially altered the structure of the Canadian regime. The most obvious change is the fact that courts now decide many questions that were formerly decided by parliaments, governments, and legislatures. In other words, the Charter has made the courts more powerful and more active political players. Numerous examples of this change could be cited. We shall limit ourselves here to a few of the most celebrated.

In 1988, the Supreme Court of Canada handed down what is perhaps its most famous Charter decision to date, *The Queen v. Morgentaler*. This case dealt with the politically explosive issue of abortion. Parliament had legislated what it thought was a compromise solution to the abortion issue: abortions were made an offence under the Criminal Code unless they were performed in accredited hospitals on the recommendation of a therapeutic abortion committee. The law was challenged by Dr. Henry Morgentaler, who sought an unrestricted right to perform abortions in his own clinics. In *Morgentaler*, the Supreme Court held by a 5–2 vote that Parliament's law was a violation of Section 7 of the Charter and that it could not be sustained under Section 1. It is interesting to note that the court's position was quite fragmented. Four separate opinions were written. One claimed that the law should be struck down on the grounds that Section 7 made it unconstitutional to restrict abortions except, perhaps, in the latest stages of pregnancy. Two other opinions suggested that the law was unconstitutional but only because its specific regulations were in one way or another procedurally unfair. Contrary to the first three opinions, the fourth claimed that the law should be upheld. In this opinion it was argued that the government had every right to regulate abortion and that the specific terms of the law in question were not tainted by a lack of procedural fairness.

Though the judges had difficulty agreeing on how to apply the Charter to abortion law, there was no ambiguity about the effect of their decision: the law was struck down, and Dr. Morgentaler was free to perform abortions in his clinics. It is worth noting that the decision in *Morgentaler* did not preclude the introduction of a new abortion law, since the majority of the judges had indicated that they would not oppose a law that was "procedurally fair." The Mulroney government proposed to Parliament a bill it thought would satisfy the judges, but it was narrowly defeated in the Senate. The Supreme Court's decision in *Morgentaler* has thus turned out to be the decisive factor in the reversal of Canada's abortion law.

Our judges have had a significant impact on many other policy questions. In the 1988 case of **Québec v. Ford**, the Supreme Court struck down Québec's law prohibiting signs in languages other than French. The court's decision touched off a political storm, culminating in the adoption of Bill 178 and, some would say, the defeat of the Meech Lake Accord. In the 1985 case of *Singh v. Minister of Employment and Immigration*, the Supreme Court declared that Canada would have to change its policy on the handling of refugee claims, despite the fact that that policy had been praised by the United Nations as a model for the rest of the world. On the basis of Section 7 of the Charter, the judges held that all persons claiming refugee status must be given a full hearing. The federal government was forced to introduce new regulations to comply with this judicial order, thereby creating the most open and liberal procedures in the world for the handling of refugee applications. In the 2001 case of *United States v. Burns*, the court declared that prisoners may not be extradited to states that use the death penalty unless the minister of justice receives assurances that the death penalty will not be sought. In so doing, the court appears to have closed the door to any future reintroduction of capital punishment as a violation of Section 7 of the Charter. In the 1999 case of **M. v. H.**, the Court held that governments may not deny gay and lesbian couples benefits that are provided to heterosexual spouses. To most experts, the reasoning of the Court in that case implied that federal laws restricting the definition of marriage to heterosexual couples probably would not withstand constitutional scrutiny if and when they were tested in the courts. When the Martin government legalized same-sex marriage in 2005, part of its argument was that it had no choice: if Parliament did not change the law on its own, the Supreme Court would inevitably force it to do so.

These cases demonstrate how the adoption of the Charter has entailed a substantial transfer of policy-making power from elected bodies to judges. The student of Canadian government is therefore compelled to pay ever closer attention to the role and conduct of our judiciary. As we shall see in Chapter 8.6, some scholars now speak of the emergence in our regime of a "Court Party," a collection of interest groups who work with the judiciary to use the Charter in order to win through the courts changes they would be unlikely to win in the political arena.[12] More generally, people are raising questions about whether the arrangements we have made for the judiciary do not need to be changed now that the judges have a much more important role in the formulation of public policy. It is frequently suggested, for example, that we need to change our procedures for appointing the justices of the Supreme Court in order to provide for more democratic control over our policy-making judges.[13]

The adoption of the Canadian Charter of Rights and Freedoms has thus introduced a whole new range of questions for the student of Canada's regime to ponder.

Key Terms

charter of rights

human rights codes

Hunter v. Southam

Section 52 remedy

reading in

Bill of Rights

notwithstanding clause

Section 1

Oakes test

Morgentaler

Québec v. Ford

M. v. H.

Discussion Question

1. Should the notwithstanding clause be deleted from the Charter?

---

12   F.L. Morton and Rainer Knopff, *The Charter Revolution and the Court Party* (Peterborough, ON: Broadview Press, 2000).

13   See Chapter 8.5 below.

PART THREE

INSTITUTIONS

THE CROWN AND ITS SERVANTS

6.1 The Crown

6.2 The Governor General

6.3 The Functions of the Governor General

6.4 The Cabinet

6.5 The Cabinet Committee System

6.6 The Prime Minister

6.7 Prime Ministerial Government?

6.8 The Civil Service

Canadians usually refer to those who exercise political power in this country as "the government." But "government" is a very imprecise term. For some, it appears to refer to a specific team of ministers—"the Harper government" or "the Chrétien government," for example. For others, the term "government" includes a large number of public servants, such as the person who processes your passport application.

The source of the confusion here is the fact that "government" is an informal and unofficial term. Our Constitution nowhere defines the meaning of "government" because, strictly speaking, there is no such institution in the Canadian regime. What Canadians loosely refer to as "the government" is in fact a complex web of independent but interrelated institutions: the Crown, the prime minister, the cabinet, and the civil service. Our purpose in this chapter is to explain what those institutions are and how they are related.

6.1 The Crown

We have seen that the preamble to *CA 1867* stipulates that Canada is to have "a Constitution similar in principle to that of the United Kingdom." This implies that in Canada, as in Britain, governmental power is technically in the hands of the "Crown" and that our head of state is the reigning queen or king. To understand this fact, it helps to keep in mind the peculiar evolution of British constitutional practice. Centuries ago, when Britain was a full-fledged monarchy, all governmental power was vested in the Crown. Over time, in response to the demands of their people for a more democratic regime, British monarchs began to "delegate" certain of their powers to other people or bodies. Legislative power was delegated to the body that came to be known as Parliament. Today Parliament is the real seat of legislative power. Yet even today Parliament's decisions do not have the force of law until they have received royal assent; this indicates that the legislative power is still technically, in part, a power of the Crown. The same is true of executive power. As early as the seventeenth century, British monarchs began to delegate the Crown's executive power to a prime minister and cabinet. Today, the prime minister and cabinet have virtually complete control of executive power. In principle, however, this power remains a power of the Crown, and those who exercise it are deemed to do so as servants of His or Her Majesty. Their executive decisions are, in principle, merely "advice" to the Crown and have no force or effect until they receive royal assent. The British regime is thus described as a **constitutional monarchy**, a regime that is monarchical by law but democratic by convention. The Canadian Constitution is very much like the British Constitution on this point.

Section 9 of *CA 1867* stipulates that "The Executive Government and Authority of and over Canada is hereby declared to continue and be vested in the Queen." Of course, the Queen would no more exercise this executive power of government here in Canada than she does in Britain. By constitutional convention, she delegates her executive power to certain elected representatives of the people—the prime minister and cabinet. In law, however, the executive power of government is a power of the Crown. In other words, all executive decisions must have the assent of the Crown and must be carried out in the Crown's name. This explains why those who prosecute criminals in Canada are called "Crown Attorneys" and why the cases they prosecute have names like *The Queen v. Oakes*. Queen Elizabeth was not personally involved in the trial of David Oakes; rather, when the officials of the Department of Justice prosecuted him, they were exercising executive power that had been delegated to the department by the Queen.

A similar pattern is evident in the way the Canadian Constitution deals with legislative power. Section 17 of *CA 1867* establishes that Canada shall have a Parliament consisting of "the Queen, an Upper House styled the Senate, and the House of Commons." The Constitution does not spell out the role of each of these three elements in the legislative process; these are covered by the preamble's reference to British constitutional practice. In the case of legislative power, the Queen asks "Her" parliament to send Her bills for Her consideration. These bills do not become law until they have obtained royal assent and are "proclaimed" by the Crown. Royal assent is still necessary for any bill to become law, but in order to guarantee the triumph of the democratic principle, a convention has evolved stipulating that royal assent cannot be withheld.

These constitutional arrangements appear to be exceedingly complicated. Yet, as we shall explain in Section 6.3, below, there are important reasons for constructing our regime this way.

6.2 The Governor General

The powers, rights, and privileges of the Canadian Crown are vested in the Queen or King of Canada. Our monarch is by law the same person who serves as monarch of Britain, but it is important to note that this person is serving in two distinct positions. One might say that Elizabeth II wears a number of different crowns: a British crown, a Canadian crown, an Australian crown, and so on. She is a monarch with many dominions. The important point is that, with respect to Canada, she is the **Queen of Canada**.

Now because Canada's monarch is also a British monarch who resides principally in Britain, it is practically impossible for her to serve actively here in Canada. Therefore, Section 10 of *CA 1867* provides that she shall have a permanent representative in this country, the Governor General.[1] Given that the Governor General is the Queen's representative in Canada, she is technically the one who appoints this official. The term of office is generally five to seven years.

In the early years of Confederation, when Canada was not yet entirely independent of Britain, the Governor General was seen as the British government's representative in this country. Our first governors–general were therefore always British nobles, appointed by the queen or king on the recommendation of the

---

[1]   The role of the Governor General is played by the lieutenant-governors in the provincial governments.

British government. After World War I, the advice of the Canadian prime minister was sought as well. Only in 1952 did the Crown begin to appoint Canadian citizens to the position. At first, our prime ministers recommended non-political figures such as diplomats Vincent Massey (1952–59) and Jules Léger (1974–79) or the distinguished military leader Georges Vanier (1959–67). There followed a period in which the tendency was to appoint retired politicians, including Ed Schreyer (1979–84), Jeanne Sauvé (1984–90), Ray Hnatyshyn (1990–95), and Roméo Leblanc (1995–99). More recently, the trend has been to appoint media celebrities like Adrienne Clarkson (1999–2005) and Michaëlle Jean (2005–10). The current Governor General is David Johnston, a former university president.

There are obvious advantages in appointing former politicians: because the Governor General is responsible for some potentially significant political decisions, it makes sense to appoint people with political experience. On the other hand, there are also some disadvantages to nominating politicians for the office. Three of the four governors-general who had been politicians—Sauvé, Hnatyshyn, and Leblanc—had served as cabinet ministers with or under the prime minister who nominated them. The danger in such appointments is that they may be perceived as partisan, or even "patronage," appointments. Such a perception is prejudicial to the dignity and independence of the office.

6.3 The Functions of the Governor General

In terms of constitutional law, the Governor General, as the Crown's representative in Canada, has very extensive powers. By constitutional convention, however, most of that power is exercised by other officials. While the Crown has to assent to any exercise of legislative power, it is well established that the Governor General must approve any bill that is passed by Parliament. And while executive power is explicitly granted to the Crown in Section 9 of *CA 1867*, Section 11 stipulates that the Governor General shall have certain official "advisers"—the prime minister and cabinet. By constitutional convention, the Crown's executive power is used only on the "advice" of these democratically elected officials.[2] Since cabinet decisions are in legal terms "advice" to the Crown, the Governor General

---

2   The Governor General would refuse to follow the advice of a prime minister on the exercise of executive power only if the prime minister attempted to offer advice after having lost the confidence of the House. After his clear defeat in the 1896 elections, Prime Minister Charles Tupper tried to take advantage of his last few days in office to have the Governor General appoint a number of senators and judges. The Governor General refused on the grounds that Tupper did not have the confidence of the House and therefore had no mandate to offer such advice.

must always be kept well-advised of cabinet's activities and intentions. On behalf of the cabinet, the prime minister meets regularly with the Governor General to keep him or her abreast of the government's plans. Although in theory it is the Governor General who is being advised by the prime minister, it is sometimes true that the prime minister will take advantage of these sessions to privately seek advice on matters that cannot be discussed with cabinet colleagues or other advisers. As the Crown's representative in the regime, and one whose impartiality cannot be questioned, the Governor General is occasionally a useful sounding board for a prime minister with a difficult problem.

Because the Crown no longer has any meaningful legislative or executive power, the office of Governor General is sometimes referred to in colloquial terms as a mere "rubber stamp." While it is true that he or she normally exercises no power of any great consequence, the Governor General nonetheless plays two important roles in the Canadian regime: guardian of responsible government and representative for the Queen, our **head of state.**

We saw in Chapter 3 that our system of responsible government is rather complicated. We do not directly elect anyone to run our governments; we elect parliaments out of which democratically accountable governments must be constructed. Those governments do not simply construct themselves. The one indispensable role of the Governor General is to serve as the **guardian of responsible government**, the official who ensures that we have a government that enjoys the confidence of the House. Governors-general carry out this function through the use of three **reserve powers** (powers they reserve the right to use on their own initiative).

The *first reserve power* is the power to appoint the prime minister. Since the voters do not elect a prime minister, it is essential to give someone the authority to appoint one when the position is vacant. In Canada, that person is the Governor General. It is essential to remember that the Governor General's choice is governed by one single criterion: the prime minister will be the person with the best chance of commanding the confidence of the House of Commons. Historically, that choice has been so easy that almost anyone could be entrusted to make it. Canada has highly disciplined political parties and an electoral system that usually gives one of those parties a majority of seats. If a prime minister resigns because the electorate has given a different party a majority of seats, the leader of that other party is the obvious choice for prime minister. And even where no party has a majority, if a prime minister resigns, it has thus far in our history always been obvious who the alternative is. Still, it is conceivable that parliamentary elections could produce a fragmented House of Commons, in which no party has a majority of seats and it is not evident which party is most likely to lead a minority government. In such a situation, the Governor General's power to name the prime minister would be essential to the smooth functioning of responsible government.

The *second reserve power* is the power to dismiss a prime minister who attempts to govern without the confidence of the House of Commons. This power has never been used at the federal level and has not been used by a lieutenant-governor at the provincial level since the beginning of the twentieth century. Still, the power does exist and is essential to the proper functioning of responsible government. Without it, there would be no way to prevent a prime minister and cabinet from clinging to office when, under the rules of responsible government, they are supposed to resign or ask for elections. The fact that this second reserve power is used so infrequently is more a proof of its efficacy than its irrelevance. If the Governor General did not have it, we would quickly regret its absence.

The *third reserve power* is the power to dissolve Parliament and call elections. Normally governors-general follow whatever advice is given them by their prime minister, yet there have been occasions when such advice has been refused. In 1926, Prime Minister Mackenzie King, realizing that his minority government was about to be defeated on a motion censuring the government for corruption, asked Governor General Lord Byng to dissolve Parliament and call new elections. Byng refused, instead calling upon Arthur Meighen, the Conservative leader, to form a new ministry. There is a great deal of disagreement as to whether Byng's decision was a good one,[3] but there is no doubt that the Governor General needs the reserve power to refuse dissolution in circumstances where elections have been held recently and there is a clear alternative choice for prime minister in the House.

This relatively obscure point of constitutional procedure came to the country's attention during the parliamentary crisis of December 2008. When the Liberals, NDP, and Bloc announced their intention to vote non-confidence in the Conservative government and offer a Liberal-NDP coalition to replace it, there was some speculation that Mr. Harper might attempt to prevent such a move by asking Governor General Michaëlle Jean for a dissolution (and therefore an election) if the House expressed a lack of confidence in his government. Since a general election had been held a mere two months earlier, and since the Liberal leader Stéphane Dion would obviously have the confidence of the House, the Governor General would almost certainly have been correct to refuse any request from Mr. Harper for a dissolution. Instead, Mr. Harper blocked the opposition's strategy by asking the Governor General to prorogue Parliament (that is, declare a temporary

---

3   See J.R. Mallory, *The Structure of Canadian Government* (Toronto: Gage Publishing, 1984), 52–55.

CHAPTER SIX · THE CROWN AND ITS SERVANTS

recess) for six weeks. Some observers argued that the Governor General should have refused this request on the grounds the Mr. Harper was merely trying to prevent the opposition from exercising its right to express non-confidence.

However, it is probably a mistake to suggest that the Governor General has a reserve power to deny a request to prorogue. Governors-general traditionally take whatever advice the prime minister offers with respect to proroguing, and there is no reason for them to have any discretionary authority in this area. After all, Mr. Harper was merely postponing the vote, not preventing it.

While wielding the reserve powers is the most essential function of the Governor General, the most common functions of the office are ceremonial. As the official representative for the Queen, our head of state, the Governor General represents the Crown in a number of ways. First, the Governor General must preside over a number of important political ceremonies, such as the opening of Parliament, and represents Canada at a wide variety of events where official representation is necessary—welcoming certain foreign dignitaries, presenting awards, and attending state funerals in foreign countries. Of particular note is the fact that the Governor General is the official head of our armed forces.

The Governor General's role as *de facto* head of state frees the prime minister to concentrate more fully on the business of governing. More important, however, is the symbolic value of having someone other than the prime minister serve as the highest representative of our regime. In his influential book *The Crown in Canada*,[4] Frank MacKinnon argues that the Crown strengthens democracy by keeping potentially arrogant politicians in their place: the ceremonial work of the Governor General is a constant reminder to politicians that they are servants of the Crown (and hence servants of the people) rather than political masters. Because the office of Governor General stands above party politics, it represents all the people of Canada rather than just those who voted for the party in power. This gives the citizens of the regime (and its military) a non-partisan focus for their loyalty. They can be loyal to the regime, as embodied in the Governor General, without necessarily supporting the politicians who run the government at any given point in time. For these reasons, MacKinnon argues, the Crown is a useful institution for keeping our powerful politicians a little more humble.

6.4 The Cabinet

As we saw in Chapter 3, the real seat of government power in a system of responsible government is a body known as the "cabinet." In constitutional practice (as

---

4   Frank MacKinnon, *The Crown in Canada* (Calgary: Glenbow-Alberta Institute, 1976).

opposed to constitutional law) it is this cabinet that exercises executive power. The cabinet also has decisive control over legislative power, especially in situations of majority government. But what, exactly, is the cabinet, and what is the constitutional basis of its power?

To answer these questions, we must turn, once again, to the text of the Constitution. Section 11 of *CA 1867* creates a body called **The Queen's Privy Council for Canada**, which is given the all-important right to "advise" the Governor General in the exercise of his or her powers. As "advisers," the privy councillors are, strictly speaking, mere servants of the Crown. As we have seen, however, under the rules of responsible government, "advice" given to the Governor General is the equivalent of an order. The Queen's Privy Council for Canada is thus a very powerful body, for it controls virtually all those powers granted by the Constitution to the Crown or the Governor General.

Section 11 states that the privy councillors are appointed by the Governor General, but constitutional convention stipulates that the Governor General will make these appointments on the "advice" of the person he or she has asked to serve as prime minister. Although the Constitution does allow for the possibility that the Governor General might "remove" a member of the Privy Council, appointments to that body are in practice appointments for life. This means that the Privy Council includes every living person who has ever been named to that body. Privy councillors nominated by former prime ministers Mulroney, Chrétien, and Martin are thus still members of the Privy Council.

Of course, in a democratic regime, it would be unthinkable to have privy councillors who had been nominated by a defeated government continue to exercise political power. We therefore have a convention stipulating that the power to "advise" the Governor General will be exercised only by a small subset of privy councillors: those who have been nominated by (and have maintained the confidence of) the current prime minister. It is this subset of the Privy Council that we call the "cabinet," and we may therefore define the cabinet as those privy councillors who have the power to advise the Crown. The size of the cabinet is determined by the prime minister. Mulroney's cabinet had as many as 40 ministers and Chrétien's had as few as 28. The cabinet appointed after the 2011 election had 39.[5] A number of MPs will also be appointed **parliamentary secretaries** to these ministers. A parliamentary secretary will sometimes answer questions in the House on behalf of a minister and generally serves as a kind of assistant or even apprentice to the minister. Indeed, the position of parliamentary secretary

---

5   The membership of the current cabinet is listed on the website of the prime minister: http://www.pm.gc.ca.

is frequently used as a way of auditioning newer MPs for subsequent promotion to cabinet.

While it is technically correct to refer to the members of the cabinet as privy councillors, it is more common to call them "ministers." This is because most members of the cabinet will spend most of their time "advising" the Crown on the work of one of its "ministries" or departments. For instance, the Minister of Energy and Natural Resources will spend most of his or her time developing new policy for that ministry and ensuring that existing policy is being executed effectively and efficiently. (More will be said about this work in Section 6.8 below.)

But the cabinet is much more than a collection of individual ministers. An essential element of our system of responsible government is the principle of **collective responsibility**—the idea that cabinet must function *as a team* to develop, implement, and take responsibility for public policy. This principle follows logically from the conventions of responsible government: it is not individual ministers who must maintain the confidence of the House or resign, it is the cabinet (including the prime minister) as a whole. To the extent that it is the cabinet that has the mandate to govern, rather than a collection of individuals, responsibility for the exercise of power must logically rest with the cabinet as a team rather than with individual ministers.

The principle of collective responsibility means that whenever ministers have an idea for new legislation in their area, their proposal must win the approval of the cabinet before it can be taken to Parliament. It also means that certain important executive decisions (for example, which of several companies should be awarded a lucrative contract to build frigates for the navy) will be made by the cabinet as a whole rather than by the single minister in charge of that area. For reasons outlined in Sections 6.5 and 6.7, it is increasingly the case that executive and legislative decisions that require cabinet approval are in fact being made by cabinet committees or even by the prime minister. Under the principles of responsible government, such practice is legitimate only to the extent that those making the decisions have a mandate to speak for the cabinet.

Under the doctrine of collective responsibility, any decision made by the cabinet as a whole must be defended by each and every one of its members, and, by convention, a cabinet minister who is not prepared to defend a position taken by cabinet must resign. This explains why cabinet discussions must always be confidential and secret. Ministers have to be able to freely and vigorously debate proposed measures before they decide on them, but they would not be able to defend a cabinet decision in public if it were revealed that they had spoken against it in the course of cabinet deliberations.[6]

Because the cabinet plays such a central role in the exercise of political power, it is essential that it be as representative of the country as possible. By tradition, it will have at least one member from each of the country's ten provinces, with the possible exception of Prince Edward Island. The various regions of the country are normally represented in some sort of proportion to their population, but deviations will occur if particular regions have elected few government members. There must be a representative number of French Canadians. It is also important to ensure strong representation for women and at least some representation for those Canadians who are visible minorities. The formation of the cabinet must, in the final analysis, take into consideration the way in which Canadians identify the fundamentally important political distinctions of provinces, regions, ethnicity, and gender.

6.5   The Cabinet Committee System

In Canada's first century, the cabinet could handle its business by meeting once a week, usually on Friday afternoons. By the 1960s, however, the growth of the welfare state had expanded the workload of governments dramatically. This was reflected in the fact that the cabinet had grown from 12 ministers under Sir John A. Macdonald to over 30 under Pierre Trudeau. Because of the volume of business to be conducted, as well as the number of participants involved, the traditional cabinet meeting was no longer an adequate forum for making the kinds of decisions that it needed to make. For this reason, prime ministers Pearson and Trudeau developed a system of cabinet committees that revolutionized the way cabinet does its business.

Each prime minister has the authority to organize the cabinet committee system however he or she likes, and since the Pearson/Trudeau years, a number of substantially different models have been used. It therefore makes little sense to describe any particular model in detail, but each of the systems we have seen thus far is characterized by a number of essential features.

---

6   In an attempt to appear more "democratic," BC Premier Gordon Campbell occasionally held televised cabinet meetings when he was first elected. The kindest interpretation one can give to this kind of exercise is to characterize it as token. No meaningful cabinet decision could ever be made publicly because cabinet ministers could not make serious criticisms of proposals during the meeting and then defend them publicly afterwards.

The basic idea of the system is to divide the cabinet's work and assign it to a number of smaller groups—the cabinet committees. The cabinet's work is done more efficiently because five groups of six people can do five times as much work in an hour as one group of 30 people. Most cabinet committee systems will be composed of between five and 12 such committees, which are usually organized around a particular policy area (for instance, economic development or social policy). Each committee will study all of the problems or questions that arise in its particular area and make recommendations to the full cabinet. For the system to function, the cabinet must normally approve a committee's recommendations without too much debate; otherwise, it would end up doing the committee's work all over again. Still, individual ministers who are not members of the committee have every right to raise questions and objections at the cabinet level and sometimes succeed in having questions sent back to the committee for further study. Most cabinet committee systems have contained one "super-committee," usually called the Priorities and Planning Committee. Chaired by the prime minister, this committee is usually responsible for determining the broad lines of government policy.

As of December 2011, Prime Minister Harper's cabinet had seven standing committees. The two most important are Priorities and Planning (chaired by Mr. Harper) and Operations, which provides day-to-day coordination of the government's agenda. There are also cabinet committees with responsibility for social affairs, economic growth, foreign affairs, and national security. As always, the Treasury Board is a cabinet committee that oversees personnel, administrative, and expenditure management.[7]

6.6 The Prime Minister

Canadians know that the prime minister is the most powerful political figure in our regime, yet very few of us understand the basis for this power. Our written Constitution gives us little help in this regard. The office of prime minister is not mentioned in *CA 1867*, and it is mentioned only in passing in *CA 1982*. Thus, the powers of the prime minister are all based on constitutional convention. Let us think for a minute about the title of the office: the "prime" minister is literally the "first" minister. This title makes sense because, in seeking out a group of advisers,

---

[7]   The organization of the cabinet and its committees is at the discretion of the prime minister. For the latest organization of the cabinet and its committees, see the website of the Privy Council Office: http://www.pco-bcp.gc.ca.

the Governor General first names a prime minister, who then offers advice on the appointment of the other ministers.

It is this right to advise the Crown on the assignment of cabinet posts that constitutes the core of the prime minister's power. We have seen that in a regime based on responsible government, the cabinet is the centre of legislative and executive power. The office of prime minister carries with it no specific departmental responsibilities, and today, prime ministers rarely reserve a specific ministry for themselves.[8] The fact that they control the membership of the cabinet gives prime ministers a tremendous amount of influence over all the other members of that most powerful body. Ministers who prove to be a thorn in the side of their prime minister may well be demoted to a less attractive portfolio or dropped from the cabinet altogether. Conversely, ministers who support the prime minister's views may improve their chances of promotion to a more important cabinet post. As a result, few ministers are willing to resist a prime minister when he or she has strong opinions on some question.

Prime ministers chair the meetings of the cabinet, and this provides them with an important opportunity to exercise their leadership. Because the cabinet has to act together as a team, its decisions must be based on consensus. One of the prime minister's great tasks is to cultivate this consensus. In order to succeed at this task, prime ministers need great skill; they must know when to postpone discussion and when to continue it; when to paper over disagreements and when to have them argued out; and, above all, when and how to use their own influence to settle a particularly divisive question. Moreover, it is up to the prime minister to determine whether consensus has been reached (there is no formal voting in cabinet) and to define what the consensus is. This prerogative is another source of significant political influence.

The other major task of the prime minister is to serve as the leading spokesperson for the cabinet. Individual ministers take responsibility for public relations in most matters relevant to their particular departments. If the issue is a particularly important one, however, the prime minister will often be the person who makes the cabinet's case to the public. This is especially true during election campaigns, when the public's attention is focused almost exclusively on the prime minister and the leaders of the opposition parties.

In addition to their right to advise the Governor General on the composition of the cabinet, Canada's prime ministers wield a number of other specific powers. The most important of these are the right to advise the Governor

---

8   This was done frequently in the first century of Confederation. John A. Macdonald, for example, was both Prime Minister and Minister of Justice.

General on the dissolution of Parliament and the holding of elections; the right to advise the Governor General on a number of key appointments, including appointments to the Senate and to the judiciary; and the right to organize the machinery of government, including the number and composition of departments and the nature of the cabinet committee system.

Prime ministers have a number of people who help them in the performance of their duties. First are the members of the **Prime Minister's Office (PMO)**. Originally, the PMO was a small secretariat that took responsibility for organizing the prime minister's schedule, answering mail, and other routine tasks. The office was greatly expanded by Prime Ministers Trudeau and Mulroney. Today's PMO has a staff well in excess of 100; it is responsible for monitoring the general political situation and giving the prime minister political advice. The members of the staff (led by the Principal Secretary) are for the most part partisan political activists rather than career civil servants.

Just the opposite is true of a second secretariat, the **Privy Council Office (PCO)**, which is staffed by non-partisan career civil servants. As its name suggests, the PCO serves as a secretariat to the cabinet and is thus responsible to the chair of the cabinet, the prime minister. The PCO facilitates the collective work of the cabinet by organizing and providing logistical support for its meetings and its committees. It has also, since the Trudeau years, served as an agency that can give policy advice to the prime minister and cabinet (as distinct from the political advice that emanates from the PMO). The PCO is headed by the Chief Clerk of the Privy Council, who is the highest ranking civil servant in the country.

Prime ministers are usually assisted in their duties by a **deputy prime minister**, a member of the cabinet who has a portfolio of his or her own, but who also serves as a kind of second-in-command to the prime minister. Through most of our history, being deputy prime minister conferred little real power. At most, it meant filling in for the prime minister when he or she was absent or indisposed. Since the time of the Mulroney government, however, the position of deputy prime minister has become more significant. Prime Minister Mulroney actually delegated much of his day-to-day work to his deputy, Don Mazankowski, in order to free himself to concentrate on two or three particularly important issues, such as the Constitution and free trade. In Martin's government, Deputy Prime Minister Anne McLellan played a similar role, chairing the Operations Committee of Cabinet. Mr. Harper has been the great exception in this respect: his government has no deputy prime minister.

6.7 Prime Ministerial Government?

It is sometimes argued that the Canadian regime is moving away from cabinet government and toward "prime ministerial" government.[9] There can be no doubt that the office of prime minister has grown substantially more powerful in recent years. In this television age, the prime minister's role as the chief spokesperson for the government gives him or her a public profile that dwarfs the profile of the cabinet. Moreover, the decentralizing tendencies of the cabinet committee system have had the effect of fragmenting the collective power of the cabinet. To a large extent, it has been the prime minister, with the assistance of the PMO and PCO, who has stepped into the gap. In recent years, a series of prime ministers have used their authority to transfer more and more of the cabinet's power in their own hands. The trend is now so strong that Jean Chrétien could make the astonishing observation that cabinet has become little more than a "focus group" for the prime minister.[10]

Stephen Harper's first term in office suggests that he runs a government that is at least as "prime ministerial" as those of his immediate predecessors—and probably more so. His handling of the issue of Québec's status as a nation provides one of the most striking illustrations of the degree to which he controls his government. In late 2006, Mr. Harper caught everyone off guard by announcing that his government would introduce and support a resolution declaring that Quebeckers constitute a "nation" within a united Canada. No one was more surprised by this announcement than Michael Chong. As the Minister of Intergovernmental Affairs, Mr. Chong was the person in cabinet responsible for policy in this area, but Mr. Harper did not even bother to inform (let alone consult) Mr. Chong before embarking on this significant change in policy. Mr. Chong subsequently resigned in protest.

There are several other indications of a strengthening of prime ministerial government under Mr. Harper. He has laid down rigid restrictions about when and where cabinet ministers can speak and what they can say. He has also taken personal control over the appointment of the chairs of the committees of the House of Commons, something that has traditionally been left to the committees themselves.

---

9   For a discussion of this thesis, see Donald Savoie, *Governing From the Centre: The Concentration of Power in Canadian Politics* (Toronto: University of Toronto Press, 1999).

10   Donald Savoie, "The Canadian Prime Minister: Revisiting *Primus* in Canadian Politics," in Thomas Bateman, ed., *Braving the New World,* 3rd ed. (Toronto: Thomson-Nelson, 2004) 209–23.

For some, it is ironic that these extensions of prime ministerial government should be taken by Mr. Harper. After all, his political roots are in the Reform Party, which originally stood for more open, democratic, and accountable government. Perhaps what the case of Mr. Harper shows is that the tendency toward prime ministerial government is a function of the regime itself rather than simply the product of a few individual prime ministers.

Still, one must be careful not to overestimate the power of the prime minister. It should never be forgotten that prime ministers are not directly elected to their position by the people. Because they are ultimately dependent on the confidence of the House of Commons, they cannot afford to alienate key sources of support such as the cabinet. Indeed, a united cabinet, through the threat of collective resignation, could probably force the resignation of any prime minister. Moreover, in most federal cabinets, there are some ministers whose support within their party (or with the general public) is so strong that they are not easily intimidated by a prime minister. A perfect illustration of this phenomenon would be the influence wielded by Paul Martin in the years he served as Jean Chrétien's Minister of Finance. Martin's influence over the Liberal Party was so great that it seriously rivalled that of the prime minister. Indeed, some would argue that Martin's supporters within the party actually forced Chrétien out of office. This may be too strong a statement, but there is little doubt that the influence of Martin as Minister of Finance constituted a substantial limitation on the authority of his prime minister.

In the final analysis, the "strength" of any particular prime minister will depend as much on political circumstances as on the rules of the Constitution. The prime minister is invited to form a government because he or she is the leader of the party that is most likely to have the confidence of the House of Commons. The prime minister's power as prime minister will therefore be directly related to the control he or she has over that party. This control of the party will be influenced by a number of factors. One is the process used by the party to choose its leader.[11] Another is party unity: the prime minister will have trouble dominating the government if the party in power is divided into factions. The most important factor, however, is the prime minister's popularity with the voters. Popular prime ministers who are poised to lead their party to victory will command great support in their party. On the other hand, prime ministers whose personal unpopularity threatens to lead to electoral defeat may have a difficult time keeping their cabinet and caucus in line.

---

11   This is discussed below in Chapter 10.

6.8 The Civil Service

Section 9 of *CA 1867* invests the executive power of government in the Crown. We have seen that under the terms of responsible government, the Crown exercises its executive power on the advice of a small number of servants (its ministers) who are accountable to the elected representatives of the people. But the tasks associated with the exercise of executive power are too numerous and complex to be handled by such a small group of people. The Crown therefore needs many other servants to carry out its executive tasks. These people are known as the Crown's "civil" servants (as opposed to its military servants). In 2010, the federal government employed about 180,000 of them. They are non-partisan professionals, hired on the basis of merit (rather than their political connections), in most cases by the politically neutral Public Service Commission (PSC).[12]

The civil service may be divided into two branches. The majority work in what are known as **line departments**, ministries like Transportation, Health, or Foreign Affairs, which provide services of some sort to the general public. A smaller group are employed by the so-called **central agencies**, such as the PSC or the Treasury Board.[13] These are bodies that engage in the coordination of government policy rather than in the delivery of particular services to the public. Many of these civil servants wield a substantial amount of power. The civil servants who work as officers for Canada Customs, for instance, have a good deal of authority when it comes to searching the cars of Canadians returning from visits to the United States. In order to prevent abuses of that power, it is essential to ensure that all civil servants will be accountable for the way in which they carry out their duties. Under responsible government, this accountability is achieved through the principle of **ministerial responsibility**.

According to this principle, the minister who heads each department must be accountable to the House of Commons for the conduct of each and every civil servant working in that department. On the most basic level, such accountability implies that the ministers may be asked in the House to investigate allegations of incompetence or impropriety in their departments and to take appropriate measures. If the incompetence or impropriety is substantial and may be attributed to serious mismanagement by the minister, the convention

---

12   The public service includes both the civil service and all other employees of the national government who fall under the Public Service Employment Act. A full accounting of all these employees is provided by the Public Service Commission at http://www.psc-cfp.gc.ca

13   The Treasury Board is a special committee of the cabinet, established by statute, which reviews all proposed expenditures and which serves as the official employer of the civil service.

of ministerial responsibility requires the minister to resign, but resignations for reasons of egregious mismanagement have rarely occurred at the federal level.[14] In 1985, Fisheries Minister John Fraser was compelled to resign after it became known that he personally ordered officials in his ministry to approve the sale of tuna that departmental officials had deemed unsafe for human consumption. In 2005, Immigration Minister Judy Sgro resigned amid public concerns over her department's practice of providing visas to exotic dancers.

It is common, in our parliamentary system, for opposition members to demand a minister's resignation for much less serious matters or for matters where the minister was less directly implicated. One of our most famous controversies regarding ministerial responsibility took place in 1988 when the budget of Finance Minister Michael Wilson was leaked to the press the day before it was due to be released. The leaking of a budget is a serious problem because those who have advance knowledge of certain changes in the government's fiscal policy can take advantage of that knowledge to make substantial profits by buying or selling stocks, bonds, currencies, or other commodities. When Wilson's budget was leaked to the press, members of the opposition immediately called for his resignation. Wilson refused to resign, arguing that he could not be held personally accountable for the actions of an unknown person or persons who may have leaked the budget for criminal or malicious reasons. Wilson's argument was a reasonable one: to take a more stringent view of the meaning of ministerial responsibility would make each and every minister the hostage of any disaffected civil servant who wanted to see the minister fired. Under the convention of ministerial responsibility, Wilson would have been required to resign had the leak occurred due to gross personal negligence on his part, but it is well-established that a minister cannot be required to resign for mistakes that are not his or her own. To be sure, ministers would be *politically* accountable to the House of Commons for such mistakes—that is, they must ensure that appropriate disciplinary and corrective measures be taken—but they are not *personally* accountable for mistakes made by others.

---

14   S.L. Sutherland, "Responsible Government and Ministerial Responsibility: Every Reform Is Its Own Problem," *Canadian Journal of Political Science* XXIV, 1 (March 1991): 100–105.

Figure 6.1: Ministerial Responsibility

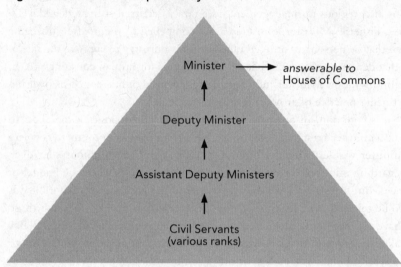

Some observers argue that it is unrealistic or simplistic to say that ministers are in charge of their departments. The civil servants in each department are divided into various ranks. At the top of the ladder in each department is an official known as the deputy minister, a career civil servant who usually has advanced technical training and a good deal of civil service experience. In most cases, the deputy minister will know far more about the business of the department than will the minister. In theory, the deputy minister is merely the minister's chief adviser; in practice, however, the deputy's superiority in knowledge can lead to a situation where he or she is really the one who runs the department. This is particularly true in situations where one has a strong and experienced deputy working for a weak or inexperienced minister.

The Commission of Inquiry into the Sponsorship Scandal (informally known as the Gomery Commission) filed its second and final report in February 2006. In that report, Justice Gomery suggested that the "sponsorship scandal" was in many respects a failure of ministerial responsibility. Responsible government is based on the principle that those who exercise the power of government (the prime minister and cabinet) are responsible to the House of Commons, that is, accountable to the House for their actions. Justice Gomery found that the misconduct that took place in the sponsorship scandal was facilitated by an absence of appropriate mechanisms to keep the prime minister and cabinet fully accountable to the House. His report recommended a number of reforms including:

- in order to make the civil service more independent of the prime minister and cabinet, the deputy ministers should be appointed independently rather than by the prime minister;
- cabinet ministers should be made accountable to the House for the actions not only of their civil servants but also of their political staff (e.g., executive assistants, chief-of-staff);
- strengthening parliamentary committees, especially the Public Accounts Committee, which reviews government expenditures;
- placing all secret contingency funds (such as the notorious "Unity Reserve" that Prime Minister Chrétien used to fund the sponsorship activities) under the direction of central agencies where they will be subject to greater transparency.

As part of its *Federal Accountability Act*, the Conservative government acted upon the third and fourth of these reforms, but it has expressed no interest in the first two.

Key Terms

constitutional monarchy	collective responsibility
Queen of Canada	Prime Minister's Office (PMO)
head of state	Privy Council Office (PCO)
guardian of responsible government	deputy prime minister
reserve powers	line departments
Queen's Privy Council for Canada	central agencies
parliamentary secretaries	ministerial responsibility

Discussion Questions

1. Given that Canada is a democracy, should the Governor General not be elected?

2. Are prime ministers and premiers too powerful? If so, what could be done about it?

CHAPTER SEVEN

PARLIAMENT

7.1   The Role of Parliament

7.2   The Parliamentary Calendar

7.3   The House of Commons: Membership and Officers

7.4   The Business of the House of Commons

7.5   The Rules of Procedure of the House of Commons

7.6   The Backbencher

7.7   House of Commons Reform

7.8   The Senate

7.9   Senate Reform

Under the heading "Legislative Power," Section 17 of *CA 1867* declares that Canada shall have a "Parliament" consisting of a House of Commons, a Senate, and the Queen. Since Canada's senators are appointed and the Queen has her position by heredity, only the House of Commons can claim to be a democratic institution. By constitutional convention, then, it is the House of Commons that takes the predominant role in the exercise of Parliament's powers, and this in turn explains why people commonly equate "Parliament" with the House of Commons.

The Constitution says relatively little about the structure, role, or powers of Parliament. Yet that lacuna does not leave us without guidance. The statement in the preamble of *CA 1867* stipulating that Canada is to have "a Constitution similar in principle to that of the United Kingdom" establishes that, unless otherwise specified, our Parliament is to be a Canadian version of the British Parliament at Westminster. Of course, we have seen that the British Constitution is one that is in continual evolution. This means that the place of Parliament in the British regime has changed greatly over the years. Before we begin to describe the specific workings of Canada's Parliament, it will be necessary to explain briefly the role of that institution in modern times.

7.1   The Role of Parliament

British constitutional history is the history of the development of parliamentary democracy. Originally, Parliament served as a body that advised the Crown in its exercise of legislative power. It was called a "parliament" (from the French word *parler,* to speak) because it was in essence a deliberative body, that is, a body designed to engage in speech about what should be done. Over time, Parliament's advice came to be understood as binding on the monarch so that it was in effect in control of the legislative activity of government. As democratic ideas developed further, the British adopted the principle of responsible government—the idea that those exercising executive power must have the confidence of the people's representatives in Parliament. By the early nineteenth century, Parliament was in what is sometimes called its "golden age." With full control over legislative power, and a tight grip on those exercising executive power, Parliament was the most important political institution in British politics.

By the end of the nineteenth century, however, the power of Parliament had begun to wane because of the rise of highly disciplined political parties whose members could be counted on to vote in accordance with the wishes of their party leaders. In the "golden age" of Parliament, what was said or done in that body was often of decisive importance. Great speeches might make or break legislative proposals, or force a cabinet to resign. But once Britain's parliamentarians had all joined parties that were able to control the way their members voted, real power was transferred to the cabinet; since the cabinet constituted the leadership of the party that had control of Parliament, it had effective control over that body. One might say that Parliament lost much of its influence because what was *said* there rarely affected what was *done* there. Party discipline guaranteed that the cabinet would always have enough votes to protect its own position in power and to get its legislation adopted.

This is the situation that now prevails in Canada. In the Canadian regime, it is Parliament that adopts legislation, and, formally, it is Parliament that determines whether a cabinet has the right to govern. But the existence of highly disciplined parliamentary parties means that Parliament rarely uses its power in these matters. When it adopts legislation, Parliament is in most cases merely ratifying legislative decisions that have in effect been made by the prime minister and cabinet. Nor does Parliament often exercise much real power when it comes to determining whether a government should continue in office. For a cabinet supported by a party with a parliamentary majority is virtually guaranteed the "confidence" of the House of Commons.

Since 2004, Canadians have three times elected parliaments where no party has a majority. In some respects, Parliament then plays a more important role in these minority situations. Governments cannot simply legislate as they please and must sometimes work out compromises if they wish to avoid new elections. Pundits and politicians speculate endlessly about whether or when the House will vote to bring down the government. Yet even in the case of minority government, it is not the debate in the House that determines what the House will do; if the House votes to withdraw confidence in a government, it is just formalizing a decision made by two or more of the opposition parties to force new elections.[1]

In order to understand properly the role of Parliament in the Canadian regime, it is necessary to look at that institution in light of the changes that have followed from the emergence of disciplined political parties. Though Parliament is still a legislative body, and the House of Commons still has the power to make or break a government, the development of party discipline and the resulting transfer of parliamentary power to the cabinet have left Parliament with a new role. *The primary purpose of the modern parliament is to make the cabinet accountable for its actions to the public.* Parliament provides a forum in which opposition members can criticize the government, offer constructive alternatives, and perhaps even succeed in pressuring the government to make changes to a bill or even withdraw it. The opposition cannot prevent a cabinet with a parliamentary majority from doing as it pleases, since the party in power will by definition be able to outvote the parties in opposition. But effective criticism of a government's policy in a high-profile setting such as Parliament can be very damaging to the governing party's chances in the next elections. By allowing opposition members to

---

1   One rare exception was a vote of confidence in May 2005 when the number of votes held by the parties supporting the Martin government (Liberal and NDP) appeared to be equal to the number of votes held by the parties opposing it (Conservative and Bloc). The fate of the government therefore appeared to depend on the vote of independent MP Chuck Cadman. Cadman was very coy about which way he intended to vote, and many Canadians tuned in to watch this dramatic, but exceptional, vote on television.

scrutinize and criticize the cabinet's conduct or policy, then, Parliament plays an essential role in keeping the government sensitive to the concerns of the voters.

7.2 The Parliamentary Calendar

To understand how Parliament works, one must begin with some basic information about the parliamentary calendar.

Parliament is not an institution that works on a permanent ongoing basis. The parliamentary calendar divides the work of that body into distinct units called "Parliaments." Each time general elections are held, the new contingent of MPs forms a new Parliament. These Parliaments are thus numbered in tandem with the country's elections. In 1867, Canadians elected the first Parliament. Our 41st Parliament was elected in 2011. Each Parliament is broken down into smaller time units known as **sessions** of Parliament. The session is its basic work unit. Any legislative work begun in one session (for instance, the adoption of new youth crime legislation) has to be completed in that session. If it is not, and those sponsoring the legislation wish to try again in a new session, they must start all over from scratch.

It is the Governor General, on the advice of the prime minister, who decides when the session should begin. Similarly, it is the Governor General, on the advice of the prime minister, who declares an end to the session (the technical term for this is **prorogation**). Thus, there is no set length of time for a parliamentary session; sessions will run until the prime minister is satisfied with what Parliament has accomplished. For most of our history, sessions have typically been about a year in length. Since elections are normally held about every four years, this means that each Parliament usually has four sessions. There is no fixed rule on this matter, however; the first session of the 32nd Parliament, in which the Trudeau government proposed a number of controversial pieces of legislation (including the National Energy Policy and the plan for *CA 1982*), lasted almost four years.

Each session begins with a **Throne Speech**, delivered to the members of both the House and the Senate, assembled together in the Senate chamber. This speech is read by the Governor General, but it is prepared by the prime minister's staff. The speech outlines the legislative program that the government intends to propose to Parliament. That program, and the government's general performance, are then debated for a few days in the House of Commons.

When the prime minister decides that it is time to terminate not only a session but the Parliament as well, he or she asks the Governor General for a **dissolution** of Parliament. Dissolution automatically entails the holding of general elections to select another Parliament.

7.3 The House of Commons: Membership and Officers

The House of Commons currently consists of 308 Members of Parliament (or MPs). Each MP has been elected to represent one territorially based constituency known as a riding. In general, ridings are constructed in accordance with the principle of representation by population, so that the percentage of "seats" each province has in the House will be roughly equivalent to its percentage of the national population. There are some minor institutionalized deviations from this principle. Some of the smaller provinces (especially Prince Edward Island) are overrepresented in the House because of Section 51A of *CA 1867*, which guarantees every province at least as many seats in the House as it has in the Senate. The three territories are also overrepresented in the House in that their modest populations are all less than the average population of a Canadian riding. These deviations serve to improve dramatically the representation of the smaller partners in Confederation, yet do not seriously weaken the influence of the larger provinces.

The number of seats per province is adjusted after each decennial census in order to ensure that the distribution keeps pace with changes in population. In 1985, a somewhat complicated formula to govern this redistribution was developed. It was not entirely effective at maintaining proportionality because it under-compensated rapidly growing provinces such as BC and Alberta. Not surprisingly, the Conservative Party, which is strong in these areas, was keen to change the formula. In 2011, the 41st Parliament revised the formula by way of legislation called the Fair Representation Act. As a result, in the next general election the total number of seats in the House of Commons will increase by 30 to 338. The new formula will give Alberta and British Columbia each six more seats, Ontario fifteen, and Québec three—numbers much more in line with their current populations.

The fundamental distinction among MPs is that some are "government members" (that is, they belong to the party that forms the cabinet) and the rest are members of the "opposition." Within the ranks of the opposition, there is a further distinction: the largest of the opposition parties becomes "Her Majesty's Loyal Opposition" or the "Official Opposition," as it is sometimes called. Under parliamentary rules, this Official Opposition is entitled to certain privileges that are not extended to the other opposition parties: its leader is granted special speaking privileges in the House and even has a special residence provided at taxpayers' expense (Stornoway). The conferral of these privileges and titles on a politician who, in effect, lost the election, is indicative of how vital a role the opposition plays in Parliament. Because the central task of the modern parliament is to make the government accountable to the public, the opposition is an extremely important component of that body.

The layout of the House reflects the importance of this adversarial government-opposition relationship in a regime based on responsible government. While most legislative chambers in the world seat all members together, facing a central podium, the Canadian House of Commons (like the British House in Westminster) has the government and opposition members facing each other like the offensive and defensive lines of a football team. Moreover, the prime minister and cabinet are always seated directly opposite the Official Opposition. Figure 7.1 provides a sketch of the layout of the House.

Figure 7.1: Plan of House of Commons, 41st Parliament

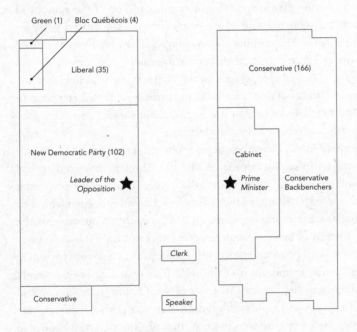

The most important parliamentary officer of the House of Commons is the **Speaker**. The Speaker is an MP elected by the House at the beginning of each Parliament to preside over its debates and to take responsibility for its administration. The person chosen as Speaker will, of course, have been elected to the House as a partisan politician—usually as an MP for the governing party. Once installed in office, however, Speakers must maintain a strict impartiality. They never take part in parliamentary debate and are permitted to vote only when it is necessary to break a tie.

The House has a number of other officers. The **Clerk of the House**, who sits at a table in the middle of the floor directly in front of the Speaker, takes responsibility for doing the official paperwork of the House and provides procedural advice to the Speaker when this is necessary. The **Sergeant-at-Arms**, usually a distinguished military figure, is responsible for the security of the House. Recording secretaries are also present in the House to keep an official record of its debates (commonly known as *Hansard*). There are also two special officers with a kind of "watchdog" function, the Auditor General and the Ethics Commissioner. The primary responsibility of the **Auditor General** is to review government spending. The importance of this particular position became quite evident to Canadians in 2003 when Auditor General Sheila Fraser tabled a report suggesting that the Chrétien government had seriously mismanaged the $500 million Canada Unity Fund. Among other things, it appeared that up to $100 million of the money had been given to advertising firms with strong connections to the Liberal Party for work of little or no value. The ensuing "Sponsorship Scandal" led to the removal of several prominent Liberals from their top management positions in Crown corporations and to criminal charges against the civil servant who managed the sponsorship dossier. It also played a key role in turning what had appeared to be an easy Liberal majority victory in the 2004 elections into a mere minority government—a stinging rebuke from the electorate.

The position of **Ethics Commissioner** is a newer one and has been a source of some controversy in the past decade. While the Chrétien government had promised in 1993 to create an independent ethics commissioner, the position it actually created was widely criticized for being insufficiently independent. The problem was that the Ethics Commissioner was originally accountable to the prime minister instead of being an independent officer of the House. In cases where that officer was asked to investigate ethical propriety of actions involving cabinet members or the prime minister himself, there was, rightly or wrongly, widespread doubt about his capacity to proceed with appropriate vigour and independence. In response to public dissatisfaction with these arrangements, Parliament created two new positions in 2004: that of Ethics Commissioner to deal with questions of conduct by members of the House of Commons, and that of Senate Ethics Officer to handle similar questions in relation to senators. The terms of office for these positions were set at five years and were made non-renewable to avoid any suspicion that incumbents might go easy on parliamentarians in order to win reappointment.

7.4 The Business of the House of Commons

The work of the House is complex and varied, but four main elements of its business may be identified.

The first, and most important business of the House, is the adoption of **bills**. Bills are legislative proposals. Any MP has the right to introduce a bill for the consideration of the House, but, for reasons discussed below in Section 7.6, **private members' bills**, though numerous, are rarely adopted. Most of Parliament's legislative activity is focused on **government bills**, legislative proposals presented to the House by a minister. These proposals have in most cases been generated by some combination of civil service, minister, and cabinet, and they are referred to as government bills because they normally will have received cabinet approval before they are brought to the House. Only a minister can introduce legislation that entails new taxes or the expenditure of public monies.

Parliament has an elaborate procedure for considering bills, but the complexities of the procedure are there for good reasons. A bill is adopted only after it has passed three "readings." In order to discourage hastiness, the rules stipulate that each of these readings must take place on different days.[2] Moreover, in order to facilitate an orderly consideration of bills, each reading has a distinct focus or purpose. The point of the **first reading** is merely to introduce the bill to the House and to give its members (and the public) a chance to acquaint themselves with its provisions. Some time later, the minister sponsoring the bill will move that it be given **second reading**. The second reading focuses on the basic purpose or principles of the bill. This gives the House an opportunity to endorse the general thrust of the proposal without getting bogged down in debate about details. Once a bill passes second reading, it is sent to one of the House's committees for careful study of its specific provisions. At the **report stage**, the committee presents the House with the results of its study. The report normally includes proposals for amending some of the bill's provisions, and these amendments are voted on by the House. The bill is then presented to the House for final approval in a **third reading**. From here, the bill proceeds to the Senate, where it must go through the same stages. Once the bill has passed all three readings in the Senate, it is presented to the Governor General for **royal assent**, which is a constitutional formality. Only at this stage may the bill be **proclaimed**, that is, transformed from a legislative proposal into a binding law or "statute."

---

2   The House of Commons may, on occasion, vote to suspend this rule if it deems immediate action on a bill necessary.

A second type of business conducted in the House is the adoption of **resolutions**. A resolution differs from a bill in that it merely expresses the opinion of the House; it does not result in the adoption of a new law or policy. What, then, is the point of a resolution? Resolutions are essentially a means of allowing for public debate on issues. The opposition might move a resolution that "this House condemn the government's handling of the economy" in order to try to persuade the public that the government's economic policy is inadequate. The government, on the other hand, might propose a resolution designed to test the public's reaction to some course of action it is considering.

A third type of business conducted in the House is the **scrutiny of public expenditure**. This scrutiny comes in two stages, before and after the expenditure. Before any money is spent by a governmental department, the department must present its **estimates** (its proposed expenditures for the coming year) to whichever of the House's standing committees has jurisdiction in that area of government. This process presents MPs with an opportunity for a detailed examination of proposed government spending, and not a penny of public money may be spent by a department without prior approval by the House. Public expenditures are also scrutinized after the fact. The House's Public Accounts Committee, which is usually chaired by a member of the opposition, examines the finances of each department to ensure that the public's money has been spent wisely. The committee is assisted in its efforts by the Auditor General.

The fourth major type of business conducted in the House is the provision of information. In order to hold government accountable for its work, MPs must have access to relevant information. The procedures of the House allow members to submit written questions or requests for information. The government tables its responses to such questions or requests with the Clerk, and they are subsequently recorded in *Hansard*. MPs also have the chance to pose impromptu questions orally in the Question Period. As most Canadians will know, however, the questions asked in this forum are rarely asked in good faith. Opposition members often ask questions that are designed not to elicit information but to embarrass the government; indeed, the "questions" that are posed are often not questions at all but barely camouflaged speeches. The ministers to whom the questions are directed therefore respond in kind: questions are frequently evaded or used as an opportunity to attack the opposition.

Many Canadians have a negative impression of Question Period because of the highly partisan and frequently hyperbolic character of the exchanges that take place during it. Yet, while there are good reasons to be critical of some of the excesses of Question Period, no other forum allows for such intense and powerful criticism of government policy; it is no coincidence that almost all the footage of parliamentary debate one sees on the television news is drawn from that source. For all its faults, then, Question Period is an essential device for allowing Parliament to perform its crucial role of keeping the government accountable to the public.

7.5 The Rules of Procedure of the House of Commons

The proceedings of the House of Commons are governed by two types of rules. First, Parliament has codified basic regulations concerning the organization of its business and the conduct of its debates in a body of rules known as the **Standing Orders**. The House may amend these Standing Orders by a simple majority vote, and there have been numerous changes to them over the years. In addition to its Standing Orders, the House also recognizes a large number of rules that derive from British (or in some cases, Canadian) parliamentary tradition. It is useful to think of these rules as something like a parliamentary equivalent of constitutional conventions: while not carved in stone, they are respected because years of experience have shown them to be useful.

To the outside observer, many of the rules of procedure followed by the House may seem somewhat quaint. But rules that at first glance appear arbitrary or even whimsical often turn out, on closer inspection, to be both rational and valuable. The House of Commons is meant to be an adversarial chamber. In one way or another, most parliamentary rules are designed either to facilitate or to regulate the adversarial relationship between government and opposition. Notice, for example, how the seating arrangements in the House of Commons promote an adversarial mentality: government and opposition members are seated facing each other, ready to do battle. At the same time, however, the House follows certain rules that are designed to ensure that the battle between the two sides remains civil: comments must always be addressed to the Speaker, rather than directly to one's opponent, and to prevent disagreements from becoming personal, colleagues are addressed as "the Honourable Member from X" rather than by name.

Among the most important rules are those governing the use of House time. In the House of Commons, time is a precious commodity for it takes a good deal of time for the government to get its program through. Though the opposition rarely has enough votes to block government measures, it can exert great pressure on the government by tying up House time and stalling the government's legislative agenda. The House therefore has a number of rules regarding the use of time that are carefully designed to strike a reasonable balance between the government's need to get its business through the House and the opposition's role as a check on the government. Speeches are normally limited to 20 minutes in length, and each member may speak only once on a given motion. Twenty minutes per member per motion is enough to allow the opposition members to cause substantial headaches for the government, but not enough time to stall legislation indefinitely. There is also a rule under the Standing Orders known as **closure**, which permits the government to cut off debate if it decides that the opposition is taking too much time. On paper, the closure provision would seem to deprive the opposition of a fair share in the control of the House's time. One must keep in mind, however, that closure is a suppression of debate. When the rule was first developed, it was assumed that governments would resort to it only in extreme cases, for suppressing debate might be perceived by the public as anti-democratic. During Canada's first century, the closure rule was indeed used rarely and often at great cost to the popularity of the government. More recently, however, it seems that a decline in public attention to Parliament has permitted governments to invoke closure more indiscriminately.

7.6 The Backbencher

In describing the roles of MPs, a distinction is often drawn between the "front benches" and the "back benches." The front benches on the government side of the House are taken by the members of the cabinet. The front benches on the opposition side are occupied by the "shadow cabinet," members who have been assigned a responsibility for criticizing a particular minister. It is the members occupying the front benches who monopolize most of the responsibility, power, and publicity in Canadian politics. The "**backbenchers**," on the other hand, serve in relative anonymity. Indeed, they are often dismissed as "trained seals" whose only job is to vote when and how their leaders tell them to.

Yet it would be a great mistake to think that backbenchers are without influence. Parliament provides three major opportunities for them to voice their concerns. The first is the weekly caucus meeting. Whenever the House is in session, Wednesday mornings are reserved for meetings of the caucus—the MPs (and senators, if they wish) of each party. These meetings are held behind closed doors so that caucus members may speak frankly but without damaging party unity. In opposition caucus meetings, the backbenchers wield a great deal of influence. In government caucus meetings, the backbenchers are less powerful; to a large extent, these meetings are used by the prime minister and cabinet as a means of informing the backbenchers of what they have already decided to do. Still, the prime minister and cabinet can remain in office only as long as they have the confidence of the House, and this gives the government backbenchers a certain amount of leverage; concerted opposition on their part to cabinet proposals will force the cabinet to reconsider.

A second venue in which backbenchers may exert influence is the House of Commons committees. Chief among these are the "standing" (that is, permanent) committees, each of which focuses on some particular area of public policy. The members of these committees, almost all of whom are backbenchers, may thus develop a certain expertise in that area. The committees are responsible for the clause-by-clause examination of bills that takes place after second reading and for the examination of departmental estimates. They may also take responsibility for carrying out studies or investigations on topics relevant to their jurisdiction, sometimes holding hearings across the country. Standing committees have 12 members, assigned by party affiliation in proportion to each party's strength in the House. Each committee has a Chair who runs its meetings and decides all questions of order and procedure. On most committees, the Chair is one of the government members. A few, however—the Public Accounts Committee and the Ethics Committee, for instance—are always chaired by an opposition member since the role of those committees is to serve as a check on the actions of the government. Party discipline is normally much less rigid in committees than it is in the House itself, giving committee members an opportunity to exert some personal influence on the business of Parliament. However in the 39th Parliament, where most standing committees had Conservative chairs but opposition majorities, committees sometimes became ferociously partisan. The government accused the opposition members of using their majorities to conduct witch hunts; the opposition accused the government of purposely trying to make the committees dysfunctional.

The third means for backbenchers to voice their concerns is the private member's bill. Any member of the House may introduce a bill for first reading on any topic, provided that the proposal does not require the expenditure of public money. The rules of the House allot very little time for discussion of private members' bills, and few are ever adopted. But these bills do afford backbenchers an opportunity to put their ideas before the public, and it is not uncommon for some of those ideas to be picked up by the government and reintroduced later on in the form of a government bill. Private members' bills have a better chance of being adopted in a minority parliament where the government has a diminished capacity to control the agenda of the House. In the 39th Parliament, for instance, the House passed a private member's bill sponsored by Liberal Dan McTeague and backed by all three opposition parties creating more favourable tax arrangements for Registered Education Savings Plans.[3]

---

3   The bill, which both surprised and outraged the Conservatives, was effectively overturned a week later as part of a more comprehensive budget motion.

7.7 House of Commons Reform

One of the most common complaints by Canadians about their government is that their elected representatives do not effectively represent them. MPs are routinely criticized for being too subservient to their party leaders. They seem to do a better job of representing the party in Parliament than of representing their constituents. This criticism has been the underlying cause behind numerous attempts to reform the rules and structure of the House of Commons. Attempts at reform have focused on three areas in which the power of individual members might be increased: the standing committees, private members' bills, and free votes.

With respect to the standing committees, reform proposals generally focus on providing the committees with more substantial research resources and increasing the prestige of committee chairs. In a 2008 study of the subject, for example, Tom Axworthy of Queen's University advocated giving committee chairs the same salaries and perks as cabinet ministers and providing each committee with five or six full-time research officers rather than the one they typically have now.[4]

A second reform that is often discussed is the idea of allowing greater opportunities for the introduction and consideration of private members' bills. By providing more time for the debate of such bills, the power of individual MPs to bring forward issues relevant to their particular constituents would be increased.

Finally, it is proposed that MPs should be given more opportunity to vote against their own party. This freedom could be accomplished by relaxing the fairly strict rule governing confidence. One possibility would be that motions of non-confidence in the government would have to be explicit. No longer would defeat of government bills be tantamount to a motion of non-confidence, so government MPs would be able to vote against their party without fear that such a vote would bring down the government.

Prior to becoming prime minister, Paul Martin indicated that reducing what he called the "democratic deficit" would be one of his many priorities. A large part of what he meant by "democratic deficit" was the perceived lack of influence of backbench MPs. At Martin's suggestion, then, the rules surrounding questions of confidence were changed to provide government MPs with greater independence from the party leadership. House of Commons votes are now divided into three categories. Matters the government regards as a vote of confidence are called "three-line votes," and all government members are expected to

---

4   Tom Axworthy, *Everything Old is New Again: Observations on Parliamentary Reform* (Kingston: Centre for the Study of Democracy, Queen's University, April 2008).

vote with the government. "Two-line votes" are matters on which the government has a formal position, but they are not seen as matters of confidence. Here all cabinet ministers and those parliamentary secretaries whose ministers have a stake in the matter being discussed are expected to support the government's position; all other government members are free to vote as they wish. Finally, for votes that do not constitute a question of confidence in the government and on which the government takes no official position, all government members are free to vote as they wish; this is called a "**one-line vote.**"

This change in voting procedures will certainly give backbench MPs a more active role in the management of public affairs. On the other hand, like most proposals for reforming the House of Commons, there are potential drawbacks. Relaxing the confidence rule will encourage MPs from the government side to vote with the opposition. It is unlikely, however, that such a change would alter the way the opposition MPs vote. We may therefore find ourselves frequently confronted by an apparently divided government party and completely united opposition parties. This might turn out to be a recipe for weak government.

In the final analysis, one has to ask whether the defects of parliamentary government are not outweighed by its advantages. Parliamentary government runs smoothly and efficiently because it is, in the main, cabinet government and not government of 308 individual MPs. Cabinet government allows us to clearly establish who is responsible for government legislation and current public policy. The prime minister, the cabinet, and, ultimately, the governing party will be held accountable by the electorate at the next elections. Parliamentary government may not be ideal in every respect, but its advantages should not be taken lightly.

7.8 The Senate

The purpose of the Senate is to serve as a chamber of "sober second thought," which reviews legislative proposals emanating from the House of Commons. It was originally hoped that in performing this function, the Senate would look at legislation from a perspective that differed from that of the House of Commons in two distinct ways. First, the Fathers of Confederation worried that a House of Commons elected on the democratic principle might fail to respect the rights of property; the poor majority might use its democratic power to despoil the rich minority. Thus, the Senate was meant to be a body that would stand up for property rights. This is reflected in the fact that Section 23 of *CA 1867* specifies that senators must possess assets, above and beyond their personal liabilities, in excess of $4,000. The sum of $4,000 does not seem like much today, but in 1867 a relatively small proportion of Canadians could have claimed to be that wealthy.

Second, the Senate was intended to pay special attention to the concerns of the less populous regions of the country. While the principle for allocating seats in the House of Commons was representation by population (making the larger provinces of Ontario and Québec dominant in that body), the principle for allocating Senate seats was equality of the regions. *CA 1867* originally granted 24 seats to each of the three regions that first formed the country: Ontario, Québec, and the Maritimes. The subsequent entry of other provinces into Confederation led to some minor deviations from the principle of regional equality, but Senate representation is still, in essence, based on that principle.[5]

In law, the powers of the Senate are almost the same as those of the House of Commons.[6] In practice, however, the Senate almost never makes full use of its powers, because senators are not elected. Section 24 of *CA 1867* provides that senators are to be "summoned" to that body by the Governor General; in practice, this means that they are appointed by the prime minister. From the very beginning of Confederation, it was recognized that an appointed body like the Senate would have to defer to the leadership of the elected House of Commons. Over the course of our history, the prestige of the Senate has declined steadily, in part because Canadians, whose political ideas are increasingly democratic, have become less tolerant of non-elected officials. However, the decline is also a result of the fact that so many of the appointments made to the Senate by our prime ministers have been patronage appointments designed to reward service to the prime minister's party. By the middle of the twentieth century, it had become a convention of our Constitution that the Senate must not oppose a bill that has the support of the House of Commons. Though senators still carried out their responsibilities for reviewing legislation, they restricted themselves to making recommendations for minor improvements to the bills sent to them by the House. Occasionally such "recommendations" can have major effects. In recent years, for example, government efforts to adopt new legislation in relation to cruelty

---

5   The Senate currently has 105 seats: Ontario and Québec have 24 each; the West has 24 seats (six per province); the Maritimes still have 24, but Nova Scotia and New Brunswick each gave up two to Prince Edward Island when that province entered Confederation in 1873. Newfoundland was granted six Senate seats when it joined Canada in 1949. This is the principal deviation from the principle of regional equality. The Yukon, Nunavut, and the Northwest Territories have one Senate seat each.

6   There are two exceptions. Section 53 of *CA 1867* specifies that the House of Commons is to take the leading role in the adoption of "money bills" (legislation raising or spending public funds). Section 47(1) of *CA 1982* specifies that the Senate has only a suspensory veto over constitutional amendments proposed by the House of Commons.

to animals have been repeatedly stalled as the Senate sends each bill back to the Commons with amendments the government deems unacceptable.

The Senate has also, on occasion, demonstrated a willingness to confront the House of Commons more directly. When the PC government came to power in 1984, the Liberals had been in office for 16 years. In that period, the vast majority of Senate appointees had been card-carrying Liberals, and the Liberals thus had a comfortable majority there. When the PC-dominated House adopted a bill implementing the controversial Free Trade Agreement with the United States, the Liberal-dominated Senate refused to go along. By withholding their approval of the bill, the Liberal senators forced the PCs to call a general election, thereby giving the voters an opportunity to express their views on the issue. Shortly after the PCs won that election, they introduced legislation in the House to create the controversial Goods and Services Tax (GST). Again, after the legislation was passed by the House, the Liberal senators threatened to deny the bill their approval. Prime Minister Mulroney responded by using Section 26 of *CA 1867,* which gives the government the authority to appoint four or eight additional senators (one or two per region) when this is necessary to break a deadlock between the two houses of Parliament. Mulroney appointed eight new senators, all of them PCs, and this was enough to ensure that the upper house passed the government's bill.

These episodes provide an interesting illustration of how constitutional conventions work. We saw in Chapter 2 that conventions depend for their enforcement on public reaction. In these cases, the Liberal senators gambled that public opinion would support them. They argued that their actions were consistent with the spirit, if not the letter, of the convention in question, for the purpose of the convention subordinating the Senate to the House of Commons was to ensure that power would be exercised democratically, and the polls indicated that the majority of voters wanted an election on free trade and the defeat of the GST. Whether the argument was good or not, the Liberals got away with it. The only way to enforce a convention is for the voters to punish those who violate it. In the 1993 elections, however, the voters gave the Liberals a strong majority.

7.9 Senate Reform

Canadians have long been dissatisfied with the Senate. **Senate reform** is thus a perennial theme of Canadian political discourse. It includes ideas about changing the way one becomes a senator, about the powers of the Senate, and about the relationship between the Senate and the House of Commons.

A substantial body of opinion suggests that the best way to reform the Senate is to abolish it. Many Canadians believe that senators do little or no productive work and that the institution is nothing but a great waste of money. This is an overly simplistic view, but it is a popular one nonetheless. A more sophisticated case for abolition is made by those who point out that to the extent that senators have an influence on legislation, it is often an undesirable influence. The Senate was intended to be a body that would represent the interests of property. Although the vast majority of today's Canadians would be able to meet the Constitution's requirement that senators possess $4,000 in property, that body is still not representative of the socio-economic majority; even today, many (if not most) senators are very closely linked to Canada's business elite. Colin Campbell has argued that the Senate has operated as a "lobby" for big business, reworking legislation to the advantage of banks and other large corporations.[7] It is because of the close link between the Senate and corporate Canada that the NDP has traditionally supported Senate abolition.

Most advocates of Senate reform prefer to keep the Senate but seek to restructure it so as to give more effective parliamentary representation to Canada's less populous regions. The most common proposal along these lines is to transform the upper house into an elected legislative body. Drawing inspiration largely from the Senate of the United States, reformers argue that in a federal union, the legislative body of the national government should have one house based on representation by population and a second, equally powerful house based on the principle of the equality of the provinces or regions of the country. On this view, the key to making Canada's Senate effective is to elect its members so that they will have as much democratic legitimacy as the members of the House of Commons.

Other observers argue that the Senate should be left pretty much as it is. These analysts reject the proposal for electing senators on the grounds that it could lead to parliamentary paralysis in cases where the two chambers are dominated by different parties. They also reject abolition, arguing that the Senate is more useful than people realize: it cleans up errors or oversights in bills passed by the House of Commons; it serves as a source of cabinet ministers in cases where a prime minister has no MPs from a particular province;[8] and it serves as a convenient place to which a prime minister might "promote" cabinet ministers

---

7   Colin Campbell, *The Canadian Senate: A Lobby From Within* (Toronto: Macmillan, 1978).

8   After winning the 1979 elections with almost no seats from Québec, Prime Minister Joe Clark used the Senate to strengthen his cabinet's representation from that province. After the 1980 elections, which left incoming Liberals with no seats west of Winnipeg, Prime Minister Trudeau did

whose services are no longer required. Defenders of the status quo argue that since the operation of the Senate costs each Canadian only about a dollar a year, it would make more sense to make minor improvements to the institution than to abolish it.[9]

Senate Reform has long been an issue dear to the hearts of many Western Canadians who see a more powerful Senate as a vehicle for better protecting Western interests against a House of Commons that is heavily dominated by Central Canada. It was an especially important issue for the Reform Party, of which Mr. Harper was once a member. Since Mr. Harper became Prime Minister, he has attempted to move the Senate reform agenda forward incrementally. Having gained a majority in the 2011 election, Prime Minister Harper introduced new legislation—the Senate Reform Act—into the 41st Parliament. The new legislation would change the Senate in two important ways. First, it would limit the terms of senators to nine years, while maintaining the mandatory retirement age of 75. Second, the Act would allow for the provinces to hold elections for recommendation to the Crown. The prime minister would be obligated to consider these recommendations before advising the Governor General on new appointments. Providing for an elected Senate has proven difficult for the following reason: Section 24 of *CA 1867* stipulates that senators are appointed and Section 42(1)(b) of *CA 1982* stipulates that changes to the "method of selecting Senators" requires a constitutional amendment by the 7/50 formula. The Conservative legislation is designed to work around the Constitution by using the concept of "senators-in-waiting" first implemented by the Province of Alberta. Since 1990, Alberta has held elections for "senators-in-waiting" in conjunction with its regular legislative elections. Originally, the idea was to create a pool of people who have been elected by Albertans as their democratic choices and to hope that the prime minister would be shamed into nominating new senators from that pool rather than his or her own choices. Since that time, only twice has a prime minister cooperated with the scheme, but Mr. Harper is keen to use the approach systematically. Perhaps most interesting is that the new legislation is aimed at putting a new constitutional convention in place.

The Harper government's approach to Senate reform has been criticized not only by the opposition parties but by some long-time advocates of reform. In both cases the argument being made is that piecemeal reform is inadequate and

---

the same thing. With a relatively small pool of MPs from Québec in 2006, and none from Montreal, Mr. Harper appointed Michael Fortier to the Senate and named him to the cabinet.

9   Darcy Wudel, "A Job Description for Senators," *Policy Options* 7, 3 (April 1986); J. Lemco and P. Regenstreif, "Let the Senate Be," *Policy Options* 6, 4 (May 1985).

may entrench even more deeply some of the problems associated with the Senate. For instance, a more democratic and hence more powerful Senate is not a good thing from the point of view of those provinces or regions that believe they have less than their fair share of senators; yet any change to the number of senators a province has can be made only through the general amending formula of the Constitution, which Mr. Harper concedes is extremely unlikely.

Key Terms

sessions	first reading
prorogation	second reading
Throne Speech	report stage
dissolution	third reading
riding	royal assent
Speaker	proclamation
Clerk of the House	resolutions
Sergeant-at-Arms	scrutiny of public expenditure
Hansard	estimates
Auditor General	Standing Orders
Ethics Commissioner	closure
bills	backbenchers
private members' bills	one-line vote
government bills	Senate reform

Discussion Question

1. If Mr. Harper succeeds in his bid to transform the Senate into an elected body, what will be the effects of that change on Canadian government and politics?

CHAPTER EIGHT
THE JUDICIARY

8.1   The Role of the Judiciary
8.2   The Fundamental Principles of the Canadian Judiciary
8.3   Canada's Courts
8.4   The Supreme Court of Canada
8.5   The Politics of Judicial Appointments
8.6   The "Court Party" Thesis

8.1   The Role of the Judiciary

The first thing that students of the Constitution should notice about the provisions of *CA 1867* governing "the judicature" is the location of those provisions. As we have seen, the sections governing executive and legislative power occupy a prominent position close to the beginning of *CA 1867*. Judicial power, on the other hand, is not discussed until Part VII, three-quarters of the way through the *Act*. To some extent, this is a consequence of the fact that Canada's judicial system has a federal dimension to it, a fact that makes it reasonable to outline the provisions governing judicial power only after the provisions governing federalism have been laid down. But the relatively late discussion of judicial power is also a reflection of the fact that the Fathers of Confederation viewed judicial power as substantially less important than the legislative and executive powers.

Such a view would be untenable today, for the role of the judiciary has expanded far beyond its original limits. In 1867, most observers would have ascribed to the judiciary two basic tasks: the adjudication of legal disputes between private parties and the adjudication of cases in public law. Today's judges regularly engage in two additional activities: the direction of royal commissions of inquiry and judicial review of the Constitution. Judicial review, in particular, has magnified the importance of the judiciary far beyond anything the Fathers of Confederation had expected. These four tasks can be summed up as follows.

1. *Adjudicating legal disputes between private parties.* According to the liberal philosopher John Locke, the primary reason why human beings create political regimes is that they need someone to settle their disputes in an authoritative and impartial manner. Locke believed in certain universal and permanent principles of justice, which he called natural laws, and he thought that all human beings could in principle understand the validity of those laws. But Locke doubted that human beings would respect those laws consistently. He also doubted their ability to apply and enforce them impartially. In their natural state of freedom, then, men would inevitably be drawn into an ever-escalating cycle of injustice and vengeance. Reasonable human beings are therefore willing to renounce their natural freedom and put themselves under the command of a political regime that will be able to resolve disputes before they turn violent.

In order to accomplish this objective, the political regime will adopt laws to govern the most common private disputes and establish courts to settle such disputes according to the principles laid down in those laws. The regime will still permit, and may even encourage, individuals to employ a number of private mechanisms to settle their disputes. The most common of these are negotiation, mediation (a process in which a third party is brought in to facilitate negotiations between the disputants), and arbitration (where the disputants agree to allow a third party to impose a settlement on them). But the effectiveness of these three mechanisms is largely dependent on the fact that disputants know that unresolved disputes can, and normally will, be taken to the courts for decisive resolution.

At the time of Confederation, it was deemed necessary to put responsibility for "private law"—laws governing matters such as property rights, contracts, and torts—in the hands of the provincial governments. Section 92.13 of *CA 1867* thus reserves "property and civil rights" as an exclusive jurisdiction of the legislatures of the provinces. The reason for this was that New Brunswick, Nova Scotia, and Ontario embodied their private law in one format while Québec traditionally had used another.

Private law in Québec is embodied in a statute called the civil code, a detailed and comprehensive compendium of all the rules governing matters of property and civil rights. This practice, used by most legislative jurisdictions in the world today, was one that Québec had adopted when it was a French colony, and in 1774 the British government guaranteed Québeckers the right to retain their code. The other colonies, more British in heritage, had always followed the British practice of embodying much of their private law in a form known as "common law." Common law is judge-made law, as opposed to statutes adopted by legislative bodies. In late medieval England, royally appointed judges slowly began to take control of what hitherto had been a patchwork system of justice. In order to impose some order and consistency on that system, they adopted the practice of deciding cases involving matters like property or contracts on the basis of **precedents** (previous judicial decisions on the same point of law). Where no precedent existed, judges were free to decide cases in the manner that seemed most consistent with the underlying principles of the case law that existed. By virtue of the principle of **stare decisis** ("to stand by what has been decided"), however, judges were required to respect any precedent that had been endorsed by courts of authority superior to their own. By following these basic rules, England's judges were able, over time, to develop a single system of private law "common" to the whole country.

2. *Adjudicating cases in public law.* Judges also have substantial authority in matters of "public law." The difference between public and private law is that while private law governs relationships between two or more private parties, public law creates and regulates relationships between private parties and the government. This difference is reflected in the names of the cases heard under each type of law: while a typical case in private law might be titled *Jones v. Smith*, cases in public law will feature the Queen, or some officer of the Crown, in their title—*Russell v. The Queen, Ford v. Attorney General of Québec.*

The two main areas of public law are criminal law and administrative law. Section 91.27 of *CA 1867* declares criminal law to be an exclusive jurisdiction of Parliament (that is, Ottawa). Our criminal law is contained primarily in the Criminal Code of Canada, which prohibits a wide variety of actions by declaring them to be criminal offences—assault, sexual assault, fraud, murder, and hateful speech, to name but a few. In addition to offering a legal definition of these crimes, the Criminal Code establishes appropriate ranges of punishment for each of them. It is the judges of Canada's courts, however, who decide on the specific sentence, and in most cases the Criminal Code grants them a good deal of latitude. This constitutes a very substantial form of political power.

The term "administrative law" refers to any regulatory legislation that does not involve the application of criminal sanctions. Administrative law thus covers a very wide range of topics at both levels of government, from traffic regulations (a provincial matter) to old age pensions (a federal jurisdiction). Because of the tremendous number of administrative law decisions that need to be made by today's governments, a good deal of administrative law is now applied by administrative tribunals (for example, the Workers' Compensation Board) rather than courts. However, the judiciary still hears many types of administrative law cases and will often have the power to overrule decisions made by administrative tribunals.

3. *Judicial commissions of inquiry.* In recent decades it has become increasingly common for governments to ask judges to take charge of royal commissions investigating either problematic areas of public policy or alleged misconduct in some part of the public sector. Judges have been asked to lead investigations into the "sponsorship scandal," alleged racism in the justice system of Nova Scotia, alleged illegal activities by the Royal Canadian Mounted Police (RCMP), and Canada's medicare system, among other subjects. As a rule, the recommendations of these commissions carry a good deal of weight with the governments that create them. The individual judges who head such commissions are thus able to exert a substantial amount of influence on specific political issues.

Governments are not obligated to place the direction of royal commissions in the hands of judges. In fact, many such commissions have been led by non-judicial figures. There are two reasons why governments frequently look to the judiciary for their royal commissions. First, judges have professional experience in organizing hearings in which parties are able to present evidence in a procedurally fair manner. Second (and probably more importantly), judges have a reputation for impartiality. However, Peter Russell, a leading expert on the Canadian judiciary, argues that it is precisely because of their impartiality that judges should be spared from such work:

> The participation of judges in these commissions is bound to contribute to the politicization of the judiciary and will likely diminish the aura of impartiality—which is one of the reasons for appointing judges to royal commissions in the first place. If this resulted merely in fewer royal commissions or fewer judicial royal commissioners, there would be no serious loss; there are other means of conducting inquiries into government misconduct and public policy. The more serious danger is to the judicial branch of government itself

and its capacity for effectively performing its essential function of adjudication.[1]

4. *Judicial review of the Constitution.* We have seen in Chapter 2 that the terms of the Constitution require interpretation and that it is the courts that take responsibility for that task. We have also seen, in Chapters 4 and 5, that this function of judicial review has given Canada's judiciary substantial political power. Judges now decide, or decisively influence, a number of important questions of principle and policy: How extensive are the powers of the federal government? Is it permissible for either level of government to restrict access to abortions? Are laws prohibiting the use of marijuana acceptable? These types of issues are now routinely decided by the courts rather than by legislatures.

It is important to note, however, that the judiciary does not become involved in such questions on its own initiative. Most of the time, judicial review of the Constitution is triggered by specific cases in private or public law where a ruling on the meaning of some part of the Constitution is necessary for the adjudication of the dispute in question. Let us take as an example the case of *Big M Drug Mart v. The Queen, 1985.* In this case, Big M Drug Mart was charged with violating a federal statute, *The Lord's Day Act*, which prohibited commercial establishments like Big M from doing business on Sunday. In court, Big M did not deny that it was open on Sundays in violation of the law, but it argued that it should not be punished because the law itself was in violation of Section 2(a) of the Charter of Rights and Freedoms, which guarantees "freedom of religion." In order to determine whether or not Big M should be punished, the courts that heard this case (including, in the end, the Supreme Court of Canada) were required to make a ruling on the meaning of Section 2(a). Does the right to freedom of religion make it unconstitutional for governments to prohibit shopping on "the Lord's day"? If it does, Big M is innocent. If it does not, Big M must be punished in accordance with the law.

The second mechanism for triggering judicial review of the Constitution is the **reference procedure**. When the federal government created the Supreme Court of Canada, it provided that the court could be called on to give its opinion on the constitutionality of specific decisions or statutes referred to it by the governor-in-council. Originally, the government's intention was to use this reference procedure to help it decide whether specific provincial statutes should be

---

1   Peter Russell, *The Judiciary in Canada: The Third Branch of Government* (Toronto: McGraw-Hill Ryerson, 1987) 13.

disallowed. Eventually, however, the reference procedure came to be used as a means of obtaining quick rulings on the constitutionality of proposed legislation. (Waiting for the constitutionality of a law to be challenged by private parties and appealed through the judicial system might take as long as ten years.) In the 1930s, for example, the government was able to refer the "New Deal" legislation proposed by R.B. Bennett to the courts and to learn in relatively short order that most of the legislation was *ultra vires*—beyond the jurisdiction—of the federal government. The provincial governments soon recognized the value of the reference procedure and established comparable mechanisms in their own courts. Today most judicial review of the Constitution arises from the adjudication of cases rather than reference questions, but the reference procedure is the source of some of the more interesting and important cases—the patriation reference, for example (discussed in Chapter 2, p. 25).

8.2 The Fundamental Principles of the Canadian Judiciary

There are three fundamental principles that govern the Canadian judiciary in its efforts to carry out the tasks described above: impartiality, independence, and equality before the law. Each of these principles has been inherited from the British judiciary. Indeed, it is plausible to argue that the authoritative status of these three principles is implied by the statement in the preamble to *CA 1867* that Canada is to have "a Constitution similar in principle to that of the United Kingdom." As we shall see, however, the Constitution entrenches these principles in other places as well.

1. *Impartiality.* Section 11(d) of the Charter of Rights and Freedoms guarantees that any person charged in Canada with some offence has a right to a "fair" trial before an "impartial tribunal." There is nothing surprising in this, for the requirement that judges be impartial is more or less implicit in the very concept of adjudication.

The general meaning of the principle of **impartiality** is relatively straightforward: judges must be free from prejudice for or against any party appearing before them. It may, of course, be impossible for human beings to refrain from showing at least some prejudice in their judgement about things, but our regime assumes that its judges will be reasonably impartial and for the most part leaves it up to individual judges to police themselves in this regard. It does, however, attempt to promote impartiality by means of three specific provisions.

The first is the right of parties to appeal a judge's decision to a higher court. The right of appeal promotes impartiality in two ways: knowing that their judgements may be subjected to the scrutiny of a higher court gives individual judges great incentive to be fair and objective, and parties who have been victims of judicial bias get a second hearing. It is important to note, however, that the right to appeal is not unlimited. In the first place, it is not automatic. One generally has to ask the court to which one seeks to appeal a decision for permission (or "leave") to appeal. Appeal courts will grant such leave only if they have serious doubts about the ruling of the lower court. Moreover, not every aspect of a case is subject to appeal. When judges adjudicate disputes, they engage in two distinct processes: they must first decide the facts of the situation in dispute—what exactly happened—and they must then determine what the law says about these situations. Appeal courts will grant leave to appeal if there appear to be problems in what a judge has said about the law or perhaps if the judge has made procedural errors, but, as a rule, they do not hear appeals of a judge's decision about the facts of a case.

Another feature of Canada's judicial regime that serves to promote impartiality is its "adversarial" character. In many countries, judges will play a very active role in the judicial process, taking responsibility for fact-finding and then settling the disputes in accordance with their understanding of the law. Such arrangements are not consistent with our regime's suspicion of public power and its emphasis on individual liberty and responsibility. In Canada, we follow the British practice of giving judges a more passive role. We place the responsibility for establishing facts and presenting arguments with the adversaries themselves, and our judges serve as referees rather than inquisitors. Instead of seeking out facts and arguments, they restrict themselves to making rulings on the basis of the facts and arguments presented to them by individual litigants. This has the effect of minimizing judges' latitude for imposing their own views on the contending parties.

The third provision is the doctrine of political neutrality. This doctrine, which we also inherited from Britain, decrees that judges must keep silent about political matters. They may not be members of political parties, they may not speak on political topics, and they must not display public preference for any particular political views. The reason for this doctrine is not hard to see. Judges will often be called upon to hear cases in which they will make decisions of political importance. If they have taken a public stand on a particular issue—if, for instance, a judge proclaims herself to be an ardent opponent of abortion—it will be difficult to persuade the public that both sides in a case involving abortion will get a fair hearing from her. Moreover, as Peter Russell points out, if judges start attacking politicians, it is inevitable that politicians will fight back. This would only serve to undermine the authority and independence of the courts.[2]

---

2   Russell 88–89.

In 1981, Canadians witnessed an interesting example of the doctrine of political neutrality. Justice Thomas Berger of the BC Supreme Court publicly attacked the constitutional accord which formed the basis of *CA 1982* because it did not contain a veto for Québec and because it did not entrench certain rights for Aboriginal Canadians. A committee of the Canadian Judicial Council, which investigated Berger's conduct, reported that his comments might serve to undermine the public's perception of the judiciary's impartiality:

> It is apparent that some of the native peoples are unhappy with s.35 of the Canadian Charter of Rights and Freedoms. If Justice Berger should be called upon to interpret that section, for example, the meaning to be given to the word "existing" in "the existing aboriginal and treaty rights of the aboriginal peoples of Canada," would the general public have confidence now in his impartiality? After Justice Berger spoke publicly on the necessity for Québec retaining a veto, his brother judges in Québec were called on to determine whether such a right existed.[3]

The committee found that Berger's remarks were sufficiently indiscreet to justify removing him from the bench but thought that a warning would be more appropriate. Berger rejected these findings but resigned from his position a year later.

It is sometimes alleged that the judiciary is not truly impartial because it tends, on the whole, to be moderate or even conservative in its politics. Stephen Brooks, for example, complains that judges are never "radical critics of society." He notes that they "rarely concern themselves with the distribution of power in society" and are generally "insensitive to the structural inequalities that exist in society and in the economy." This, he argues, is due to a number of factors. One is that judges tend to come from middle- or upper-middle-class backgrounds. Another is that they are appointed by governments, which, as a rule, do not want to see political radicals on the judicial bench. Most important, however, is the fact that the law itself is riddled with inherently conservative premises such as "individualism" and property rights. This means that anyone schooled in the law, as judges must be, will almost inevitably have acquired conservative political prejudices.[4]

---

3   Cited in F.L. Morton, *Law, Politics, and the Judicial Process in Canada* (Calgary: University of Calgary Press, 1990) 111.

4   Stephen Brooks, *Canadian Democracy: An Introduction* (Toronto: McClelland and Stewart, 1993) 196–97.

It is certainly important for students of Canadian politics to understand the political implications of judicial decision-making, and it is possible to argue, as Brooks does, that the judiciary's political impact is in a sense conservative. Yet to claim that this constitutes a lack of impartiality is unfair to our judges. In the Canadian regime, the primary task of the judiciary is to apply the law, not to make it. In those cases where they in effect "make the law" by giving concrete meaning to imprecise legislative language, it is entirely reasonable to expect them to formulate their interpretations in light of the basic principles of the existing regime. It is perfectly legitimate for Canadians to seek modifications to the existing regime by pressuring their politicians to introduce the appropriate legislative changes, but it would be inconsistent with the principle of responsible government to expect the judiciary to act as agents of radical political change.

2. *Judicial independence.* In addition to guaranteeing a right to a trial before an "impartial" tribunal, Section 11(d) of the Charter of Rights and Freedoms also guarantees that the tribunal shall be "independent." While the terms "independent" and "impartial" sound alike, they do not mean the same thing. Strictly speaking, the principle of **judicial independence** is a kind of subset of the principle of impartiality.

When we say that the judiciary must be independent, we mean that it must be independent of the executive branch of the regime. The reason for this is quite simple. In many, if not most cases before the courts, the executive will be a party to the dispute. *Big M Drug Mart v. The Queen* is actually a dispute between Big M and the Attorney-General of Alberta (a member of the provincial executive) who, in taking Big M to court, is attempting to execute his duties under the law by prosecuting a party alleged to have violated a federal statute. The judiciary would have difficulty being impartial if it were subject to the control of an executive that, of necessity, frequently appears before it as a litigant. The principle of judicial independence thus entails certain conditions to guarantee that judges will be free of pressure from the political executive.

In a 1985 case entitled *Valente v. The Queen*, the Supreme Court of Canada had an opportunity to articulate those conditions in an authoritative fashion. The first is that judges must have security of tenure. In other words, the executive must not be able to fire judges merely because it dislikes their rulings. Secondly, the salaries of judges must be fixed by law, for, if the judiciary is not financially independent of the executive, the executive might try to influence judges by increasing or decreasing their salaries. The third and final condition is that judges must have control over those aspects of the administration of their courts that have an impact on judicial decision-making (the scheduling of cases, for example).

Using the Supreme Court's three conditions as a standard, it may be said that Canada's judiciary is highly independent. Section 99 of *CA 1867* explicitly guarantees the judges of our superior courts security of tenure until the age of 75 "during good behaviour." This is a traditional way of saying that judges may be removed from office only if they are physically or mentally incapable of performing their duties or if they have engaged in activities that might bring the administration of justice into disrepute (for example, selling drugs or driving under the influence of alcohol). In other words, judges may not be fired for making decisions that the executive does not like or even for making mistakes. The tenure of the judges of Canada's other courts is protected by similar provisions in the statutes creating those courts.

Section 100 of *CA 1867* entrenches the principle that the remuneration of the judges of our superior courts shall be fixed by law. This protects the salaries of individual judges from manipulation by the executive. Once again, the judges of our other courts are protected by similar provisions in the statutes creating those courts.

The third condition of judicial independence set down by the Supreme Court in *Valente* is not entrenched anywhere in the Constitution. For the most part, however, Canada's judges have ample authority over those aspects of courtroom administration that are essential to their adjudicative work.

The importance Canadians attribute to the principle of judicial independence may be seen in an incident known as "The Judges Affair." In March 1976, the Chief Justice of the Québec Superior Court, Jules Deschenes, wrote to the federal minister of justice to complain that on separate occasions three of Prime Minister Trudeau's cabinet ministers had contacted judges concerning cases they were hearing. None of the ministers resigned over the allegations, but the prime minister made it clear that similar conduct would not be tolerated in the future. Two years later, when it was reported that Labour Minister John Munro had contacted a judge to discuss the sentencing of one of his constituents, he was forced to resign. A decade later, Jean Charest was forced to resign from the Mulroney cabinet for having called a judge on behalf of a voter from his riding.

3. *Equality before the law.* The third fundamental principle of Canada's judicial regime is that everyone is equal before the law. This principle is explicitly entrenched in Section 15(1) of the Charter of Rights and Freedoms. It is also implicit in the preamble to the Charter, which stipulates that "Canada is founded on principles that recognize the supremacy of . . . the rule of law." One aspect of "the rule of law" is the principle that the law must be applied to all people equally.

Though Canada's courts are in principle committed to such equality, problems arise from the fact that legal proceedings are often very costly for those engaged in them. Provincial governments maintain legal aid programs to ensure that defendants in criminal cases who cannot afford to pay a lawyer will be provided with one. In non-criminal cases, however, the assistance offered under such programs is spotty. As a result, people who are entitled to some kind of redress under the law often are not able to pursue their claims because they cannot afford to. Moreover, even those who can pay a lawyer may find that they cannot afford full justice. In a judicial system that relies almost exclusively on the adversarial process for the presentation of facts and the articulation of arguments, the quality of one's legal representation can make the difference between winning and losing one's case. It is often true that the more money one has for legal fees, the better one is represented. This is not simply because high-priced lawyers are sometimes more effective than less expensive lawyers. It is also a function of the fact that the litigants with more money can afford expensive legal research and can drag cases on so long with appeals or procedural disputes that their adversaries can no longer afford the fight.

8.3 Canada's Courts

At first glance, Canada appears to have a bewildering array of courts, some of which have odd, or even quaint, names. But there is a logic to the structure of Canada's court system that is easily understood if one keeps in mind a small number of basic principles.

The first of these principles is hierarchy. Court systems are almost by definition stratified into different layers with some courts deemed superior to others, and one court labelled "supreme." There are several reasons for this. One is the division of judicial activity into trials (where a case is heard for the first time) and appeals (where the decision reached in the trial stage is re-examined). Logic dictates that if an appeal court is going to have the authority to overturn a decision reached by a trial court, it will have to be of higher status. Moreover, if litigants are to have a right to appeal the decision of the appeal court, there must be a court of higher authority than the appeal court—hence, at some point, there must be a final court of appeal, which is "supreme."

Another reason why court systems are organized in hierarchical fashion is that some subjects of adjudication are inherently more important than others. Murder cases are very important, for example, because those found guilty of murder are subject to very severe penalties. Cases of illegal parking, on the other hand, generally involve relatively light sentences and are thus not as important as murder cases. It therefore makes sense to divide a judicial system into **superior courts**, which will in theory have the most able judges, and **inferior courts**, which may have more informal procedures, depending on the type of case they handle.

One may thus sketch a simple, hypothetical hierarchy of courts something like the diagram in Figure 8.1. Here we find inferior courts specializing in traffic violations or small claims, "superior" trial courts to handle crimes like murder or assault and battery, a Court of Appeal to hear appeals from both the inferior and superior trial courts, and a "Supreme Court" to hear appeals from the Court of Appeal.

The second principle we must keep in mind in order to understand Canada's court system is federalism. The system sketched in Figure 8.1 would work well in a unitary regime like that of Britain. In a federal regime, however, the design of a court system becomes more complicated because one has to accommodate the claims of two layers of government. As we saw in Chapter 4, the United States was the first great model of a federal regime. In planning a judicial system for their federation, the Americans thought it best to create what is called a "dual" system. In this approach, there are two distinct networks of courts: a federal network for the adjudication of cases under federal law and a separate network in each state for adjudicating cases involving state law. The sole unifying feature in this dual system is that the Supreme Court of the United States sits in appeal of cases from both networks. Figure 8.2 provides a simple outline of the American "dual" system.

Figure 8.1: Hierarchy of Courts in Canada

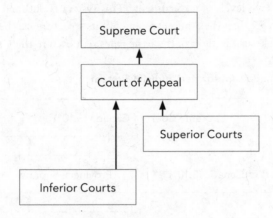

Figure 8.2: Dual Court System of the United States

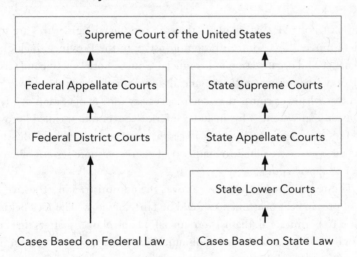

It is not surprising that the Americans opted for a dual system with a separate network of state courts, for their regime was originally designed to be a strongly decentralized federation with highly independent state governments. As we have seen, however, our Fathers of Confederation thought that the Americans had made a grave mistake in giving so much authority to their state governments. Accordingly, in planning Canada's judicial system, they sought an approach that would combine the diversity required by federalism and the uniformity that comes from a single centralized system. This led them to create what Peter

Russell has called an **integrated judicial system**: a single system under the joint custody of the two levels of government.[5] This system is outlined in Figure 8.3. It is more complex than the American one, but its structure can be easily understood if one looks at it in light of the basic rules set down in the Constitution.

Figure 8.3: Canada's Integrated Judicial System

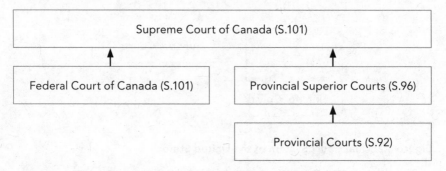

Section 92.14 of *CA 1867* stipulates that the provincial legislatures are to have jurisdiction over "the Administration of Justice in the Province, including the maintenance and organization of Provincial Courts, both of Civil and Criminal Jurisdiction." In other words, provincial governments have the power to create and run whatever courts they deem necessary for the operation of a fair and efficient judicial system. This includes **inferior courts** (often called "provincial courts") such as traffic, family, or small claims courts. It also includes the **superior courts** that, as we have noted, are either trial courts for more serious offences and disputes or appeal courts.

The reason for placing control over the administration of justice in the hands of provincial governments should be fairly obvious. The idea behind federalism is to permit local (that is, "provincial") control over matters that are best dealt with locally. The administration of justice is such a matter for a number of reasons. One is the difference between the civil code system of Québec and the common law system in use in the rest of the provinces, a difference that might reasonably place different demands on their respective judicial systems. Another is that different provinces may find that situational factors as mundane as size could make a system appropriate for one province but inappropriate for another: while a large province might find it necessary to have "district" courts to give service to all areas of the province, such a system might be unnecessary in a small province. In any event, the colonies that united in 1867 to form Canada already

---

5   Russell ch.3.

had their own distinctive judicial systems in place, each of which was tailored to meet local needs, and there was no pressing reason to replace them.

There was, however, a need to modify the rules for appointing judges. While the federal principle requires local control over local matters, it also dictates that matters of national interest be handled nationally. The Fathers of Confederation decided that criminal law was a national matter (although the Americans had left it in the hands of the state governments) and should therefore be handled by the federal government. But the objective of having a single criminal law for all Canadians would have been undermined had its enforcement been left in the hands of a provincially controlled judiciary. Judges have a good deal of discretion when it comes to the sentencing of offenders, and courts in one province might have consistently imposed lighter or harsher sentences than judges in other provinces. In order to ensure that Canada's criminal law would be applied with some degree of consistency, it was stipulated in Section 96 of *CA 1867* that the federal government was to have the authority to appoint the judges of all superior courts (which would handle the most important aspects of criminal law). Further to this end, Section 100 provides that the salaries of those judges are to be set and paid by the federal Parliament. While Canada's inferior courts are completely under provincial control, then, we have a network of superior courts under shared jurisdiction: the provinces create and maintain the courts according to local need, but Ottawa appoints and pays the judges to ensure national consistency of judicial decision-making. These two types of court are often referred to as **Section 92 courts** (inferior) and **Section 96 courts** (superior).

The Constitution also provides for a third type of court: federally created courts with federally appointed judges, sometimes called **Section 101 Courts**. Section 101 of *CA 1867* grants Parliament the authority to establish special courts for "the better administration" of federal law, as well as a "General Court of Appeal for Canada." Parliament has made use of both branches of its powers under Section 101. In 1875, it created the Exchequer Court as a special court for the "better administration" of certain areas of federal law. In 1970, this court was significantly restructured and then renamed the Federal Court of Canada. The Federal Court hears cases in specialized areas of federal law (for example, maritime law and patent and copyright law) as well as appeals of decisions made by federal regulatory agencies and administrative tribunals.

In 1875, Parliament also used its powers under Section 101 to create the Supreme Court of Canada. The Supreme Court has the authority to hear appeals from provincial courts of appeal and from the Federal Court of Canada. The fact that this measure was not taken until seven years into the history of the Dominion does not mean that Canada was without a supreme court during that initial period. The Fathers of Confederation assumed that Canadians would use Britain's highest court, the **Judicial Committee of the Privy Council (JCPC)** as their final court of appeal. The creation of the Supreme Court of Canada did not immediately change that practice: decisions of the provincial court of appeal could be appealed to the JCPC rather than to the Supreme Court. Indeed, the decisions of the Supreme Court could themselves be appealed to the JCPC. In short, the Supreme Court was at first not truly "supreme." One might say that it was the supreme court *in* Canada, but not the supreme court *for* Canada. It was not until after World War II that this quasi-colonial situation was terminated. In 1949, with the blessing of the JCPC itself, Parliament abolished the right to appeal cases to the JCPC. Only then did the Supreme Court of Canada become truly supreme.

8.4 The Supreme Court of Canada

The Supreme Court now consists of nine judges, appointed by the prime minister. According to the terms of the *Supreme Court Act,* three of these judges must come from Québec to ensure that the court will have at least three judges who are familiar with Québec's civil law system. By tradition, at least one judge is always from Atlantic Canada, and a minimum of two must be from the West. Under normal circumstances, three of the judges will be from Ontario, although on occasion that province has had only two.

The court now hears about 100 cases a year. In some of these cases, the right to such a hearing is automatic (for example, in certain criminal cases where the appeal court has overturned the decision of the trial court). For the most part, however, the court is now in control of its own docket. Those who wish to appeal a case to it must persuade at least two members of a three-judge panel that the case deserves to be heard. The judges will want to hear a case if it appears there has been a serious error in the lower court's decision or if it raises an important legal or constitutional issue that needs to be settled by the country's highest court.

In order to avoid deadlock, cases are heard by odd-number panels of judges. There can be as few as five judges on a panel, though exceptionally important cases will be heard by all nine. Most, however, are heard by a panel of seven judges. After the case has been heard, the judges retire to discuss it. While in the Supreme Court of the United States it is the most senior judges who speak first in these discussions, in Canada it is customary to have the judges speak in reverse order of seniority. This is meant to ensure that the newer judges will not feel pressured to go along with the views of their more senior colleagues. In the vast majority of cases, the judges arrive at a unanimous verdict, and one of them is assigned to write a "decision" which explains the verdict and the reasons for it. When the court is not unanimous, one judge will author the **majority opinion** while another will write a **dissenting opinion**. Occasionally judges may agree on a verdict on the basis of different reasons. In such cases there will be a majority opinion, but individual judges may write their own **concurring opinions**.

Perhaps the most peculiar feature of the Supreme Court is the fact that it exists by virtue of an organic statute—*The Supreme Court of Canada Act, 1875*—rather than a constitutional law. The amending formula set out in Section 41 stipulates that the "composition of the Supreme Court of Canada" may not be amended without the consent of Parliament and all ten provincial legislatures. Apart from this, the structure, operation, and perhaps even the existence of the court depend on the will of the federal Parliament. Some observers have argued that a political institution as important as the Supreme Court should be entrenched in the Constitution, and provision was made to do so in the Meech Lake and Charlottetown Accords. The failure of those accords leaves the court a creature of organic statute.

8.5 The Politics of Judicial Appointments

Canada's judiciary was designed to be professional and non-political. Our judges are not elected to their positions, they are appointed by the executive from the ranks of practising lawyers and legal specialists. Moreover, the principles of judicial independence and impartiality have served to keep our judges at arm's length from partisan politics. In recent decades, however, the process for selecting our federally appointed judges (of which there are approximately 1,100) has become something of a political issue.

Originally, the movement to reform the process for judicial appointments was in the direction of making that process less political than it is. The target of reformers was the partisan character of the appointment process. It has always been the case that the party in power tends to appoint a disproportionate number of its own supporters to the bench. This tendency is less pronounced now than it was 50 years ago, but it is still significant. Reformers have not been able to eliminate the partisan character of judicial appointments, but they have managed to curb the most serious abuses. Since 1988, input on these appointments has been provided by a number of regional Judicial Advisory Committees (JACs). Ottawa appoints three members of each JAC and an additional four members are named by the Canadian Bar Association, the provincial government, the provincial law society, and the provincial judges. The JACs rank candidates as highly qualified, qualified, or not qualified; appointments would normally go only to those who are deemed highly qualified. One change implemented by the Harper government was to have the JACs declare the candidates to be merely qualified or not qualified. The effect of this change will likely be to give the government greater discretion to select the candidates it prefers and thus to reduce the real influence of the JACs. The other innovation introduced by the Conservatives was to change the composition of each JAC. It has added a federally appointed representative of police forces to each committee and allows the member appointed by the judges to vote only in the case of a deadlock. These two changes shift control of each committee away from the four externally appointed members to the four members appointed by Ottawa and consequently weaken the thrust of the 1988 reforms.

With respect to the Supreme Court, the reform movement has been quite different. While the aim of the reforms described above has been to make the appointment process less political, when it comes to Supreme Court appointments, reformers seek to make the process more political. Observers of the judiciary are quick to point out that much of the time, especially in cases involving judicial review of the Constitution, judges are making decisions that have significant political consequences. Moreover, as we saw in Chapter 5, it appears that many of these decisions are of necessity made on political (or moral-political) rather than legal grounds. This leads many observers to ask why a small number of unelected (and largely unknown) Supreme Court judges should have the power to make fundamental, and often irrevocable, political decisions for Canada. That in turn leads them to press for changes to the appointment process.

For example, it has now been conceded by all relevant parties that provincial governments ought to have some input into the appointment of Supreme Court justices. As we saw in Chapter 4, those judges have to make rulings about the respective powers of the federal and provincial governments under Sections 91 and 92 of *CA 1867*. In the past it was assumed that Supreme Court judges were non-partisan professionals who could be trusted to make those rulings in an impartial manner, even though they owed their positions on the court to the federal government. Now, however, it is generally supposed that division of powers cases are at least to some extent inherently political rather than legal matters. This fact makes it necessary to alter a regime in which one of the parties to those cases—the federal government—has exclusive control over appointments to the court that has the final say on those cases. It was only logical that in both the Meech Lake and Charlottetown Accords, it was agreed that Ottawa should share the power of Supreme Court appointments with the provincial governments. This process would allow each level of government to veto the appointment to the court of anyone whose views on federalism were unacceptable to it.

But it is the adoption of the Charter of Rights and Freedoms that has led to the most radical calls for politicizing the appointment of the judiciary. In Charter cases, judges have decided whether Canada should have laws against euthanasia, whether Sunday shopping should be permitted, whether the government should be allowed to permit cruise missile testing, and other similar questions. Because these are questions to which there may be only political answers, it is now frequently suggested that the judges who make those decisions must somehow be politically accountable. The most radical means of achieving political accountability is to make the judges directly responsible to the voters by making their positions elected rather than appointed. This option has few supporters because it is generally recognized that an elected judiciary would have little independence from voters and would thus be less than fully impartial. A more common proposal is to copy the American practice of subjecting nominees for Supreme Court positions to examination by the legislative branch of the regime. In theory, this is meant to allow the public to find out ahead of time what political views the nominee would bring to the bench and to block the appointment of nominees whose views are deemed undesirable.

As part of his response to what he called Canada's "democratic deficit," Prime Minister Martin expressed support for some kind of public review process for Supreme Court appointments. When two vacancies had to be filled in the summer of 2004, an ad hoc committee, including both parliamentarians and members of the legal community, was given an opportunity to review the credentials of the two nominees, Louise Charron and Rosalie Abella. Martin indicated that the use of this ad hoc committee was a temporary expedient and that he hoped in the future to develop a more permanent arrangement for reviewing Supreme Court appointments. When Mr. Harper became prime minister in 2006, he took a slightly different approach. He required his first Supreme Court appointee, Marshall Rothstein, to appear before a committee of parliamentarians for a three-hour televised interview. Committee members were able to express their opinions regarding the suitability of the nominee to Mr. Harper, but the decision to appoint remained entirely in the hands of the prime minister. This practice of having potential appointees appear before a parliamentary committee has continued even though the Conservative Party gained a majority in the House of Commons in 2011.

While it is generally desirable to promote openness and transparency in government, the idea of reviewing nominations to the Supreme Court is not without its problems. In the first place, it is not clear that parliamentarians will be able to find out exactly what a nominee's political views are. As the American experience indicates, potential judges are reluctant to commit themselves to specific positions in response to hypothetical questions, for they realize that this will compromise their ability to deal with particular cases in an impartial fashion. They therefore tend to be highly evasive when answering such questions before screening committees. Moreover, one has to consider how the American approach would work in the substantially different Canadian system. The United States has a relatively weak party system in that Democrats will often vote for Republican proposals and vice versa. It is therefore common for the Supreme Court nominees of a Democratic president to be supported by Republican senators and vice versa. In Canada's highly disciplined party system, on the other hand, MPs almost always vote according to a party line. Might this not lead to a partisan examination of Canadian Supreme Court nominees in which government members automatically vote for the nominee and opposition members automatically vote against? If so, what purpose would the process serve? Finally, one has to wonder if such a process would not serve to make the judges themselves politically partisan. After all, if Parliament has examined their political beliefs and found them acceptable, why should they feel any restraint about imposing those beliefs on Canadians when they make their rulings?

8.6 The "Court Party" Thesis

One of the most interesting features of the judiciary as a political institution is that it is the only institution in our regime that has the power to decide unilaterally just how much power it will have. Under Section 52(1) of *CA 1982,* our courts have an obligation to strike down any law that denies a Charter right. A law that prohibited Catholics from voting would clearly be a violation of both Section 2(a) and Section 15.1 of the Charter, and the judiciary would have a clear obligation to declare it unconstitutional. But what about a provincial law prohibiting privately funded health care? A Québec doctor named Jacques Chaoulli argued that Québec's ban on private health insurance infringed the right to "security of the person" in Section 7 of the Charter because it denied people access to speedy private medical care, forcing them to spend time on long wait-lists for public medical care. In the Supreme Court's 2005 *Chaoulli* decision, four justices of the Supreme Court declared that Québec's law was an infringement of Section 7—but three justices declared it was not. Significantly, one of the concerns expressed by the minority in this case was that the issue before the Court was really a question of social policy. In the view of the minority, policy questions of this sort are best left in the hands of legislative bodies where the relevant cost/benefit tradeoffs can be made by officials who are democratically accountable to the people.

The view articulated by the minority in *Chaoulli* might be characterized by the term **judicial restraint**. Those who favour judicial restraint argue that when courts apply an entrenched bill of rights such as the Charter, they should give the benefit of the doubt to the legislature that enacted the law in question and should use their power to strike a law down only when the infringement of the right is clear-cut. **Judicial activism**, on the other hand, is the approach that favours pushing the power of judicial review vigorously, beyond the black-and-white issues and deep into the grey. The term "judicial activism" is frequently used in a manner that suggests the judge or judges in question are using their judicial power to advance a specific political agenda.

When the adoption of the Charter was first being debated, it was frequently suggested that Canada's judiciary would probably exercise restraint in its application of the Charter since it had always been very restrained in its handling of the Canadian Bill of Rights. What has the record shown 26 years later? Depending on their own political perspective, experts disagree somewhat as to how activist our courts have been, but most would likely characterize their record as at least moderately activist. Indeed, some political scientists who specialize in the study of Canada's judiciary go so far as to argue that judicial activism has been systematically promoted by the "**Court Party**," a collection of advocacy groups with a partisan interest in the judicialization of politics. Morton and Knopf have suggested that interest groups that have not been successful at lobbying elected politicians have turned to the courts as a more effective vehicle for advancing their agendas. Drawing on funding provided by governments or foundations, they pursue long-term litigation strategies designed to expand the reach of the Charter and shape its interpretation so as to promote their particular causes. In some cases, they also work through JACs to influence the appointment of judges and even host "judicial education seminars" for newly appointed judges. The Court Party thus serves to encourage the judiciary as an institution to play a larger and more active role in the Canadian political process.[6]

---

6   F.L. Morton and Rainer Knopf, *The Charter Revolution and the Court Party* (Peterborough: Broadview Press, 2000).

Key Terms

precedents	Section 96 courts
stare decisis	Section 101 courts
reference procedure	Judicial Committee of the Privy Council (JCPC)
impartiality	majority opinion
judicial independence	dissenting opinion
integrated judicial system	concurring opinion
inferior courts	judicial restraint
superior courts	judicial activism
Section 92 courts	Court Party

Discussion Questions

1. Should the House of Commons be given the authority to reject a prime minister's nominee to the Supreme Court?

2. Which is more in keeping with the principles of liberal democratic regime: judicial activism or judicial restraint?

PART FOUR

PARTICIPATION

CHAPTER NINE

ELECTIONS

9.1 Elections and Representation

9.2 Canada's Electoral System

9.3 The Effects of SMP

9.4 Proportional Representation

9.5 Single Transferable Vote

9.6 Voting in Canada

9.1 Elections and Representation

We learned in Chapter 1 that the Canadian regime is not a direct democracy but a representative democracy. This means that the central democratic mechanism of our regime is elections. Section 3 of *CA 1982* entrenches the most important of our democratic rights in the following language:

> Every citizen of Canada has a right to vote in an election of members of the House of Commons or of a legislative assembly and to be qualified for membership therein.

To understand the significance of these rights, it is important to consider them in light of the basic principles of responsible government. We have seen that in responsible government, the regime obtains its democratic legitimacy by virtue of the fact that those who exercise political authority are in some way accountable to the citizens who form the electorate. Our members of Parliament are directly accountable to us in that they must be periodically re-elected in order to remain in office. The prime minister and cabinet are accountable to us indirectly in that they must always maintain the confidence of the House of Commons we have elected directly. Elections to the House of Commons thus constitute the democratic linchpin of the regime because they ensure that those who make political decisions will in some sense represent the will or interests of the electorate.

But how exactly do the politicians "represent" the voters? What exactly is meant by the term representation? It is important to consider these questions with some care if we are to understand properly the logic of our elections. In democratic theory, there are at least three main concepts of representation. According to the first view, elected representatives are seen as **delegates**, that is, spokespersons who faithfully transmit the views of the majority of the people who elect them. A second interpretation treats representatives as **trustees**, people to whom we "entrust" the responsibilities of government. In this view, our representatives are elected for their character and judgement and are free to decide for themselves how to vote on each issue. A third concept of representation emphasizes the role of the representative as a **party member**. According to this view, the task of our representatives is to be loyal supporters of the policies advocated by their party. It should be obvious that these three concepts of representation are to some extent contradictory. On any given issue, it is likely that an MP would vote one way as a loyal party member and a different way as a delegate speaking for his or her local constituents. Acting as a trustee and voting according to his or her conscience, the MP might favour yet another alternative.

Which of these models of representation do we use in Canada? This is a question for which there is no simple answer and that perhaps explains why Canadians are often confused about it. Some will tell you that they vote for the party (or perhaps the party leader), while others claim to vote based on the personal qualities of their local candidates. Still, consideration of the logic of responsible government will allow us to draw some general inferences about how our representatives are supposed to represent us.

We know that responsible government turns out, in practice, to be government by a cabinet that is accountable to the House of Commons. Because the cabinet is not elected directly by the voters, it is important that we elect the House of Commons in such a way as to draw the strongest link possible between the voters and the cabinet. This means that our representation must, for the most part, be party representation. The idea of party representation forms the basis of the concept of a **mandate**. If it is assumed that the voters elected their MPs primarily on the basis of party affiliation, then the party that is called on to form the government may reasonably infer that the electorate has endorsed the general line of policy that it proposed in the election campaign. The party may thus claim that it has a "democratic mandate" to carry out that line of policy. If our MPs were elected primarily as delegates or trustees, there would be no such mandate. The strongest link between the electorate and its government would be severed, leaving the government less accountable to the people than we think it should be.[1]

This is not to say, however, that there is no room for the delegate and trustee models of representation in Canada. It should not be forgotten that MPs have an opportunity for full and free debate on matters within the parliamentary caucus. Voters may therefore reasonably expect their MP to speak in accordance with his or her judgement (trustee model) or on behalf of the constituents (delegate model) in that setting. But they probably should not expect their MP to vote against a position taken by his or her party once the caucus has made up its mind. Canada's approach to representation should therefore be understood as a mixture of the delegate, trustee, and party member theories, but it probably puts the heaviest emphasis on the party member theory.

The complexity of our approach to representation in Canada becomes evident whenever there is an incident of **"floor-crossing"** in the House of Commons. Immediately after the 2006 election, David Emerson, who had been elected in Vancouver-Kingsway as a Liberal candidate, "crossed the floor" of the House of Commons to join the Conservative caucus and become a minister in the Harper government. Many voters of Vancouver-Kingsway were outraged by this move. How could someone who had just been elected as a Liberal unilaterally defect to the Conservatives? Wasn't Mr. Emerson cheating all those who had voted Liberal of their democratic rights? From the point of view of the "party member" theory of representation he most certainly was. On the other hand, floor-crossing is perfectly consistent with the trustee theory of representation. As the "trustee" of the voters of Vancouver-Kingsway, Mr. Emerson could argue that the voters had elected him as an individual and had given him the authority to do what he thought best for the riding and for the country. And that was essentially Mr. Emerson's argument: since Vancouver needed to have a voice in the cabinet, and

---

1   We suggested, in Chapter 1, that the Fathers of Confederation would not have insisted on maintaining such a direct link between the voters and the government. It is obvious that Canadians' thinking on this point has evolved over time. While Canadians maintain a belief in the virtues of indirect (representative) government, we do insist that the government should be accountable to the electorate in a meaningful way.

since the Vancouver area had not elected any Conservatives, it would be in the best interests of Vancouverites for him to switch to the Conservatives and provide a voice for Vancouver in the corridors of power.

Another issue that emerges when we consider the matter of representation is the question of who can represent us. According to the **microcosm theory of representation**, legislative bodies are fully representative *only* if the assembly is a microcosm of society as a whole. For example, if 51 per cent of the population is female, then 51 per cent of the representatives ought to be female. Similarly, if the population is composed of diverse ethnic groups, the assembly should reflect that diversity. The microcosm theory has always played some role in the Canadian regime. As we saw in Chapter 6, the prime minister is expected to form a cabinet that reflects our country's diversity not only in geographic terms but also in terms of religion, ethnicity, language, and gender. The microcosm theory is also becoming increasingly influential in deciding who is to be selected to serve on the Supreme Court of Canada. In recent times, there has been some discussion of reforming our electoral system in order to have our Parliament mirror more closely the social composition of the regime. During the negotiations leading to the Charlottetown Accord, for example, it was proposed that half the seats in any elected Senate should be reserved for women.

There are, however, some serious questions to be raised about the microcosm theory of representation. First, who would decide what the politically relevant characteristics of society are? How do we determine which groups get special representation and which do not? Second, how is a system to be designed to ensure that those characteristics are indeed represented? It would be easy enough to ensure there is an equal number of men and women in Parliament; we could simply elect one of each in every riding. But what about other groups? Finally, there is a deeper philosophical question: is it true that the interests of various groups can be represented only by members of those groups?

9.2 Canada's Electoral System

Political institutions are not neutral. They affect the way politics is conducted. Electoral institutions, in particular, can play a substantial role in determining who wins and who loses an election, how strong different parties will be, and what types of party are likely to succeed. It is therefore important to understand what kind of electoral system Canada uses and to consider what impact that system might have on the country's political life. We take up the former point in this section and the latter in Section 9.3.

The design of an electoral system will depend on three main factors. The first is the question of electoral districts. Will the country be divided up into a number of electoral districts, or will the voters all vote in a single national election? Second is the number of representatives. What is the optimum number of representatives for the legislative body? If there are too few, that body may not be sufficiently representative of the population. If there are too many, it may become dysfunctional. (Imagine a House of Commons with 10,000 MPs!) Furthermore, if the electoral system is based on multiple districts, one has to ask if there will be one member elected per district or multiple-member districts. (One might want double-member districts to ensure that each district is represented by one man and one woman, for example, or by more than one party.) Finally, there is the question of the method of electing representatives. How is the actual voting to be structured? Does the person with the most votes (a **plurality**) win, or must the winner have a majority of votes? Does the elector simply choose one candidate, or does the voter rank the candidates in order of preference?

The preamble to *CA 1867* specifies that Canada is to have "a Constitution similar in Principle to that of the United Kingdom." In addition to this Constitution, we also adopted the same type of electoral system. Like Britain, then, Canada adopted what is usually referred to as the **single-member plurality (SMP)** system. This is an electoral system in which the country is divided into a number of electoral districts (informally called **ridings** or **constituencies**), each of which has one representative. That representative is elected by a plurality of votes rather than a majority. A winning candidate will therefore often have less than 50 per cent of the votes cast in the district. For this reason, the system is sometimes referred to as **first-past-the-post**: you don't have to have a majority to win; you nearly need to get to the finish line ahead of all the other candidates.

Section 37 of *CA 1867* specifies how many MPs there will be from each province. By extension, this should tell us how many electoral districts there will be. But Sections 51 and 52 provide for a readjustment of these numbers after each decennial census of the population. The current distribution of seats/electoral districts is indicated in Figure 9.1.

Figure 9.1: Distribution of Seats in the House of Commons (to take effect in 2013)

Atlantic Canada		**32**
	Prince Edward Island	4
	Nova Scotia	11
	New Brunswick	10
	Newfoundland and Labrador	7
Central Canada		**199**
	Ontario	121
	Québec	78
Western Canada		**104**
	Manitoba	14
	Saskatchewan	14
	Alberta	34
	British Columbia	42
Northern Canada		**3**
	Northwest Territories	1
	Nunavut	1
	Yukon	1
Total		**338**

In order to respect the democratic principle of "one-person, one vote," Canada's electoral districts are designed to be roughly equal in population. At the last redistribution of seats, the average electoral district had about 80,000 people. But it is impossible, and even undesirable, to insist that every constituency be exactly the same size. Notice, for example, that making the electoral districts equal in population will make them unequal in size. One will find 80,000 people in a very small area in Toronto, but it may take the northern third of Saskatchewan to create a district with that population. A constituency of that geographical size may be too large for an individual MP to represent effectively. In order to keep the geographical size of constituencies reasonable, it is not uncommon to create electoral districts with smaller than average populations in remote areas. Deviations in the size of electoral districts are also imposed by Section 51A of *CA 1867*. Designed to provide protection for the smaller provinces, this section declares that no province shall have fewer MPs than its number of senators. Because of Section 51A, Prince Edward Island is guaranteed four MPs (though in terms of population, it deserves only one). Similarly, New Brunswick must always have ten MPs, though its current population would warrant only seven.[2]

9.3 The Effects of SMP

Our use of a single-member plurality system has important consequences for electoral politics in Canada. SMP divides our voting into 308 separate elections. It then awards seats in the House of Commons only to those who come first in each of the electoral districts. These arrangements will generally produce results marked by a wide discrepancy between the distribution of votes and the distribution of seats.

To see how this may be so, let us consider a hypothetical example. Imagine a Canadian election with only three parties, Parties A, B, and C. Suppose that on voting day, Party A gets 34 per cent of the total votes in Canada, Party B gets 33 per cent, and Party C also gets 33 per cent. This would appear to be the closest election in Canadian history. But what happens if the overall ratio of support (34/33/33) is consistent right across the country? Under our SMP system, Party A would end up with all 308 seats (it would win each constituency 34–33–33) and Parties B and C would get none! Under SMP, then, one party could get 100 per cent of the seats in the House of Commons even though a large majority of the electorate (66 per cent) voted for someone else. Furthermore, the votes of those 66 per cent would, in a manner of speaking, be wasted.

The example cited above is an extreme one, but Canadian political history contains cases that are similar in principle. In the 1987 provincial election in New Brunswick, for example, the Liberal Party under the leadership of Frank McKenna received about 60 per cent of the total vote. Because that support was relatively consistent across the province, the Liberals won all 58 seats in the New Brunswick Legislature. And despite winning almost 40 per cent of the votes, the PCs and the NDP got no seats at all. This outcome demonstrates dramatically a characteristic that is typical, in lesser degree, of all Canadian elections. SMP systematically favours the leading national party with the widest distribution of voters. Such a party will almost always receive a larger percentage of seats than its percentage of the popular vote in the "winner-take-all" format of SMP.

---

2   Note that the effect of the amended Section 51 of *CA 1867* is to ensure that no province will ever have fewer seats in the House of Commons than it had in 1985, which is when this section came into force.

The historical record shows that since World War I, the leading national party generally obtains around 45 per cent of the votes. But thanks to our electoral system, 45 per cent of the vote consistently yields the leading party 60 or even 70 per cent of the seats. This is a significant fact, for it means that it is the SMP electoral system that is responsible for the creation of majority governments in Canada. Only three of the 25 elections since World War I have given a single party more than 50 per cent of the votes (1940, 1958, and 1984). Yet 16 of those elections have resulted in majority governments. Moreover, even if the leading national party does not receive enough of a boost from SMP to convert a minority of votes into a majority of seats, it will still find itself with a greater share of the seats than its share of the vote. In the 2008 election, for instance, the Conservative Party picked up 46.4 per cent of the seats—close to a majority—with only 37.6 per cent of the vote.

The impact of the SMP system is felt not only by the leading party. Obviously, if the leading party benefits from SMP, it does so at the expense of the other parties. But the other parties are not all treated the same way by SMP. Our electoral system favours small regional parties but works against the less popular national parties. A moment's reflection on the logic of SMP shows why. Because of SMP's "winner-take-all" approach, votes are wasted unless the party comes in first in an electoral district. This means that secondary parties will succeed only if their support is heavily concentrated in key areas so that they come in first in some ridings. If their support is spread evenly throughout the country, they are unlikely to win many seats. The 2008 election provides a good illustration of the point. The Green Party won almost 7 per cent of the vote but did not win a single seat. With 18 per cent of the vote, the NDP received only 12 per cent of the seats. On the other hand, the Bloc obtained far fewer votes than the NDP (10 per cent of the total as opposed to 18.2 per cent) but captured substantially more seats (49 to 37) since its support was concentrated entirely in the province of Québec.

The 2011 election again produced similar effects. The Conservative Party won a majority of the seats, winning 166 of 308 seats in the House of Commons. Their share of the vote in Canada as a whole was close to 40 per cent, but their share of the seats in the House of Commons is 54 per cent. The reverse happened to the Liberal Party, who won only 34 seats. While the Liberals won about 19 percent of the popular vote, they won only 11 per cent of the seats in the House of Commons (see Figure 9.2).

SMP strengthens regionalism in Canada not only by promoting regional parties but by intensifying regional strengths and weaknesses within our broadly national parties. Because of its "winner-take-all" rules, SMP systematically under-represents certain regions in each party caucus and over-represents others.

In the 1980 election, for example, over 20 per cent of Westerners voted for Liberal candidates. Yet because the Liberal candidates consistently came in behind the PC or NDP candidates, the Liberals ended up with only two seats in the whole region (about 3 per cent). This made it difficult for incoming Liberal Prime Minister Pierre Trudeau to give Western Canada adequate representation in his cabinet. During the same period, Mr. Trudeau would sometimes win almost every seat in Québec, even though substantial numbers of Québec voters did not support him. Consequently, the Liberal caucus of that period did not really reflect Liberal support in the country:

A look at Figure 9.3 shows that the regionalization of party representation continues today. For instance, in the 2011 election, the Liberal Party received 25 per cent of the vote in Ontario but only 10 per cent of the seats. Meanwhile, with 44 per cent of that vote in that province, the Conservatives won 69 per cent of the seats. Similarly in Western Canada, on the basis of seats, one might conclude that it is overwhelmingly Conservative and has no interest in the Liberal Party. But vote totals show that this is not true. The Conservative Party won 82 of the 92 seats in the four western provinces—a stunning 89 per cent of the seats. And yet their share of the popular vote in the region was less than 60 per cent.

To summarize, we may say that the SMP electoral system has four major effects on electoral politics. First, it rewards the largest national party with more seats than it "deserves," frequently converting a minority of votes into a majority of seats. Second, it handicaps smaller national parties such as the NDP and the Greens by giving them a smaller share of seats than their share of the popular vote. Third, it encourages regionalism by fostering the growth of parties that focus on regional interests and concerns. Fourth, it encourages regionalism by magnifying the regional strengths and weaknesses of our national parties.

Figure 9.2: General Elections of 2011, Seats Won

	Atlantic	Québec	Ontario	West	Territories	Canada
Conservative	14	5	73	72	2	166
NDP	6	59	22	15	1	103
Liberal	12	7	11	4	0	34
BQ	0	4	0	0	0	4
Green	0	0	0	1	0	1

Figure 9.3: General Election of 2011, Percentage of Votes/Percentage of Seats in Provinces

	Liberals	Conservatives	NDP	BQ	Green
NL	40/57	28/14	37/29	0/0	1/0
PEI	41/75	41/25	15/0	0/0	2/0
NS	29/36	37/36	30/27	0/0	4/0
NB	23/10	44/80	30/10	0/0	3/0
QC	14/9	17/6	43/79	23/5	2/0
ON	25/10	44/69	26/21	0/0	4/0
MB	17/7	54/79	26/14	0/0	3/0
SK	9/7	56/93	32/0	0/0	3/0
AB	9/0	67/96	17/4	0/0	5/0
BC	13/6	46/58	33/33	0/0	8/3

9.4 Proportional Representation

Political observers who are troubled by some of the effects of SMP have advocated the adoption of an alternative electoral system, called **proportional representation (PR)**. Proportional representation is used in many liberal democracies. (In fact, the pure SMP system that Canada inherited from Britain is relatively rare in the world.) PR exists in a variety of forms, some of them rather complicated. The one most commonly proposed for adoption in Canada is known as the **party list system**.

In this system, each party prepares a list of its candidates in rank order. Electoral districts are abolished, so that instead of holding 308 elections, we hold a single nationwide election. In this single election, the electorate votes for parties rather than candidates. When the results are tabulated, the number of seats each party wins is determined by the proportion of the vote it received. If, for example, Party A received 20 per cent of the vote, it would receive exactly 20 per cent of the seats available. On the assumption that we keep 308 seats, this would mean that Party A gets 61 seats. Those seats would then be awarded to the first 61 candidates on Party A's list.

Advocates of PR argue that this system is fairer than SMP. Parties get seats in proportions that mirror exactly the preferences indicated by the voters. As opposed to SMP, this electoral system does not "distort" the electorate's voting pattern by favouring certain types of parties and disadvantaging others. PR is also said to be fairer in that it eliminates the phenomenon of "wasted ballots." Under PR, every vote has an impact in shaping the composition of the House of

Commons. Figure 9.4 shows the actual allocation of seats from the 2011 election and how the seats would have been allocated under a PR system.

Figure 9.4: Results of 2011 Election Using SMP and Using PR[3]

Party	Number of Seats Using SMP	Number of Seats Using PR
Conservative	166	122
NDP	103	95
Liberal	34	58
BQ	4	18
Green	1	12
Other	0	3

Another point raised by advocates of PR is that it provides for more diverse representation within each party caucus. We have seen that SMP tends to magnify the regional strengths and weaknesses of each party. PR offers a solution to this type of problem. Because parties are free to structure their lists as they like, each party can arrange its list to ensure that all regions will have adequate representation within the caucus. Similarly, the party leadership can use its control over the composition of the list to ensure adequate representation in the House of Commons for groups that are traditionally under-represented there—women, for instance.

It should be noted, however, that PR also entails certain disadvantages. The charge most frequently levelled against it is that it leads to political instability. As we have seen, the Canadian electorate rarely gives any party a majority of votes. It is our SMP electoral system that is responsible for transforming a mere plurality of votes (nationwide) into a majority of seats in the House of Commons. Precisely because PR gives each party seats based on its proportion of the overall vote, the adoption of PR would make majority governments extremely rare. Minority governments or coalition governments, which are generally less stable, would become the norm. (Of course, minority governments have become the norm in recent times precisely because SMP has facilitated the emergence of a regional protest party, the Bloc, which by effectively removing about 50 seats from the total available to the Liberals and Conservatives, makes it very difficult for either of those parties to amass a parliamentary majority.)

---

3   Calculations here are done on the assumption that the party lists used would be national lists. One could also implement a PR system in which seats were allocated on the basis of provincial lists. The results might well be substantially different.

Connected with the concern about permanent minority government is the allegation that PR will lead to a more divisive politics by facilitating the emergence of small single-issue parties and parties with non-mainstream agendas. Such parties are generally shut out of the House of Commons by our SMP system, which awards seats only to those parties strong enough to come first in some riding. Under PR, however, it is likely that an anti-abortion party or an animal rights party—or even a frivolous group like the Rhinoceros Party—would be able to scrape together enough votes nationwide to earn a seat or two in the House of Commons. In a minority government situation where the party in power is in danger of losing a vote, the government party might have to cut a deal with one of these minor parties in order to stay in office. The tail would then wag the dog as the minor party dictated its terms to the party in power.

A third major problem with PR is that local constituencies would no longer have an MP of their own. A well-structured party list might ensure that all regions have adequate representation, but it would not guarantee an MP for each of our electoral districts. Ontario, for example, would likely be dominated by representatives from Toronto. The province of New Brunswick might have two MPs from Moncton and three from Saint John, but nobody from the other two-thirds of the province. And even in those two cities, the link between the voters and the MPs would be much weaker than it is today, for the MPs would owe their positions in the House of Commons not to the support of the local electorate but to the party bosses in Ottawa who put their names high on the party list. For these reasons, the adoption of PR would mean that Canadians would no longer be able to count on having a representative in Ottawa to listen to their concerns or to help them when they have problems with the government. It would also mean that the individuals who actually form the government would never have been elected as individuals. They would be party loyalists who owed their place in Ottawa to the leaders of their party—the people with the authority to put their name on the party's electoral list. This arrangement would almost certainly make them less responsive to the electorate and even more subordinate to party bosses. Proponents of PR have tried to address these problems by suggesting a **Mixed Member Proportional (MMP)** system which blends PR and SMP. Under MMP systems, only some of the seats would be elected on the basis of a party list system (usually one-quarter to one-half) and the rest would be elected using SMP. Voters would thus vote twice—once for their local candidate and once for the party list.

Typically, calls for the introduction of PR have come from supporters of parties that are disadvantaged by SMP, from individuals troubled by the fact that votes cast for the losing party in a given riding are "wasted," or from people who simply think it unfair that the percentage of seats a party gets does not correspond exactly to its percentage of the vote. Advocates of reform have traditionally been ignored by the parties in power because it is precisely those parties that benefit from SMP. In the past few years, however, PR has become a much more serious possibility. Oddly enough, while one might argue that the case for PR is strongest at the national level (because of the way SMP exacerbates Canadian regionalism), it is the provinces that are leading the reform movement. Governments in Prince Edward Island, New Brunswick, Ontario, and Québec have all expressed interest in introducing some form of PR at the provincial level, but no change has taken place at this point. Voters in PEI actually defeated a proposal to switch to MMP in 2005 and voters in Ontario rejected a similar proposal in 2007.

9.5 Single Transferable Vote

Another alternative to the SMP is a system known as the **single transferable vote (STV)**.

In this type of electoral system people do not vote for just one candidate, they rank all the candidates in order of preference. When the votes are counted, if no candidate has a majority of first-place votes, then first- and second-place votes are counted. If there is still no candidate with a majority, the first-, second-, and third-place votes are counted. The process continues until one candidate has a clear majority. The aim of such a system is to ensure that the candidates who are elected have the broadest base of support and a clear title to the seat. In SMP, of course, candidates usually win with a mere plurality rather than a majority. That may often mean that the winner is not really the most acceptable candidate to the riding as a whole. For instance, a Conservative candidate might win a riding with 35 per cent of the vote, just ahead of a Liberal candidate with 30 per cent, an NDP candidate with 25 per cent, and a Green candidate with 10 per cent. It may well be that those who voted for the losing candidates would have strongly preferred any of the losing candidates to the Conservative candidate. Yet even though 65 per cent of the voters see the Conservative as the least desirable candidate, the Conservative wins, thanks to SMP. By insisting on a clear majority, and by counting second, third, and fourth preferences where necessary to arrive at a clear majority, STV ensures that the candidate who is elected is the candidate with the greatest overall support.

STV is typically used in conjunction with a multi-member district system to provide a more proportional division of seats among the political parties. In a district with five seats, then, each party would have the right to nominate up to five candidates, voters would rank all of the candidates in order of preference, and the first five to reach 50 per cent (counting down from first to second to third preference and so on) would be declared elected. A multi-member STV system is more proportional than SMP in that in a district where Party A and Party B have roughly equal support, they will likely split the five seats available, instead of having one party win the only seat available while the other party gets nothing.

The citizens of British Columbia considered adopting a multi-member STV system in 2005. While 58 per cent voted in favour of the proposal, it was not adopted because the legislation providing for the referendum stipulated that major change to something as fundamental as the electoral system would require the support of at least 60 per cent of the electorate. A second referendum on the question was held in 2009, and the STV proposal was again defeated, this time by a much wider margin.

9.6   Voting in Canada

Although in constitutional law it is the Governor General who dissolves Parliament and calls new elections, he or she does so on the "advice" of the prime minister. If the prime minister's party controls only a minority of votes in the House of Commons, the House can force an election at any time by voting a lack of confidence in the government. Such a vote would compel the prime minister either to resign or, more likely, to advise the Governor General to dissolve Parliament and call elections. In the case of majority government, however, the prime minister has traditionally had a free hand to determine the timing of elections, within certain limits. Section 4(1) of *CA 1982* stipulates that no Parliament is to last longer than five years. Prime ministers have rarely waited the full five years because there is a general expectation in Canada that elections ought to be held somewhere in the fourth year of a Parliament. If a prime minister waited five years to ask for a dissolution, that was usually a sign that the government was afraid to face the electorate. On the other hand, prime ministers have sometimes been tempted to ask for a dissolution after less than four years if their government was particularly popular or the opposition was particularly weak.

As noted in Chapter 3, the Harper government, following the lead of several provincial legislatures, passed legislation providing for a "fixed" election date. Most provinces now have fixed election dates. Theoretically, our federal elections are now supposed to be held every fourth year on the third Monday in October. In theory this legislation was designed both to minimize uncertainty regarding the timing of elections and to deprive prime ministers of the opportunity to use their control over their timing to the advantage of their own party. However, the very nature of responsible government makes it impossible to stick to a fixed election date. Whenever the House expresses a lack of confidence in a government (which can happen at any time in a minority situation), an election is almost always necessary. If the House has no confidence in the Crown's ministers, then our government has no democratic mandate. Unless the leader of some other party can put together a ministry that *will* have the confidence of the House (and that is usually unlikely), the only way to restore democratic legitimacy is to hold elections for a new House, for a new House will either restore confidence in the existing government or make it clear that the prime minister must resign and make way for another leader who does have its confidence.

Mr. Harper's fixed-date legislation had to take this complication into consideration. Consequently, the wording of the legislation stipulated that the new law did not revoke the power of the Governor General to dissolve Parliament and hold elections prior to the "fixed" date. Mr. Harper took advantage of this loophole to ask the Governor General for a dissolution in September 2008, 13 months before the date set in the legislation. It is worth noting that the House had not actually declared a lack of confidence in the government. Most analysts agreed that Mr. Harper was taking advantage of the loophole in the legislation to arrange to have the elections at the time that would be most favourable to his party—the very sort of thing that the legislation was supposed to prevent.

Once the Governor General dissolves Parliament, a **general election** follows immediately. (We speak of a "general election" to describe nationwide elections. A **by-election** is held in a single constituency to fill a seat vacated midway through a Parliament by the death or resignation of an MP.) General elections are administered by a politically neutral civil servant called the **Chief Electoral Officer** who appoints a **Returning Officer** for each of the 308 electoral districts in Canada. Electoral districts are divided into smaller units called **polls**, each of which has about 250 voters. The returning officer for each electoral district will appoint a deputy returning officer and a couple of poll clerks to run the election at each poll.

The returning officer also appoints two **enumerators** for each poll; their task is to prepare the official voters' list for the poll. Under the *Canada Elections Act,* all citizens who are 18 years of age or older have the right to vote. (One notable exception is the Chief Electoral Officer, who has no vote. The returning officers are allowed to vote only in the case of a tie.) The preliminary voters' list must be ready 26 days before the election. Those who have been left off the list have 10 days to get their name added to it.

To have their names put on the ballot, candidates must present the returning officer with official nomination papers signed by 100 eligible voters from the constituency. (The candidates themselves do not have to be residents of the constituency, but it is generally a political liability to be a non-resident.) Candidates must also leave the returning officer a deposit of $1,000, a sum which is returned to all those who gain 10 per cent or more of the vote. The purpose of these two requirements is to discourage frivolous candidacies.

In order to minimize the influence that those with money might have on electoral outcomes, Canadian electoral laws place limits on the amount that a candidate may spend. They also provide substantial subsidies to those candidates who have won 15 per cent of the vote or more. The subsidies are not enough to pay for an entire campaign; candidates still need money from their national party, from local donations, and often from their own pockets, in order to mount an effective campaign. Still, these subsidies, combined with the legislated spending limits, serve to reduce the impact that candidates' private wealth (or the wealth of their supporters) might have on the electoral process. The Harper government has signalled its intention to phase out publicly funded per-vote subsidies.

A more complicated matter is the issue of third-party advertising. The problem is well illustrated by the 1988 election. It is widely believed that the victory of the Progressive Conservative Party, which backed free trade, was in some measure due to a massive advertising campaign conducted on its behalf by "big business." Parliament has attempted to limit this type of advertising. Its rationale has been that such advertising is inconsistent with the democratic principle of one person-one vote because it gives the wealthy more influence on elections than the less wealthy. Ottawa's earliest attempts to deal with third-party advertising were deemed by the courts to violate Section 2 of the Charter, but a revised law met with the approval of the Supreme Court of Canada in a 2004 decision. Under this law, third parties wishing to run ads during an election campaign must register with Elections Canada and must respect mandated spending limits. For the 2011 election, the limits were $3,765 in an individual riding and $188,250 nationally.[4] Groups such as the National Citizens Coalition continue to oppose the law, claiming that it limits freedom of expression and gives politicians and their parties an unfair monopoly on political expression during election campaigns.

Elections are normally held on a Monday. The polls are open for 12 hours in each of Canada's time zones. (The times are staggered to reduce the gap between the time the polls close on the East Coast and the time they close on the West Coast.) Lest the voters in the more Western time zones be influenced by the results of the voting in the East, our election laws forbid the broadcasting of any results in an area where the polls are still open. Due to advances in communication technology, however, this rule is becoming increasingly irrelevant.

---

4   For current information on election finances, see Elections Canada www.elections.ca

Each party is permitted to have two **scrutineers** at the poll all day long to observe the process and to keep the candidates posted on whether known supporters have voted. Upon the closing of the poll, the votes are counted by the deputy returning officer while the scrutineers look on. The deputy returning officer then seals all the votes in the ballot box and sends them to the returning officer for an official count, which takes place over the next few days. But the deputy returning officer's unofficial count is immediately communicated to the returning officer, who passes the information on to the media. The unofficial results are thus generally known within approximately half an hour.

Key Terms

delegates

trustees

party member

mandate

floor-crossing

microcosm theory of representation

plurality

single-member plurality (SMP)

ridings

constituencies

first-past-the-post

proportional representation (PR)

party list system

Mixed Member Proportional (MMP)

single transferable vote (STV)

general election

by-election

Chief Electoral Officer

Returning Officer

polls

enumerators

scrutineers

Discussion Questions

1. Which political party or parties would benefit from the introduction of STV? Which party or parties would be disadvantaged by it?

2. Is democracy enhanced by the public subsidy of political parties?

POLITICAL PARTIES

10.1 Political Parties in the Canadian Regime

10.2 The Five Functions of Political Parties

10.3 Parties and Ideology

10.4 Canada's Major Parties

10.5 The Canadian Party System

10.6 The Organization of Political Parties

10.7 Financing Political Parties

10.8 Party Government and Party Politics

10.1 Political Parties in the Canadian Regime

Political parties are publicly organized groups of people who are motivated by some common set of political ideas and whose goal is to have their particular members win public office so that those ideas can be put into practice.

It is obvious to even the most casual observer that Canadian political life is dominated by political parties. Every Canadian Parliament has been divided along party lines, and, except for a brief interlude during World War I, membership in every Canadian cabinet has been restricted to those who were members of

CHAPTER TEN · POLITICAL PARTIES

the dominant political party at the time.[1] It is worth noting, however, that the dominant role of political parties is not something mandated by the law of the Constitution. *CA 1867* and *CA 1982* do not mention political parties. Nor could one claim that the role of political parties is a matter of constitutional convention: constitutional conventions are rules, and there is no rule requiring our MPs to be members of political parties. The truth of the matter is that the dominant role of our political parties is simply a matter of need. We have political parties because they are useful (as we shall see in the next section) and because there is no law to prohibit them. One might compare the role of political parties in the Canadian regime to the role of the coach of a hockey team. There is nothing in the National Hockey League rule book that says a team must have a coach. Theoretically, a team could play without one. But, since every team finds that it is useful to have somebody directing the players, every team has a coach.

To be sure, fans will often think their team would be better off without its coach. So, too, we often hear complaints to the effect that political parties constitute an impediment to reasonable democratic political life. The "party system" is accused of limiting our choices and stifling debate. It is blamed for focusing political deliberation on partisan advantage rather than the common good. Yet while Canadians often express frustration with the "party system," they almost never take advantage of their right to elect an "independent" candidate—a candidate with no party affiliation. It is well worth pondering why that is.

A lone MP in the House of Commons exercises little political power. He or she may be able to speak on behalf of constituents' interests without having to "toe the party line." On the other hand, the "independent" MP is unlikely to accomplish much within a political institution that runs on the principle of party discipline. An independent MP would be effective only in a House that actually banned party membership, yet a rule banning party membership would certainly be in violation of the right to freedom of association guaranteed by Section 2d of the Charter.

All things considered, the existence of political parties is a sign of a healthy democratic regime. Authoritarian and totalitarian forms of government usually move quickly to extinguish political opposition by means of outlawing opposition parties. They concentrate all power in the hands of the state by means of imposing a one-party state. In Frank Underhill's words:

---

[1]   The "conscription crisis" of 1917 led to the formation of a "Union Government" that included all of the Conservative MPs and all of the Liberals who favoured conscription. Those Liberals who opposed conscription remained in opposition.

The acid test of freedom in a state is whether power and office can pass peaceably from one political party to another. "Her Majesty's Opposition" is just as necessary to free government as "Her Majesty's Government."[2]

Liberal-democratic party politics is workable because the parties agree on at least one thing: different political parties have a right to exist, and should one party win an election, it has a legitimate right to rule until the next election. Parties are "parts" of the regime. Party politics is, therefore, non-revolutionary: it works because every party agrees on the fundamental principles of the regime.[3]

10.2 The Five Functions of Political Parties

In their efforts to win political power, parties perform a number of functions that are important to the health of the regime as a whole. The **five functions of parties** are recruitment, fundraising, interest aggregation, policy development, and education.

First, parties recruit people into the party as members and, sometimes, as candidates. This recruitment function is obviously crucial, for modern democracies are constantly imperilled by apathy and lack of civic participation. The dangers of what Alexis de Tocqueville described as "individualism"—where people tend to withdraw into their individual lives of work, family, and friends, and pay little attention to political affairs—are fairly obvious. Democracy means the rule of the people, and it is endangered when the people lose their taste for politics. The parties supply us with our political leaders through national leadership conventions, our candidates by means of constituency elections, and the vast number of campaign workers needed to run all the aspects of a modern election.

Second, parties raise money for their organizations and election campaigns. This is still, by and large, a private activity. It is regulated by election finance laws. It is worth considering that if we did not have political parties to raise much of the money for elections, the costs would have to be borne by the taxpayer.

Third, parties identify, represent, and balance the diverse interests of Canadians. This process, often referred to as **interest aggregation**, is crucial to the healthy functioning of a liberal democracy. It is rare that Canadian voters have

---

2   Frank Underhill, *Canadian Political Parties* (Ottawa: The Canadian Historical Association Booklets, No. 8, 1964) 3.

3   See Giovani Sartori, *Parties and Party Systems,* Vol.1 (Cambridge: Cambridge University Press, 1976).

a single common interest. In most cases, policy that is advantageous for one group ultimately comes at the expense of others. Fiscal transfers to have-not provinces are paid for by the more prosperous provinces; companies in Winnipeg compete with companies in Montreal for lucrative government contracts. If Canada had no political parties, our MPs would be free to vote for whatever was in the best interests of their own constituents. But this would ultimately mean that the most powerful political constituencies—Ontario and Québec—would make all the rules to their own advantage. Because the major national political parties have to seek votes in all constituencies—French and English, men and women, East and West, business and labour—they are forced to hammer out compromise positions that offer a relatively fair deal to all the major categories of voters. If we did not have political parties to perform this process of interest aggregation, our regime would likely be much less successful in its pursuit of fair treatment for all Canadians.

In the process of attempting to aggregate interests and integrate them into a national whole, the parties formulate and influence public policy. Normally they design their policies at policy conventions, large gatherings of rank-and-file members who debate the current political issues and design or revise the party's main policies in light of these debates.

Finally, parties educate people about political life. Party membership provides an education in holding political office by means of providing elected offices within the party. Often a candidate has served as an elected member of a constituency organization before ever running for nomination. Parties meet to discuss policy and ideas and hold regular policy conventions. The educational function of parties thus extends beyond the party members to citizens at large, who benefit from media coverage and commercial advertising of party policy. It culminates in the way parties help to structure voter choice. The parties accomplish this by attempting to persuade voters to vote for them. One need only imagine an election without parties to see how essential their function has become.

10.3 Parties and Ideology

Parties are usually built on the basis of a loose set of fundamental political principles, commonly referred to as an **ideology**. Those principles are then used as the basis for generating ideas about the purposes of government, how it should be organized, and what public policies should be implemented.

Some might argue that this description is too "idealistic." They would instead emphasize that political parties are groups of people who are motivated primarily by the goal of winning public office so that they can obtain political power to serve their own interests. We would not disagree. Like most of us, those who enter directly into political life are rarely saints. And politics is inseparable from the desire for the benefits and honours that come with holding public office. In other words, major democratic political parties tend to be **pragmatic**. They are organizations designed to win elections, and they often compromise, if not design, their political principles to facilitate electoral success.[4]

The political parties in liberal democratic regimes are therefore best understood as attempts to serve both the ideal and the practical. They must steer a moderate middle course between the extremes of powerless idealism on the one hand and the cynically unprincipled pursuit of power on the other. There is no point in pursuing ideals that are attractive to only a very few voters. Conversely, the public will soon sour on the party or politician who is perceived to be without principles, often labelling them opportunistic and cynical. What we seem to want most are practical and pragmatic politicians who have political principles. In other words, we demand that our parties constantly manage the tension between theory and practice, between high political principle and workable public policy.

Most ideological questions turn on the issue of preservation and change. On most issues, there will always be those who favour change and those who prefer the status quo. One almost always finds those who argue that conserving what we now have is the best course of action versus those who argue that we can make progress and hence improve our present lot by following a different course. In other words, one almost always finds "conservatives" and "progressives" in any political arena.

This dichotomy between those who favour the present and those who favour change is best explained in terms of two factors. First, it seems to be a nearly universal human phenomenon that within any group you will find that some people are more inclined to have conservative dispositions than others. Some people value caution and prudence, while others are more daring and willing to take a chance. In other words, party politics seems to be rooted in the different dispositions of human beings. Second, it is often the case that there will always be those who have a vested interest in maintaining things as they are, as opposed to those whose interests would be best served by some new political arrangements. For example, it is hard to imagine professional athletes being in favour of a law that would limit their income to the salary of the highest paid police officers.

---

4   There are, of course, some parties that are uncompromisingly committed to a specific set of well-defined political ideas. But where these parties do not hold power, they often forego political success by maintaining ideological purity. Where they do hold power, they often maintain ideological purity by refusing to tolerate any meaningful debate or dissent.

These days, the main ideological division between our parties is on socio-economic matters. The dominant ideology at the time of Confederation (an ideology shared by both the Liberal and Conservative parties) might best be described as classical liberalism. Classical liberals emphasize the importance of liberty (freedom from governmental interference) and a free market economy. They also value equality, but they understand it to mean primarily equality of opportunity. In Canada, people or parties are labelled "conservative" when they are inclined to conserve the original principles of classical liberalism. The term "progressive," on the other hand, usually applies to "socialists" who advocate not only equality of opportunity, but greater equality of condition. In the Canadian context, equality of condition is pursued mainly by the redistribution of wealth through the tax system and through state funding of social programs. Because the creation of greater equality of condition usually requires intervention by government, progressives are generally less concerned about "liberty" than are conservatives. In general, they favour public regulation or even ownership of natural resources and key industries, and of economic institutions like banks.

10.4 Canada's Major Parties

Currently, there are four parties in Canada that regularly elect members to the House of Commons. Two of these parties—the Conservatives and the Liberals—date back to the days of Confederation. These are the only two parties that have ever formed a government. The NDP and the Bloc have historically also elected substantial numbers of members, and indeed, in the 2011 election, the NDP won twice as many seats as the Liberals and has, for the first time, become the Official Opposition. Finally, the Green Party of Canada has received a substantial number of votes in recent elections, and in the 2011 election it elected a Member of Parliament.

1. *The Conservative Party.* The Conservative Party developed under the leadership of Canada's first prime minister, John A. Macdonald. Macdonald was able to build his party out of a coalition of "Liberal-Conservatives" from Upper Canada (pre-Confederation Ontario) and "Bleu" politicians from Lower Canada (pre-Confederation Québec). Under Macdonald and his French-Canadian lieutenant George-Étienne Cartier, the Conservative Party dominated Canadian politics for the first 30 years after Confederation. The Conservatives put in place a "national policy" of protectionism against the United States, western expansion via the Canadian Pacific Railway, and strong central government. The party was not opposed to state intervention in the economy. Such intervention was seen as necessary for the development of Canada, and the party therefore traditionally

favoured state enterprises. In the 1940s, the Conservatives absorbed the remnants of a Western protest party called the Progressive Party and adopted the somewhat paradoxical name, the Progressive Conservative Party.

A remarkably similar story took place more recently. In the late 1980s, an Albertan named Preston Manning launched a new Western protest party called the Reform Party. Reform was both socially and fiscally conservative and therefore cut deeply into Progressive Conservative support in the West. Indeed, the emergence of Reform had much to do with the total collapse of the PCs in the 1993 election. Through most of the ensuing decade, the PCs and Reform fought a life-and-death struggle to be the right-of-centre alternative to the Liberal Party. This division of the political right made it easy for the Chrétien Liberals to win solid majorities throughout this period. In 1998, Reform reconstituted itself as the Canadian Alliance Party in the hope that the PCs would join them. A few did but not enough to put an end to the war. Finally, in the run-up to the 2004 election, fear of a huge Liberal victory finally drove the two parties into a marriage of necessity. The result was the new Conservative Party of Canada. The former Canadian Alliance/Reform forces formed the more powerful faction within the new party, and their former leader, Stephen Harper, was easily elected leader. This new party stands for lower taxes and less government control, a more decentralized federation giving more responsibility to the provinces, global free trade, and a stronger free-market economy. It experiences some divisions on social issues, with those from the former Reform/Canadian Alliance wing tending to take conservative positions on issues such as gun control, capital punishment, or same-sex marriage while many of the former PCs incline to more progressive views. In foreign affairs, the Conservative Party tends to be strongly supportive of the United States.

2. *The Liberal Party.* The second great party from the Confederation era was the Liberal Party, which emerged out of a coalition of Upper Canadian "Reformers" and the "Rouge" politicians of Québec. During the first years of Confederation, the Liberal Party was united mainly by its opposition to the Macdonald Conservatives. It was not until Wilfrid Laurier became Canada's first French-Canadian prime minister in 1896 that the Liberals developed a coherent set of political ideas based on free trade and provincial rights. The Liberal Party has long been the national representative of the rights of French Canadians and therefore developed the tradition of alternating its leadership between anglophones and francophones. The view that Canada was a compact between two nations—English and French—is one that has had far greater influence within the Liberal Party than in the various incarnations of the Conservative Party. The policies of official bilingualism and multiculturalism were instituted under Liberal

governments. In recent years, the Liberal Party has come to stand for the main-tenance of a strong national government and is generally suspicious of efforts to decentralize the Canadian federation. Like the Conservatives, the Liberals favour global free trade and a free-market economy, but they are more sympathetic to government intervention in the economy and are stronger advocates of the wel-fare state. On social issues, Liberals are generally in favour of measures such as gun control and same-sex marriage. In foreign affairs, they are more likely than the Conservatives to be critical of the United States.

3. *The New Democratic Party (NDP).* The NDP is Canada's only important demo-cratic socialist party. It originated in the regional protest politics of the Cooperative Commonwealth Federation (CCF), which began in reaction to the collapse of the prairie economy in the 1930s, for which capitalist interests, located mainly in central Canada, were deemed responsible. The reaction against free-market capi-talism and liberalism was therefore long associated with the concern that Canada was a country run by central Canada to serve the interests of central Canada. The Liberals and the PCs were thought to represent the interests of the ruling elite or capitalist class, as opposed to the working class of industrial labour and farmers. The CCF was formed as a party to represent the interests of the working class.

In 1961, the NDP was formed by combining the largely Western CCF with the Canadian Labour Congress (CLC), Canada's most important labour organization, whose great strength was in Ontario. Until the 2011 election, one could best describe the NDP as having had only modest success as a national political party, with its strongest showing in 1988 when it won 43 seats. It has done well provincially, having formed governments in five of the provinces, and has been the Official Opposition in others. Traditionally, the party has drawn its strength from Ontario and Western Canada. But in 2011, it made spectacular gains in Quebec and gained substantial support in the Maritimes. For the first time it has become the Official Opposition party in Ottawa. Although the NDP has never formed the government in Ottawa, it has had considerable influence on national policy. Over the years, many of its progressive ideas (medicare being the primary example) have been implemented by the Liberals, often as the price for NDP support during a minority government.

4. *The Bloc Québécois (the Bloc).* The Bloc Québécois is an unusual political party in that it is dedicated to achieving independence for Québec and hence to its own disappearance as a political party in Canadian politics. It came into existence after the failure of the Meech Lake Accord, when a handful of Québec MPs quit the PC and Liberal caucuses and joined together to form a new party. The 1993

election transformed the Bloc from a small group of disaffected MPs into a major political party, winning 54 seats in Québec. Because it had won more seats than any other opposition party, it even became "Her Majesty's Loyal Opposition," a somewhat ironical outcome.

Much to the surprise of many analysts, the Bloc has remained a substantial force in Ottawa. It is surprising because the Bloc is in many respects a typical regional party. Because the electoral system rewards regional party strength disproportionately, it has been able to transform a small amount of the national popular vote into a relatively large number of seats. Yet regional protest parties usually fade in influence after a meteoric rise. The anger that drives them gradually subsides, and people begin to realize that, in a parliamentary regime, one cannot achieve much from the opposition side of the House. By 2003 the Bloc appeared to be on the brink of a major decline. It may well be that the party was saved only by the eruption of the sponsorship scandal, which in Québec was of concern not simply because of the mismanagement involved but, more profoundly, because it was seen as an attempt to buy Québec's loyalty through crude propaganda. Outrage over the sponsorship scandal propelled the Bloc to an unexpectedly handsome result in the 2004 election. In the 2011 election, however, the Bloc elected only four Members of Parliament. It would not be unreasonable to interpret this result as a sign that the Bloc may be on the verge of disappearing, as is almost always the case with regional protest parties.

5. *The Green Party.* The Green Party was formed in 1983 as a Canadian version of Green parties that had emerged in countries such as Germany and New Zealand. The party ideology is rooted in the "Charter of the Global Greens," which emphasizes six principles: ecological wisdom, social justice, participatory democracy, non-violence, sustainability, and diversity. The Green Party is appealing to many voters—particularly younger voters—but it faces two massive challenges.

The first challenge for the Greens is their focus. Rightly or wrongly, the name of the party suggests that it is focused on a single issue, the environment. On the one hand, that implies to many voters that the Greens have nothing coherent to contribute in relation to the myriad non-environmental issues that a government must contend with. On the other hand, environmentalists such as David Suzuki argue that a party focused on "Green" issues does the environmental movement a disservice by diverting the political efforts of environmentalists away from the parties that actually exercise power. For Suzuki, a better strategy for environmentalists would be to make existing parties "greener."

The second challenge for the Greens is, of course, the electoral system. Whether one thinks of the Green Party as a single-issue party or as an ideological party, SMP will work against it systematically. The results of the 2008 election illustrate the point: with 7 per cent of the vote, the Greens did not win a single seat and did not even come close to winning one. In the 2011 election, however, they won only 4 per cent of the vote but elected a member from British Columbia, the province where they have the strongest regional base. One can therefore see that even with 15 per cent of the vote nationally, an ideologically based national party is unlikely to win any seats unless it has a strong regional base. So long as Canada uses SMP, it will probably prove difficult for the Green Party to establish itself as a major national party on par with the others.

10.5 The Canadian Party System

Political scientists often speak of "**party systems**." What they mean by this is the number and types of parties that a regime is likely to have given the various factors that influence parties: the electoral system, party finance rules, federalism, political culture, and so on.

For instance, because Canada has a democratic political culture, ours is a **multi-party system** rather than a **single-party system**. In many countries, only one political party is legally sanctioned. China, for example, allows no other political party than the Communist Party. The idea underlying such a system is that the public interest is best served by working out public policy within the party rather than allowing diverse parties to develop competing alternatives. Liberal democratic regimes, however, are based on the principles of freedom of thought, freedom of association, and political participation. Because they protect and promote a diversity of political opinion, liberal democracies are of necessity home to a multiplicity of political parties. Canada's multi-party system allows for the development of different parties that represent different ideological positions, represent very different political interests, and put forward different political agendas. This diversity was evident in our most recent elections. At the time of the fortieth general election in 2008, 19 political parties were legally registered by Elections Canada, including the Christian Heritage Party, the Radical Marijuana Party, the Libertarian Party, the Canada Action Party, and the Marxist-Leninist Party of Canada. Of course, the five parties just mentioned have very low profiles. Even though some of them consistently run candidates in a large number of ridings, they almost never elect anyone. So while we have a multi-party system, it is evident that our system is more hospitable to some kinds of parties than others.

Roughly speaking, we may classify political parties in four categories. First, we have **brokerage parties**: large, highly pragmatic parties that espouse middle-of-the-road ideologies and try to appeal to every region, every ethnic group, and every social class. The Liberals and the Conservatives are brokerage parties. Then there are **ideological parties** such as the Marxist-Leninists or the Christian Heritage Party. These parties espouse ideological views that are outside of the mainstream and are more concerned with promoting those views than with winning seats. **Single-issue parties** resemble ideological parties in that they are more concerned with promoting a point of view than with electoral success, but in this case the point of view relates to a single issue rather thàn an ideology. The Radical Marijuana Party would be an example of a single-issue party. Finally, there are **protest parties**. These are parties that emerge from time to time among people who believe that the dominant forces in political life systematically ignore them and who are angry enough about it to use their vote as a way of expressing a protest. In some countries, protest parties are national in scope but emerge in response to a particular issue such as immigration. In Canada, where regional divisions are often quite profound, protest parties have typically been regional in character. The Reform Party would be an example of a Western-based protest party. The Bloc and the Créditistes of the 1960s are examples of Québec-based protest parties.

The Canadian regime is dominated by brokerage parties. There are two reasons for this. First, Canada's system of responsible government places a premium on being on the government side of the House of Commons. In a "separation-of-powers" regime, even small parties might have some influence in the legislative process. In our regime, legislation is controlled by the party in power. Those who are not in power will normally have significant influence only if they have a realistic hope of becoming the dominant party. The regime thus encourages a small number of large brokerage parties and discourages non-brokerage parties since they have no hope of forming a government. Of course, smaller parties might hope to exert influence in periods of minority government. Yet as we saw in Chapter 9, our SMP electoral system systematically promotes majority governments by over-rewarding the large national brokerage parties. It is SMP, more than anything else, that shapes our party system. SMP systematically thwarts new national parties (for instance, the Canada Action Party or the Green Party), single-issue parties, and national parties with non-centrist ideologies (the NDP). On the other hand, SMP does encourage regional protest parties when conditions for such parties are ripe because it rewards parties that concentrate their votes in a small number of ridings rather than dispersing them across the country.

In the early stages of Canadian history, the Liberals and the Conservatives were the only two parties in Canada. One might refer to this period as the "two-party phase" in our multi-party system. In every election since World War I, one or more "third parties" has tried to break their monopoly. The emergence of third parties led to what was commonly called a "two-and-a-half party" phase in our multi-party system. In the 1921 election, for example, a Western-based protest party called the Progressive Party actually won more seats than the Conservatives. But regional protest parties are by their very nature short-term phenomena. Because they are merely regional, they cannot hope to win a majority. Their supporters eventually realize that in a regime based on responsible government it is not terribly useful to be constantly sitting on the opposition side of the House of Commons. Support for the Progressives declined dramatically over the next few elections. By 1935, they were unable to elect a single member, and the remnants of the party merged with the Conservatives a few years later. The 1935 election marked the emergence of another "third party," the CCF. The CCF was to some extent a regional protest party, but it was also a party with a distinct ideology—democratic socialism. This party and its successor, the NDP, have been the leading third party for much of the last 60 years. However, because of their non-mainstream ideology, they have never been serious contenders for national power, and their lack of popularity has been compounded by our SMP electoral system, under which they have always received a smaller proportion of parliamentary seats than their proportion of the vote.

The general election of 1993 brought a significant change to Canada's party system. In that election, one of the traditional brokerage parties (the Liberals) won a solid majority (though not a majority of votes) but the other was handed a stunning defeat: the PCs came in fifth, winning a mere two seats. Two new regional parties had bolted ahead. In second place was the Bloc with 54 seats, followed closely by the Reform Party with 52. The PCs again finished fifth in both the 1997 and 2000 elections. At the time of the 1993 election, and in much of the ensuing decade, some observers predicted that the emergence of Reform and the Bloc spelled the end of the "two-and-a-half" party system that had characterized Canada for most of the twentieth century. But that judgement was rash. Even at the time, it was easy to see that at least some of the changes that took place in 1993 would be temporary. Because responsible government and SMP place such a premium on victory, it was almost inevitable that the PCs and the Reform Party would resolve their differences so as to create a national alternative to the Liberals. Given the nature of the Canadian regime, competition between two dominant national brokerage parties will probably remain the key feature of our party system.

The success of the Bloc between 1993 and 2011 created a temporary deviation from this model, but when one considers the underlying forces that shape our party system, it should not have come as a surprise that the system eventually reverted to its more typical state. While the Bloc is essentially a regional protest party, its base in a single province, which understands itself to be a distinct nation, probably made it somewhat more durable than most protest parties. And to some extent, it succeeded precisely because of its success. When the Bloc was pulling roughly 50 seats out of the electoral equation, neither the Liberals nor the Conservatives were able to amass a sufficient number of seats to form a majority government. The minority governments that ensued often needed support from the Bloc to remain in power, and Bloc leader Gilles Duceppe took advantage of this situation to win concessions from them. He could then in turn present these "victories" to the Québec electorate as proof that voting for the Bloc was a better way of advancing their interests than electing MPs from the other parties. But once the Conservative Party demonstrated its capacity to form a majority government without the support of the Bloc, its appeal collapsed and Canada reverted to its typical system of competition between two large national parties.

The question for the next decade is who the alternative to the Conservatives will be. The NDP displaced the Liberals as the Official Opposition and now has a strong base in Québec to complement its traditional bases in Western Canada and in parts of Ontario. The Liberal Party is at a historical low in terms of the number of seats it holds, and in regional terms its base has been contracting for decades. The forces that drive our party system—responsible government and SMP—make it very inhospitable to brokerage parties like the Liberals if they do not have any real prospect of winning power. If the Liberals are unable to reclaim their status as the true alternative to the Conservatives, those forces will likely drive them either into a merger with the NDP or into irrelevance.

Should the main competition in the next decade be between the Conservatives and the NDP, we might reasonably expect the party system to take on a more ideological character, but it is important not to overstate that factor. The competition for government will force the NDP to behave more like a brokerage party and less like an ideological party, and that will be especially true if it merges with the Liberals.

10.6 The Organization of Political Parties

You will recall that a national election in Canada is really a collection of 308 separate simultaneous elections in the various electoral constituencies. Political parties are therefore organized at the constituency level. Each of Canada's major national parties has 308 local constituency organizations, which are set up for a number of purposes: attracting members into the party; raising money for the next election; choosing a candidate to run in the riding; and sending members to the provincial and national conventions to debate policy ideas, elect party officials, and choose the party leader.

Each constituency has its own party association, with a constitution and an executive charged with responsibility for the association's ongoing business. Between elections, the association's full membership may meet merely once or twice a year. Constituency organizations become more active at times when they must select delegates to a national convention or when an election is approaching.

Because Canada's parties are designed primarily for winning elections, they are organized in a way that gives the party leadership the power to set election strategy. The party leader usually plays the key role in providing the campaign platform, choosing the campaign strategy, and setting the party's course for the election campaign. Thus, the leader is usually the one who gets the credit for electoral success and who usually pays the price for electoral defeat. It is not unusual that a major defeat will soon be followed by a reorganization of the party, which often includes a leadership convention.

How party leaders are chosen affects how much political power they wield over the party. At the turn of the century, the parties still chose their leaders in a caucus meeting. Those members who were elected to Parliament would meet and choose who would lead them. This process of caucus leadership selection left individual MPs with some power over their leader, since he owed his position to them.

With the advent of the party leadership convention, the power of party leaders has grown considerably. The leadership convention process is one in which the party sends a fixed number of delegates to a convention and they in turn elect a leader. Many delegates will be representatives of their constituency associations. Others may be delegates representing various party associations. Still others will be MPs, senators, and elected members from provincial assemblies. All told, there may be 4,000 to 5,000 delegates at a convention. By a process of secret ballot, they vote on a leader from among a number of candidates. The usual procedure is for successive votes in which the field is reduced by dropping the candidate who has the fewest votes from the ballot until one candidate wins a majority.

The convention model greatly increases the power of the party leader over his or her caucus. Because the party leader no longer owes her position to the caucus but to the party organization as a whole, she can speak for the party over and against the caucus members who speak only for their individual constituencies. This system has been the dominant mode of leadership selection for most of this century. Recently, however, a new and allegedly more democratic process of selecting a leader has begun to be used: the all-member vote. This process resembles what the Americans call a "primary." Instead of a convention in which delegates represent the views of all the party's members, parties have elections in which each member gets to vote directly for a leadership candidate. The all-member vote system thus marks a continuation of the trend toward making the leadership selection process more democratic. Whether this new process is more likely to produce better or more popular leaders remains to be seen, but there can be no doubt that it strengthens the hand of the leader relative to other officials in the party because leaders chosen in this mode owe their position to the party membership rather than the party's elite. Whether having increasingly powerful leaders makes parties more democratic is an open question.

Of the three levels of government—federal, provincial, and local—the only level where party politics does not dominate is the local. Even there, party politics has slowly crept in. In some cities, we now find slates of candidates running under the banner of a political party, and one often finds that there are close behind-the-scene links between civic politicians and provincial parties.

For the most part, however, Canada's parties are organized at both the provincial and federal levels. In some parties, the organizational links between the different levels are strong; in others the federal and provincial parties are completely independent of each other. It is also important to note that it is not unusual for a party to be politically successful in a provincial election but not in a federal election even within the same province. Voters often distinguish between the provincial and federal wings of the same party and may at the same time like one and reject the other. In the 2000 federal election, for example, the PCs did not elect a single member in Ontario even though the Ontario PCs controlled the provincial legislature.

At each level, the party organization consists of two component parts: the parliamentary wing and the extra-parliamentary wing. The former consists of all those party members who have a seat in Parliament; the latter is made up of the party executive at the constituency, provincial, and national levels (see Figure 10.1).

Figure 10.1: Party Organization

Parliamentary Wing	Extra-Parliamentary Wing
Parliamentary Leader	Party President
Caucus	National Executive
	Constituency Association

In Canadian political parties, the parliamentary wing wields power that far exceeds its size. This disproportion is to be expected, for the elected MPs necessarily view the party's policies and public positions in terms of what is conducive to being re-elected. Moreover, they must respond to the ongoing political events in the House of Commons. Therefore, the parliamentary wing of the party is forced to formulate policies and take positions long before the next policy convention can decide party policy. Thus, while parties never cease discussing ways and means of making the parliamentary wing more responsive to the extra-parliamentary wing, such reforms will always be blunted by the reality of electoral politics. Canada's parties are electoral machines designed primarily for the purpose of winning elections. To the extent that the parliamentary wing of the party is best positioned to guide the party toward electoral success, it will continue to exercise a dominating role within the party.

10.7 Financing Political Parties

A substantial amount of money is necessary to run a successful national party. Major expenses are incurred for offices and staffing, for advertising, and for running leadership and electoral campaigns. Where does this money come from? Where should it come from? The way in which we respond to these questions can have an important impact on what kinds of parties we have and what kinds of parties succeed.

In the early years of Canadian democracy, parties relied heavily on donations from wealthy individuals and large corporations. Of course, this approach made bribery and corruption a problem; in fact, two of our most successful prime ministers (John A. Macdonald and Mackenzie King) were defeated after soliciting large donations from business interests in exchange for government favours. Through much of the twentieth century, party leaders tried to keep their hands clean by shifting the responsibility for fundraising to "bag-men"—low-profile but well-connected individuals who could solicit large donations more discreetly.

The contemporary situation is substantially different thanks to reforms introduced by Jean Chrétien and then extended by Stephen Harper. Chrétien imposed strict limits on the amount of money that corporations or unions would be permitted to donate to federal parties. To replace that revenue, parties were given an annual allowance from the federal treasury—currently $1.95 for each vote received in the previous national election. Mr. Harper extended the initiative by banning corporate and union donations altogether.

Of course, parties may still seek donations from individual Canadians. In order to prevent financial inequality from undermining political equality, no one may donate more than $5,000 annually to a party. Individual donations are encouraged by generous rebates on income taxes. Moreover, to help parties defray the costs of election campaigns, Ottawa provides substantial rebates to all candidates who obtain at least 10 per cent of the votes in their riding.

The Chrétien/Harper changes to the party financing regime did not have the same impact on each party. The Liberal Party was a major loser precisely because it had been more dependent than the other parties on corporate dona-tions and less successful than either the Conservatives or the NDP at obtaining donations from individuals. Parties like the Bloc and the Greens, which are much more successful at getting votes than getting donations, have benefited enormous-ly from the $1.95 subsidy. Indeed, it may be that the introduction of the subsidy may modify our party system slightly by providing encouragement to the parties that are typically punished by SMP. Even though the Green Party won no seats in 2008, it did receive almost a million votes and is therefore guaranteed a federal subsidy of close to $2 million per year until the next general election.

Some analysts believe that the true cause of the parliamentary crisis at the end of 2008 was Mr. Harper's proposal to abolish the $2 subsidy. While his own party receives a larger subsidy than the others (since it won the most votes in 2008), the Conservatives could easily withstand the abolition of the subsidy since they are by far the most successful party at individual fundraising. On the other hand, the abolition of the subsidy would have been a problem for the NDP and a disaster for the Liberals, the Greens, and the Bloc.

The possibility that his government would be replaced with a Liberal-NDP coalition led Mr. Harper to withdraw his proposal to abolish the subsidy, but the question remains: should parties have an automatic allowance at taxpayers' expense? Some would argue that parties should have to earn their money and that guaranteed allowances lead to wasteful expenditures on attack ads, excessive staffing, and so on. Others respond that this kind of subsidy is just part of the cost of having a stable and effective democratic system and should therefore be borne by the federal treasury. The Harper government is committed to abolishing this subsidy.

10.8 Party Government and Party Politics

Parliamentary government is party government, and Canadian politics is party politics. While we may, from time to time, complain about this, it is probably both necessary and good that it is so, for it is the clear division of MPs into par-ties that allows us to determine easily who has won a national election and will form the next government. The Governor General's obligation—to ensure that Canada has a workable government in Parliament—is thus easy to discharge. Political parties provide us both with clear outcomes to elections as well as with the parliamentary leader who will become the prime minister. One need only imagine, for a moment, a scenario in which this was all undetermined. The public would have no way of telling who the prime minister would be, and it is likely that without party discipline governments would come and go with prob-lematic frequency. Party leadership and party discipline are what make for stable parliamentary government. One is left to conclude that the only thing worse than party politics would be parliamentary politics without parties.

This is not to say that party politics is simply good. Almost any observer of Canadian politics will soon notice troubling instances where party interests appear to take priority over national interests. Is the government of the day, which consists of the leadership of a particular political party, not always looking out for its future electoral interests at least as much as it is for the national interest?

A further question is the power of party leaders, both in and out of Parliament. Within Parliament the party leader has the power to determine cabinet positions within the government. In the opposition parties, the leader has the power to assign the "shadow cabinet" positions, the high profile positions of critics who follow issues of particular government departments. An MP with such a position has a chance for frequent national media exposure as well as the opportunity to build up a specialized expertise in an area of public policy. It is not unusual for a finance critic to become a finance minister should the critic's party win the next election.

Have the party leaders become too powerful in Canadian politics? They certainly dominate both Parliament and the public view of political life, often leaving us with the impression that politics is a kind of struggle between three or four individuals (and their personal advisers). But it is important to remember that the political power of party leaders ultimately depends on public opinion. Can the leader lead the party to success, however that is conceived, in the next election? A leader's power, even a prime minister's, quickly begins to decline when those in the party begin to sense defeat. While the liberal democratic regime is not a direct democracy, the political power of its parties and leaders ultimately rests on the votes, and therefore the opinions, of the people.

Key Terms

political parties	multi-party system
five functions of political parties	single-party system
interest aggregation	brokerage parties
ideology	ideological parties
pragmatic	single-issue parties
party systems	protest parties

CHAPTER ELEVEN

INTEREST GROUPS, PUBLIC OPINION, AND DEMOCRATIC CITIZENSHIP

11.1 Forms of Political Participation

11.2 Interest Groups

11.3 Women in Politics

11.4 Public Opinion

11.5 The Media

11.6 The Question of Public Opinion Polls

11.7 Civic Education and Democratic Citizenship

11.1 Forms of Political Participation

The liberal democratic regime aims at the ideal of "government of the people, by the people, and for the people." Those who are elected to office and serve in the government are ordinary citizens like you and me. They are responsible to the people as a whole to do what is in the public interest. For the regime to have a reasonable chance of working well, there must therefore be a substantial amount of political participation on the part of its citizens. People must be willing to run for public office or take part in other aspects of electoral politics. Most importantly, all citizens require an education in politics that allows them to make reasonable judgements about who should hold public office and what constitutes good public policy. Democracy requires well-informed political participation.

What, then, are the forms of political participation in a liberal democracy? First and foremost is running for public office. Those who seek election help to generate a new political agenda; those who win participate directly in the process of making law and public policy. The second is involvement in a political party: going to party meetings, fundraising, campaigning for the party's candidate, working on election day, and so on. Thousands of Canadians are involved in this fashion. A third and even more widespread form of participation is through interest groups. Almost all of us belong to various interest groups—unions, lobby groups, volunteer organizations, community leagues, associations—all of which participate in the political process. Finally there is the ongoing process of politics, the ways in which we relate individually to government and our elected officials. We read newspapers, watch public affairs programs, attend political and civic meetings, discuss politics, write letters to editors and public officials, take part in public opinion polls, and ultimately vote in elections. The Internet and social media are making many forms of participation even easier. Whether they will lead to greater or more informed participation remains to be seen.

11.2 Interest Groups

An **interest group** may be defined as an association of people sharing a common interest. This interest may be directly political, such as a desire for free trade or a wish to legalize marijuana; or it may be less obviously political, such as belonging to a boat club or a society for showing dogs. What one soon discovers, however, is that even the least obviously political associations almost always become politically involved at some point—the point at which they attempt to preserve or promote their particular interest. An association becomes an interest group when it attempts to exert political influence to further its own interest.

One might, for example, belong to a boat club—a private organization with no obvious political ties. Its various members may belong to a number of different political parties or not belong to any. Some may be politically active, while others have no interest in politics whatsoever. The members may come from different socio-economic classes, have different ethnic backgrounds, and share no common religious affiliation. The interest they share may be nothing more than a simple love of sailing or kayaking. And yet one can well imagine that the club is likely to have a strong position on specific environmental issues, perhaps to the point of lobbying government and attempting to exert influence on how such issues might be decided. The same could be said of boating licences, government safety regulations, navigation laws, the maintenance of inland waterways, zoning regulations in the area of the club, and so on. One can imagine that meetings of the boat club would often involve discussions of political problems and ways to lobby the various levels of government to promote the group's interests.

An interest group differs from a political party in two important respects. First, the interest that unites the group is much narrower than that which unites the members of a party. The Canadian Manufacturers' Association, for example, is a large interest group with members from many different sectors of the economy. The association may have positions on a wide variety of economic issues, ranging from pay equity to tax law, protective tariffs, and monetary policy. But it is unlikely that it will have a position on capital punishment or seatbelt legislation. Political parties must take into account a far broader spectrum of interests than an interest group, and parties typically attempt to accommodate as many different interest groups as possible.

Second, while an interest group seeks to influence government, a political party seeks to occupy the elected offices of government. Whereas the former seeks only to influence policy, the latter seeks to exercise authority. Political parties thus become the means by which interest groups often operate. The latter try to influence government by offering support to parties or by threatening to withdraw support in favour of a competing party.

Interest groups often seek to influence politics by means of lobbying. **Lobbying** is the attempt to influence government officials, elected and otherwise, to secure a favourable decision on a public policy or a political appointment. This often involves direct meetings with MPs or government bureaucrats. (In fact, the process is called "lobbying" because it originally took place in the members' lobby located outside most legislative chambers.) One might best understand lobbying as a form of bargaining: the lobby group seeks the MP's support with respect to its particular interest; in return, the MP often seeks electoral support from the lobby group. Support might come in the form of campaign endorsement, campaign funds, or simply public acknowledgement from the group for the actions of the MP.

A good example of lobbying would be the Chrétien government's legislation regarding gun control. A wide variety of interest groups—those concerned about public safety and violence, police associations, sport shooters, gun collectors, and firearms dealers—wrote letters to the leaders of the various political parties, to their MPs, to government officials, and to newspapers. In some cases, they took out advertisements, hired media consultants, and even hired a professional lobbyist. They organized public meetings, protests, and marches and attempted to win over public opinion in a wide variety of ways. All of these activities are part of what interest groups normally do—anything to influence the course of politics to serve their interest.

Interest groups are obviously significant actors in Canadian politics and present a special problem. While they serve to inform and enliven political debate and policy-making, they are essentially acting to serve their own interests. Theodore White once said that the first rule of politics is that every individual and every group will want more than they deserve and demand more than they want. Interest groups are formed to serve the interests of members of a particular group. The question always remains: are those interests compatible with the public interest? Today the terms lobbying and special interests have strong negative connotations in the public mind. We are suspicious when legislators and government officials take actions that are based on secret meetings and that seem to be in the interest of a specific group rather than the public as a whole. We often wonder what the lobbyists have promised and whether we can trust our government.

It must be understood, however, that interest groups play a useful role in our liberal democratic regime. Democratic government means government that is responsive to the needs and demands of the people, at least insofar as those demands are lawful and prudent. The government must be responsive to the general will as it manifests itself through public opinion. But how is the government to know what the general will is at any given moment? And how are the people kept informed about current issues and given the necessary information so that they might have an informed opinion? Interest groups establish an essential link between the government and the people. Elected officials, political parties, and government bureaucrats all interact with various interest groups on a regular if not constant basis. Thus, interest groups play a crucial role in both providing government with a strong indication of public opinion and in providing the public with information on specific issues.

Still, interest groups pose a number of serious problems. First, they promote the idea that politics is simply a process of rewarding electoral support. A political party puts forward certain policies, an interest group supports the party, the party wins the election thanks in part to that support, and the party pays off the group by making public policy that furthers the group's interests. This cynical scenario makes politics look like nothing more than a competition of private interests in which the strong rule the weak. Any idea of the public interest or common good disappears. Second, interest groups, by seeking to exert political influence, strengthen our already strong propensity to look to government for solutions to our problems. Finally, interest groups have the ability to dominate the political agenda and set public policy priorities. The problem that arises is that there are obviously some important interests in society that may be poorly organized and far less economically powerful than others. How powerful is an interest group representing the homeless or the mentally ill likely to be in comparison to the Business Council on National Issues or the Canadian Auto Workers?

How, then, do we deal with the problem of interest groups and powerful political lobbies? There is no easy answer. We cannot outlaw such groups, for as long as we have the rights to freedom of speech and association, people will form associations to further their interests. The best we can do is to regulate their activities so as to keep their power within acceptable limits. Since 1985, all lobbyists have been required to register with a Registrar of Lobbyists, and since 1995 they have been required to provide detailed reports of their activities. To respond to concerns about a "revolving door" between government and lobbyists, the Harper government's *Accountability Act* imposed a five-year "cooling off" period on retired politicians and senior civil servants wanting to register as lobbyists. Of course, the strict limits imposed by the *Accountability Act* on corporate and union donations to political parties has also served to keep the influence of lobbyists within acceptable limits.

A second and more successful way to control the power of interest groups is to encourage their growth. This was the solution of one of the chief architects of the liberal democratic regime in the United States, James Madison. Madison argued that the real danger of politics was that a single interest might grow powerful enough to control the government to further its own narrow and private goals. The way to prevent such a danger from being realized, he argued, was to encourage the growth of a **multiplicity of interests** so that no single interest might ever be powerful enough to control the government.[1]

Finally, government can itself create and promote the growth of public interest groups. This is particularly helpful when it comes to ensuring a competition of interests that will serve to debate the issues and provide for a more informed public. Thus, we find that the Canadian government supports a wide variety of interest groups with respect to the arts, education, the rights of women, multiculturalism, and so on.

11.3 Women in Politics

While men and women have equal rights to all forms of political participation— voting, belonging to interest groups and political parties, serving on juries, running for and holding public office, and so on—it is evident that politics remains an activity in which men participate to a greater extent than women. Why this is so is complex. Tradition, societal pressures, economic disparities, career differences,

---

1   Alexander Hamilton, John Jay, James Madison, *The Federalist Papers,* no. 51.

prejudice—a host of causes are no doubt at work. Whatever the explanation, it is clear that the equal participation of men and women in Canadian politics remains more the ideal than an accomplished fact.

In terms of two of the primary forms of political participation—holding public office and organizing interest groups—women are a more visible force now than they were 30 years ago. Women have been elected leaders of major political parties in most provinces and at the national level. Five women have held the office of premier, and one woman—Kim Campbell—was briefly prime minister in 1993. This trend toward greater participation at the level of holding public office is also visible in the House of Commons. Consider the following statistics showing the number of women elected to Parliament and the percentage of MPs that are women.

Figure 11.1: Women Elected to Parliament and Percentage of MPs

	Women Elected	Percentage of Women MPs
1980	15	(5%)
1984	27	(10%)
1988	39	(13%)
1993	54	(18%)
1997	62	(20.5%)
2000	62	(20.5%)
2004	65	(21%)
2006	64	(21%)
2008	68	(22%)
2011	76	(24%)

Note, however, that the trend toward greater participation by women in national political office appears to have levelled off in the past 15 years. Although the Green Party is now led by a woman, and three provinces have female premiers, the percentage of female MPs has not changed dramatically over the past five elections. Following the election of 2011, nine of the new cabinet ministers were women.

This continuing under-representation of women has led to calls for reforming the electoral system to increase the likelihood of women seeking and winning election to public office. A system utilizing multi-member electoral districts, for example, would probably increase the number of women elected since political parties might then seek to balance their slate of nominees by having a man and a woman nominated in each constituency. As noted in Chapter 9, the adoption of a party list form of proportional representation would also serve to increase the number of women in the House since parties would be able to compose lists that are more equally balanced between men and women. Another approach is to work within the existing system and to simply focus on finding more female candidates. The Liberal Party under Stéphane Dion was committed to ensuring that 35 per cent of its candidates would be women in the 2006 election. A problem with setting fixed targets, however, is that the selection of candidates is done at the local level. To guarantee that the party will meet an overall national target, the party leadership in Ottawa has to be ready to interfere, if necessary, with the local riding associations' right to choose their own candidates. That is obviously not popular with party members. Moreover, an artificially imposed target has a tendency to foster the nomination of token female candidates in ridings the party has no chance of winning. The discrepancy between the percentage of Liberal ridings with female candidates in 2008 (37 per cent) and the percentage of Liberal winners who were female (24 per cent) suggests that this happened with some frequency.

The participation of women in politics has also increased through the formation of women's interest groups. The terms "women's issues" and "women's groups" have become part of everyday political discourse. We are now likely to assume that, like other interest groups, women should associate in voluntary organizations to pursue their interests and that the normal process of interest group politics works to deal with their political demands. This assumption obviously has some validity. But it raises an interesting question: are "women's groups" interest groups in the same way as the Canadian Manufacturers' Association or the Canadian Wildlife Association? And can we identify, in some objective and authoritative fashion, a list of "women's issues" and "women's interests"?

The National Action Committee on the Status of Women (NAC) is perhaps the most well-known "women's group" in Canada. NAC claims to speak for the interests of all Canadian women. It works to advance those interests by changing public opinion, by pressuring governments to change legislation and public policy, and by providing organizational assistance to other women's groups. But NAC is not without its critics, some of whom are women. Such critics deny that one organization can speak for all women because women's interests are just as diverse as men's. And while one response to this criticism would be that it is in the interest of all women to be treated equally with men, there remains the question of what precisely constitutes equal treatment. Does equality require affirmative action, pay equity legislation, and compensatory public policies to redress past actions? Women remain divided on these questions.

On one view, then, women have a set of issues and interests that can be objectively defined and politically advocated for the sake of all women. The alternative view is that women's interests are as diverse and politically volatile as men's. From this point of view, the proper focus for reform should be electoral politics, not interest group politics: by increasing the participation of women in electoral politics, the ideas and concerns of women will come to have an impact equal to those expressed by men.

11.4 Public Opinion

In the final analysis, the power of both political parties and interest groups depends on their ability to influence public opinion. Democratic politicians are not usually willing to support manifestly unpopular causes, for they are usually not long in office afterwards if they do. Political parties are in the business of winning elections, and their policies must have some measure of popular support.

The idea that public opinion is an essential element of democratic politics seems obvious, but the issue of democratic public opinion becomes complex upon thoughtful consideration. First, who is the "public" in public opinion? And how do we know what the public opinion is on any particular issue? In what ways is the public opinion determined by "opinion makers"? How does the process of studying public opinion affect it? Does the public have an informed and educated opinion, or is it based more on emotion and perhaps even mere prejudice?

When we speak of public opinion, we often assume we know what is meant by the term "public." But who do we mean? Do we mean all people living in Canada? All citizens? All eligible voters? Only those who vote? Only those with an opinion? Perhaps we mean simply the people that have an interest in a particular issue. The possibilities are numerous.

In fact, when we speak of public opinion we usually mean the reactions of a specific group of people to particular issues, events, and personalities. We are concerned with opinions about the important events surrounding government and politics. What we discover is that the "public" having an opinion on one issue may be a different "public" from the group formed around a different issue. I could have a strong opinion about free trade, for example, but no interest or opinion about fisheries. The opinion groups forming the "public" have an opinion that changes with the issue in question, and it is thus somewhat misleading to think of public opinion as one entity. In sum, public opinion is a convenient but somewhat misleading generalization.

When we study public opinion, we must first ask *who* has an opinion on the issue in question and *what* their opinion is. In other words, we must inquire into the *content* of public opinion. Second, we must assess the *political importance* of the issue in question to those whose opinion we study. And third, we must ascertain the *intensity* with which people hold these opinions. These three factors can be intertwined in a variety of ways, and a moment's reflection reveals how complex the question of public opinion is.

Consider the following example: the federal government is considering major changes to its policies regarding how universities are to be funded. What is the public opinion on this issue? The first thing we discover is that many people have no interest or opinion on the matter. We can simply ignore this fact and move on to consider the opinions of those who are interested. But are we not ignoring the fact that many people have the opinion that this is not an important enough issue to care about having an opinion about? Or are they merely ignorant of what is at stake and as a result have no opinion?

Let us leave this first point aside and forge ahead. We find that while there are many who have an opinion, some care very passionately about the issue, and others are not concerned. One thus has to distinguish between opinion prefer- ence or content and the intensity of the opinion. You will not learn much if you do not know both the preference and the intensity of the opinion. If we were merely to ascertain public preference without ascertaining both how important the public thinks the issue is and how intensely the public holds its opinions, we would have little meaningful direction for action.

The question of the passion with which an opinion is held raises a further question: how well-informed is the person holding the opinion? Is the passion a product of their being informed, or is it a product of their being uninformed? We have all experienced both, and we all know that passion ought not be confused with prudence. If we stick with our example about federal funding for univer- sities, we could ask how many members of the public understand the way the federal funding programs now work, how proposed changes might affect those programs, and what alternatives the federal government might have given its current fiscal position.

Political science of necessity must be interested in more than just an em- pirical description of public opinion. To the extent that political science attempts to make a reasoned evaluation of democracy's claim to be the best regime, it must consider how rational and well-informed public opinion is. Authority in a democracy is not based merely on consent, but on informed consent. When we analyze public opinion, perhaps the most important question of all is the ques- tion of how well-informed the public is and upon what basis they have formed an opinion. Like a doctor examining a patient, political scientists are measur- ing the health of the liberal democratic regime when they examine the basis of public opinion.

The **sources of public opinion** are diverse. Our parents, family life, religion, schooling and education, peer group, advertising, government, the laws, political parties, interest groups, and the media all play important parts. The influence of the media is, today, a particularly controversial issue. Fears that public opinion is now routinely manipulated and controlled by the media are widespread. But perhaps the most important source of public opinion is now public opinion itself. This may sound strange at first, but what is really at work is the phenomenon of conformism—the ways in which individuals come to conform to public opinion. This was Tocqueville's observation about democratic society:

> The smallest reproach irritates its sensibility, and the slightest joke which has any foundation in truth renders it indignant; from the form of its language up to the solid virtues of its character, every-thing must be made the subject of encomium. No writer, whatever his eminence, can escape paying this tribute of adulation to his fellow-citizens. The majority lives in perpetual utterance of self applause. . . . [2]

De Tocqueville argued that the power of democratic society to get its citizens to conform to public opinion is perhaps its greatest danger. The mass media only serves as the means, albeit an ever more powerful means, to the end of mass democratic conformism.

11.5 The Media

Is conformism more of a problem now than it was in the past? We would like to think not, given that the growth of the mass media has increased both the amount of, and access to, politically relevant information. Mass circulation news-papers and magazines, radio and television, and more recently the Internet make a huge volume of information readily available to every citizen. Citizens in con-temporary Canadian society have the ability to keep up on politics by following live debates and even committee hearings from the legislatures, press conferences, daily media interviews, and nightly news reports on the day's major political events. In addition, they can use the Internet to access newspapers, radio, televi-sion, and magazines from across the country; in most cases, this access is free. For those who wish to follow politics carefully, there has probably never been a time when so much information was so easily available to so many.

Nonetheless, there is a high degree of skepticism, if not cynicism, about the relationship between the mass media and political opinion. One reason for

---

2   Alexis de Tocqueville, *Democracy in America* (Markham, ON: NAL, 1956) 119.

this skepticism is the problem of media ownership and control. In Canada, the media is by and large privately owned. While they are regulated by government, most of the media are business ventures owned by large corporations. The major exceptions are the publicly owned and controlled radio and television networks. Therefore, we should never forget that the media in Canada must always be viewed in the context of their role in bringing in advertising revenue. News reporting is one thing, among many things, that attracts readers' and viewers' attention and hence boosts sales or ratings.

The impact of this is clear: political news is one part of news reporting in general, and the media provides much more than news. Political news reporting is, in fact, a small part of what the media supplies. Most of what it supplies is entertainment. The net effect of this situation is that political news reporting runs the risk of becoming a small part of the overall entertainment package. Where the nightly news ends and the evening's entertainment news segment begins may not always be easily distinguishable. The fact that the news must be what sells is a problem, for what is most interesting may not always be what is most important. The implications of recent changes in government policy on trade or the outcome of Supreme Court decisions are likely to be of much greater political importance than a scandal in an MP's office or whether the prime minister fell asleep at a long political ceremony overseas. But the evening news often tends to focus on these spicier tidbits than deeper issues.

The focus and content of media coverage of political news has been roundly criticized in recent decades, and there is no shortage of criticism in this regard. A more interesting question, however, is whether the media should be held solely responsible for this situation. The media sells the news like any other product, so news reports are very sensitive to consumer preferences. If the media is accused of sensationalizing or dumbing-down the news, who is to blame? If the average media consumer is freely voting with his or her channel changer, who can fault the media for giving the people what they want? They would not be in business long if they did not.

There is, however, the question of the publicly owned media. The main public broadcaster in Canada is the Canadian Broadcasting Corporation (CBC). It operates extensive media in French and English throughout the country. This helps to provide balance and competition for the private media. But just as Canadians are often cynical about the private media, many are no less skeptical about media owned and controlled by government. The idea of government-controlled media supplying citizens with the news about the government has always raised the spectre of bias in those media. Will publicly funded media provide us with a truly critical account of government activity? How could they not be affected by a concern to maintain favour with those who fund them? And how could they not have a natural bias in favour of parties that advocate providing large amounts of taxpayer money for the arts, for public health care, for public universities, and of course, for public media?

11.6 The Question of Public Opinion Polls

The issue of conformism is also at the heart of the long and heated controversy over the value and place of public opinion polls. Polling by political parties, private corporations, the media, and governments goes on constantly and has become a pervasive aspect of our lives. Polls inform us about everything from the important to the trivial, from Canadian opinions about major policy issues to how many people believe that Elvis is still alive. The interesting question is why they have become so pervasive.

One reason is that they are a useful tool of mass marketing. Mass marketing techniques for determining market demand and advertising can be successfully used in democratic politics. Interest groups, government departments and agencies, and political parties all use opinion polls in order to determine what issues are important to the public and whether a particular idea, policy, or personality could prove popular. Thus, one may argue that public opinion polling is an important resource in modern democracy. If governments and political parties are there to serve the people, they need to know what the people are thinking. Politicians can get a better read of public opinion and can give the people what they want by means of public opinion polls.

On the other hand, polls contribute to conformism by promoting the view that something is good simply because a majority in a public opinion poll think it to be good. Public opinion can easily change, especially on an emotionally charged political issue. A few grisly murders and the polls may show Canadians strongly in favour of capital punishment. Moreover, we are left to wonder how well-informed the public may be on a particular issue and hence, to put the matter bluntly, what is the value of knowing their opinion. One might ask 1,001 Canadians whether the Bank of Canada should lower its interest rate. How would they know what the reasons and repercussions of changes to the bank's policy are?

Polls thus exacerbate a danger that is unique to the democratic regime—granting a kind of superior status to the opinion of a majority. Tocqueville described the problem in the following terms:

> The moral authority of the majority is partly based upon the notion that there is more intelligence and wisdom in a number of

men united than in a single individual, and that the number of the legislators is more important than their quality.[3]

The danger is that we come to believe something is either true or good because a majority of people believe it so. Such a danger has been all too often realized with respect to issues of racial and religious tolerance.

The most common debate about public opinion polls concerns their possible effects on elections. Many argue for a ban on publication of pre-election opinion polls that attempt to measure and predict voter preference. Their argument is that in the weeks between the time Parliament is dissolved and the election takes place, Canadians should be left to make up their own minds without the "benefit" of polls.

Those who propose that the publication of public opinion polls be prohibited in the period immediately preceding an election argue that such polls undermine the electoral process in two important ways. First, the publication of pre-election polls turns elections into the equivalent of horse races: election coverage in the media often focuses more on who is ahead in the latest poll than on what the issues are. Politics is thus treated as the equivalent of a sporting event and to a great extent trivialized, with voters paying more attention to who is winning than who ought to win.

A second problem caused by pre-election polls is their effect on voting behaviour. Political parties and candidates who are shown to be badly trailing are often written off by voters, who then switch their votes to one of the two leading contenders. Often a **bandwagon effect** is created by voters who want to ensure that the winning candidate in their riding is from the party that is most likely to form the government. Whether voters switch their votes to the second-place or first-place party, the effect is the same: the SMP system's tendency to make it difficult for third parties to elect their candidates is magnified. If elections are supposed to be the average citizen's main opportunity for intelligent, public-spirited political participation, then the publication of election polls seems inconsistent with healthy democracy.

The issue of election polls points to a fundamental question for liberal democratic politics. To prohibit their publication would almost certainly be a violation of some of our most important rights—freedom of the press, for example. Yet if it can be established that polls diminish thoughtful participation in politics, then arguably they would be anti-democratic. In the final analysis, the question of public opinion polls reveals the deep tension that sometimes exists between our devotion to liberalism and our devotion to democracy.

---

3   Tocqueville 113.

11.7 Civic Education and Democratic Citizenship

For the vast majority of Canadian citizens, participation in political life consists neither in running for office nor in working for a political party or interest group but simply in voting. To ask citizens to take a few minutes every few years to cast a ballot is not to ask very much. Incredibly, however, the number of people who neglect this simple democratic duty is now almost as large as the number of those who perform it. In the 2008 election, only 59 per cent of registered voters bothered to vote. Since many Canadians who are eligible to vote have not been registered to vote, the percentage of eligible voters who participated in the 2008 election is likely below 55 per cent.

· While Canada's poor voter participation rates are not so different from those of other liberal democracies, they are much lower than they used to be. Indeed, most democracies have experienced a steady decline in voter participation rates over the past four decades. Experts disagree to some extent about the cause of this decline. The most prominent explanation is Robert Putnam's thesis that declining voter turnout is a symptom of a deeper problem, a decline in **social capital**. Putnam argues that the democratic process is healthy only in places where there is a good deal of social capital, that is, a strong sense of connectedness and responsibility between citizens. Social capital is developed through participation in clubs, societies, organizations, and even sporting leagues, all of which teach people how to interact with each other to solve problems in accordance with agreed-upon rules and procedures. Putnam notes that there has been a dramatic decline in membership in clubs, societies, organizations, and leagues since the 1950s—probably, in large part, due to television. And his research suggests that the decline in voter participation rates is a direct result of this decline in social capital.[4]

In some democracies, it is simply not acceptable for a citizen to neglect to vote. In Australia, for instance, the law requires citizens to vote and imposes fines on those who do not. Some suggest that Canada should adopt this practice. Others disagree, arguing that the country is actually better off if people who are too apathetic to vote have no influence on the outcome of our elections.

There are obviously problems with both positions. Clearly, the most desirable condition would be to have high participation rates from a well-informed public.

The question of how we create a well-informed public and hence intelligent public opinion necessarily brings us to the problem of political education.

---

4   Robert Putnam, "Bowling Alone: America's Declining Social Capital," *Journal of Democracy* 6, 1 (January 1995): 65–78.

How should we educate people to be citizens in a liberal democracy? What kind of citizen does the liberal democratic regime require if it is to remain healthy? What sort of education is most likely to produce intelligent citizens who care about politics, understand the important political issues, can make prudent decisions in their electoral choices, and ultimately can be told the truth rather than merely be flattered?

One of the keystones in such an education is the right to free speech and the freedom of the press. The free exchange of ideas is essential in a liberal democracy. Only when we hear and listen to ideas being debated can we begin to make any sort of intelligent judgement on a particular issue. Only when citizens have the right to debate political issues in an atmosphere of toleration and respect, and use that right to do so, can the liberal democratic regime be sure that public opinion is reasonably well-informed.

Such debate must go beyond the issues of the day, although it must surely include those issues. It must include the ongoing controversies that surround the very principles of the liberal democratic regime itself: equality, liberty, rights, obligations, the rule of law, constitutionalism, federalism, and so on. Only when we are capable of debating the strengths and weaknesses of these principles, of understanding the competing interpretations of them, and of seeing how these principles are often at odds with one another do we approach the education needed for the citizen of the liberal democratic regime. For only then can the citizen separate those issues that go to the question of the continued health of the regime from those that are merely transitory and ephemeral.

Finally, political education in a liberal democracy must aim to encourage political participation. Citizens are far less likely to participate if they do not understand either the important political issues or the main institutions of politics. The reason for this is that without such an understanding we tend to underestimate the value of participation. Often we hear people ask: "what difference does one vote in thousands make?" or "how can you fight the establishment?" An education in the history of Canadian politics reveals that the establishment can change very rapidly, that individuals can come out of nowhere and rise rapidly to prominence in politics, and that the political landscape is often remade within months. In 1984, the PCs won the greatest electoral victory in Canadian history. Nine years later, their party was reduced to a mere two seats and its future as a national party seemed questionable. The powerful Liberal machine that replaced the PCs looked as though it might rule for decades. Yet the elections of 2004, 2006, 2008, and 2011 have revealed it to be a party in steady decline. Such changes are wrought by the actions of thousands of ordinary citizens, who belong to political parties and interest groups, write letters, and generally act as though their actions have consequences. Political participation is thus encouraged by a strong sense that we have an obligation to take part in government, that our actions make a difference, and that we benefit both ourselves and our country when we do participate. An education in politics reveals that these beliefs are, by and large, well-founded.

Key Terms

interest group
lobbying
multiplicity of interests

sources of public opinion
bandwagon effect
social capital

Discussion Questions

1. If it were practically possible to ban all public opinion polls during election campaigns, would such a measure strengthen our democracy?

2. Should Canada imitate Australia and make voting a legal requirement?

THE CONSTITUTION ACTS 1867 AND 1982

Constitution Act, 1867

30 & 31 Victoria, c. 3. (U.K.)

(Consolidated with amendments)

An Act for the Union of Canada, Nova Scotia, and New Brunswick, and the Government thereof; and for Purposes connected therewith

[*29th March 1867.*]

Whereas the Provinces of Canada, Nova Scotia, and New Brunswick have expressed their Desire to be federally united into One Dominion under the Crown of the United Kingdom of Great Britain and Ireland, with a Constitution similar in Principle to that of the United Kingdom:

And whereas such a Union would conduce to the Welfare of the Provinces and promote the Interests of the British Empire:

And whereas on the Establishment of the Union by Authority of Parliament it is expedient, not only that the Constitution of the Legislative Authority in the Dominion be provided for, but also that the Nature of the Executive Government therein be declared:

And whereas it is expedient that Provision be made for the eventual Admission into the Union of other Parts of British North America:

I Preliminary

Short title
1 This Act may be cited as the *Constitution Act, 1867.*

[Repealed]
2 Repealed.

II Union

Declaration of Union
3 It shall be lawful for the Queen, by and with the Advice of Her Majesty's Most Honourable Privy Council, to declare by Proclamation that, on and after a Day therein appointed, not being more than Six Months after the passing of this Act, the Provinces of Canada, Nova Scotia, and New Brunswick shall form and be One Dominion under the Name of Canada; and on and after that Day those Three Provinces shall form and be One Dominion under that Name accordingly.

Construction of subsequent Provisions of Act
4 Unless it is otherwise expressed or implied, the Name Canada shall be taken to mean Canada as constituted under this Act.

Four Provinces
5 Canada shall be divided into Four Provinces, named Ontario, Québec, Nova Scotia, and New Brunswick.

Provinces of Ontario and Québec
6 The Parts of the Province of Canada (as it exists at the passing of this Act) which formerly constituted respectively the Provinces of Upper Canada and Lower Canada shall be deemed to be severed, and shall form Two separate Provinces. The Part which formerly constituted the Province of Upper Canada shall constitute the Province of Ontario; and the Part which formerly constituted the Province of Lower Canada shall constitute the Province of Québec.

Provinces of Nova Scotia and New Brunswick
7 The Provinces of Nova Scotia and New Brunswick shall have the same Limits as at the passing of this Act.

Decennial Census
8 In the general Census of the Population of Canada which is hereby required to be taken in the Year One thousand eight hundred and seventy-one, and in every Tenth Year thereafter, the respective Populations of the Four Provinces shall be distinguished.

III Executive Power

9 The Executive Government and Authority of and over Canada is hereby declared to continue and be vested in the Queen.

Declaration of Executive Power in the Queen

10 The Provisions of this Act referring to the Governor General extend and apply to the Governor General for the Time being of Canada, or other the Chief Executive Officer or Administrator for the Time being carrying on the Government of Canada on behalf and in the Name of the Queen, by whatever Title he is designated.

Application of Provisions referring to Governor General

11 There shall be a Council to aid and advise in the Government of Canada, to be styled the Queen's Privy Council for Canada; and the Persons who are to be Members of that Council shall be from Time to Time chosen and summoned by the Governor General and sworn in as Privy Councillors, and Members thereof may be from Time to Time removed by the Governor General.

Constitution of Privy Council for Canada

12 All Powers, Authorities, and Functions which under any Act of the Parliament of Great Britain, or of the Parliament of the United Kingdom of Great Britain and Ireland, or of the Legislature of Upper Canada, Lower Canada, Canada, Nova Scotia, or New Brunswick, are at the Union vested in or exerciseable by the respective Governors or Lieutenant Governors of those Provinces, with the Advice, or with the Advice and Consent, of the respective Executive Councils thereof, or in conjunction with those Councils, or with any Number of Members thereof, or by those Governors or Lieutenant Governors individually, shall, as far as the same continue in existence and capable of being exercised after the Union in relation to the Government of Canada, be vested in and exerciseable by the Governor General, with the Advice or with the Advice and Consent of or in conjunction with the Queen's Privy Council for Canada, or any Members thereof, or by the Governor General individually, as the Case requires, subject nevertheless (except with respect to such as exist under Acts of the Parliament of Great Britain or of the Parliament of the United Kingdom of Great Britain and Ireland) to be abolished or altered by the Parliament of Canada.

All Powers under Acts to be exercised by Governor General with Advice of Privy Council, or alone

Application of Provisions referring to Governor General in Council 13 The Provisions of this Act referring to the Governor General in Council shall be construed as referring to the Governor General acting by and with the Advice of the Queen's Privy Council for Canada.

Power to Her Majesty to authorize Governor General to appoint Deputies 14 It shall be lawful for the Queen, if Her Majesty thinks fit, to authorize the Governor General from Time to Time to appoint any Person or any Persons jointly or severally to be his Deputy or Deputies within any Part or Parts of Canada, and in that Capacity to exercise during the Pleasure of the Governor General such of the Powers, Authorities, and Functions of the Governor General as the Governor General deems it necessary or expedient to assign to him or them, subject to any Limitations or Directions expressed or given by the Queen; but the Appointment of such a Deputy or Deputies shall not affect the Exercise by the Governor General himself of any Power, Authority, or Function.

Command of Armed Forces to continue to be vested in the Queen 15 The Command-in-Chief of the Land and Naval Militia, and of all Naval and Military Forces, of and in Canada, is hereby declared to continue and be vested in the Queen.

Seat of Government of Canada 16 Until the Queen otherwise directs, the Seat of Government of Canada shall be Ottawa.

IV Legislative Power

Constitution of Parliament of Canada 17 There shall be One Parliament for Canada, consisting of the Queen, an Upper House styled the Senate, and the House of Commons.

Privileges, etc., of Houses 18 The privileges, immunities, and powers to be held, enjoyed, and exercised by the Senate and by the House of Commons, and by the members thereof respectively, shall be such as are from time to time defined by Act of the Parliament of Canada, but so that any Act of the Parliament of Canada defining such privileges, immunities, and powers shall not confer any privileges, immunities, or powers exceeding those at the passing of such Act held, enjoyed, and exercised by the Commons House of Parliament of the United Kingdom of Great Britain and Ireland, and by the members thereof.

First Session of the Parliament of Canada 19 The Parliament of Canada shall be called together not later than Six Months after the Union.

20 Repealed. *[Repealed]*

The Senate

21 The Senate shall, subject to the Provisions of this Act, consist of One *Number of Senators*
Hundred and five Members, who shall be styled Senators.

22 In relation to the Constitution of the Senate Canada shall be deemed to *Representation of Provinces*
consist of *Four* Divisions: *in Senate*
1. Ontario;
2. Québec;
3. The Maritime Provinces, Nova Scotia and New Brunswick, and
Prince Edward Island;
4. The Western Provinces of Manitoba, British Columbia,
Saskatchewan, and Alberta;
which Four Divisions shall (subject to the Provisions of this Act) be
equally represented in the Senate as follows: Ontario by twenty-four
senators; Québec by twenty-four senators; the Maritime Provinces
and Prince Edward Island by twenty-four senators, ten thereof representing Nova Scotia, ten thereof representing New Brunswick,
and four thereof representing Prince Edward Island; the Western
Provinces by twenty-four senators, six thereof representing Manitoba,
six thereof representing British Columbia, six thereof representing
Saskatchewan, and six thereof representing Alberta; Newfoundland
shall be entitled to be represented in the Senate by six members; the
Yukon Territory and the Northwest Territories shall be entitled to
be represented in the Senate by one member each.
In the Case of Québec each of the Twenty-four Senators represent-
ing that Province shall be appointed for One of the Twenty-four
Electoral Divisions of Lower Canada specified in Schedule A. to
Chapter One of the Consolidated Statutes of Canada.

23 The Qualifications of a Senator shall be as follows: *Qualifications of Senator*
(1) He shall be of the full age of Thirty Years:
(2) He shall be either a natural-born Subject of the Queen, or a Subject of
the Queen naturalized by an Act of the Parliament of Great Britain, or
of the Parliament of the United Kingdom of Great Britain and Ireland,
or of the Legislature of One of the Provinces of Upper Canada, Lower
Canada, Canada, Nova Scotia, or New Brunswick, before the Union,

or of the Parliament of Canada after the Union:

(3) He shall be legally or equitably seised as of Freehold for his own Use and Benefit of Lands or Tenements held in Free and Common Socage, or seised or possessed for his own Use and Benefit of Lands or Tenements held in Franc-alleu or in Roture, within the Province for which he is appointed, of the Value of Four thousand Dollars, over and above all Rents, Dues, Debts, Charges, Mortgages, and Incumbrances due or payable out of or charged on or affecting the same:

(4) His Real and Personal Property shall be together worth Four thousand Dollars over and above his Debts and Liabilities:

(5) He shall be resident in the Province for which he is appointed:

(6) In the Case of Québec he shall have his Real Property Qualification in the Electoral Division for which he is appointed, or shall be resident in that Division.

Summons of Senator 24 The Governor General shall from Time to Time, in the Queen's Name, by Instrument under the Great Seal of Canada, summon qualified Persons to the Senate; and, subject to the Provisions of this Act, every Person so summoned shall become and be a Member of the Senate and a Senator.

[Repealed] 25 Repealed.

Addition of Senators 26 If at any Time on the Recommendation of the Governor General the
in certain cases Queen thinks fit to direct that Four or Eight Members be added to the Senate, the Governor General may by Summons to Four or Eight qualified Persons (as the Case may be), representing equally the Four Divisions of Canada, add to the Senate accordingly.

Reduction of Senate 27 In case of such Addition being at any Time made, the Governor General
to normal Number shall not summon any Person to the Senate, except on a further like Direction by the Queen on the like Recommendation, to represent one of the Four Divisions until such Division is represented by Twenty-four Senators and no more.

Maximum Number 28 The Number of Senators shall not at any Time exceed One Hundred
of Senators and thirteen.

29 (1) Subject to subsection (2), a Senator shall, subject to the provisions of *Tenure of Place in Senate* this Act, hold his place in the Senate for life.

(2) A Senator who is summoned to the Senate after the coming into *Retirement upon attaining* force of this subsection shall, subject to this Act, hold his place in the *age of seventy-five years* Senate until he attains the age of seventy-five years.

30 A Senator may by Writing under his Hand addressed to the Governor *Resignation of Place in* General resign his Place in the Senate, and thereupon the same shall be *Senate* vacant.

31 The Place of a Senator shall become vacant in any of the following *Disqualification of Senators* Cases:

(1) If for Two consecutive Sessions of the Parliament he fails to give his Attendance in the Senate:

(2) If he takes an Oath or makes a Declaration or Acknowledgment of Allegiance, Obedience, or Adherence to a Foreign Power, or does an Act whereby he becomes a Subject or Citizen, or entitled to the Rights or Privileges of a Subject or Citizen, of a Foreign Power:

(3) If he is adjudged Bankrupt or Insolvent, or applies for the Benefit of any Law relating to Insolvent Debtors, or becomes a public Defaulter:

(4) If he is attainted of Treason or convicted of Felony or of any infamous Crime:

(5) If he ceases to be qualified in respect of Property or of Residence; provided, that a Senator shall not be deemed to have ceased to be qualified in respect of Residence by reason only of his residing at the Seat of the Government of Canada while holding an Office under that Government requiring his Presence there.

32 When a Vacancy happens in the Senate by Resignation, Death, or oth- *Summons on Vacancy in* erwise, the Governor General shall by Summons to a fit and qualified *Senate* Person fill the Vacancy.

33 If any Question arises respecting the Qualification of a Senator or a *Questions as to* Vacancy in the Senate the same shall be heard and determined by the *Qualifications and* Senate. *Vacancies in Senate*

Appointment of Speaker of Senate 34 The Governor General may from Time to Time, by Instrument under the Great Seal of Canada, appoint a Senator to be Speaker of the Senate, and may remove him and appoint another in his Stead.

Quorum of Senate 35 Until the Parliament of Canada otherwise provides, the Presence of at least Fifteen Senators, including the Speaker, shall be necessary to constitute a Meeting of the Senate for the Exercise of its Powers.

Voting in Senate 36 Questions arising in the Senate shall be decided by a Majority of Voices, and the Speaker shall in all Cases have a Vote, and when the Voices are equal the Decision shall be deemed to be in the Negative.

The House Of Commons

Constitution of House of Commons in Canada 37 The House of Commons shall, subject to the Provisions of this Act, consist of two hundred and ninety-five members of whom ninety-nine shall be elected for Ontario, seventy-five for Québec, eleven for Nova Scotia, ten for New Brunswick, fourteen for Manitoba, thirty-two for British Columbia, four for Prince Edward Island, twenty-six for Alberta, fourteen for Saskatchewan, seven for Newfoundland, one for the Yukon Territory and two for the Northwest Territories.

Summoning of House of Commons 38 The Governor General shall from Time to Time, in the Queen's Name, by Instrument under the Great Seal of Canada, summon and call together the House of Commons.

Senators not to sit in House of Commons 39 A Senator shall not be capable of being elected or of sitting or voting as a Member of the House of Commons.

Electoral districts of the four Provinces 40 Until the Parliament of Canada otherwise provides, Ontario, Québec, Nova Scotia, and New Brunswick shall, for the Purposes of the Election of Members to serve in the House of Commons, be divided into Electoral Districts as follows:

1. Ontario

   Ontario shall be divided into the Counties, Ridings of Counties, Cities, Parts of Cities, and Towns enumerated in the First Schedule to this Act, each whereof shall be an Electoral District, each such District as numbered in that Schedule being entitled to return One Member.

2. Québec

Québec shall be divided into Sixty-five Electoral Districts, composed of the Sixty-five Electoral Divisions into which Lower
Canada is at the passing of this Act divided under Chapter Two of
the Consolidated Statutes of Canada, Chapter Seventy-five of the
Consolidated Statutes for Lower Canada, and the Act of the Province
of Canada of the Twenty-third Year of the Queen, Chapter One,
or any other Act amending the same in force at the Union, so that
each such Electoral Division shall be for the Purposes of this Act an
Electoral District entitled to return One Member.

3. Nova Scotia

Each of the Eighteen Counties of Nova Scotia shall be an Electoral
District. The County of Halifax shall be entitled to return Two
Members, and each of the other Counties One Member.

4. New Brunswick

Each of the Fourteen Counties into which New Brunswick is divid-
ed, including the City and County of St. John, shall be an Electoral
District. The City of St. John shall also be a separate Electoral District.
Each of those Fifteen Electoral Districts shall be entitled to return
One Member.

41 Until the Parliament of Canada otherwise provides, all Laws in force *Continuance of existing*
in the several Provinces at the Union relative to the following Matters *Election Laws until*
or any of them, namely,—the Qualifications and Disqualifications *Parliament of Canada*
of Persons to be elected or to sit or vote as Members of the House *otherwise provides*
of Assembly or Legislative Assembly in the several Provinces, the
Voters at Elections of such Members, the Oaths to be taken by Voters,
the Returning Officers, their Powers and Duties, the Proceedings at
Elections, the Periods during which Elections may be continued,
the Trial of controverted Elections, and Proceedings incident thereto,
the vacating of Seats of Members, and the Execution of new Writs in
case of Seats vacated otherwise than by Dissolution,—shall respectively
apply to Elections of Members to serve in the House of Commons for
the same several Provinces.

Provided that, until the Parliament of Canada otherwise provides,
at any Election for a Member of the House of Commons for the
District of Algoma, in addition to Persons qualified by the Law of the
Province of Canada to vote, every Male British Subject, aged Twenty-
one Years or upwards, being a Householder, shall have a Vote.

[Repealed]   42   Repealed.

[Repealed]   43   Repealed.

As to Election of Speaker of   44   The House of Commons on its first assembling after a General Election
House of Commons   shall proceed with all practicable Speed to elect One of its Members to be Speaker.

As to filling up Vacancy in   45   In case of a Vacancy happening in the Office of Speaker by Death,
Office of Speaker   Resignation, or otherwise, the House of Commons shall with all practicable Speed proceed to elect another of its Members to be Speaker.

Speaker to preside   46   The Speaker shall preside at all Meetings of the House of Commons.

Provision in case of Absence   47   Until the Parliament of Canada otherwise provides, in case of the
of Speaker   Absence for any Reason of the Speaker from the Chair of the House of Commons for a Period of Forty-eight consecutive Hours, the House may elect another of its Members to act as Speaker, and the Member so elected shall during the Continuance of such Absence of the Speaker have and execute all the Powers, Privileges, and Duties of Speaker.

Quorum of House of   48   The Presence of at least Twenty Members of the House of Commons
Commons   shall be necessary to constitute a Meeting of the House for the Exercise of its Powers, and for that Purpose the Speaker shall be reckoned as a Member.

Voting in House of   49   Questions arising in the House of Commons shall be decided by a
Commons   Majority of Voices other than that of the Speaker, and when the Voices are equal, but not otherwise, the Speaker shall have a Vote.

Duration of House of   50   Every House of Commons shall continue for Five Years from the Day
Commons   of the Return of the Writs for choosing the House (subject to be sooner dissolved by the Governor General), and no longer.

51 (1) The number of members of the House of Commons and the repre- *Readjustment of*
sentation of the provinces therein shall, on the coming into force of *representation in Commons*
this subsection and thereafter on the completion of each decennial
census, be readjusted by such authority, in such manner, and from
such time as the Parliament of Canada from time to time provides,
subject and according to the following rules:

1. There shall be assigned to each of the provinces a number of mem- *Rules*
bers equal to the number obtained by dividing the total population
of the provinces by two hundred and seventy-nine and by dividing
the population of each province by the quotient so obtained, counting any remainder in excess of 0.50 as one after the said process of
division.

2. If the total number of members that would be assigned to a province
by the application of rule 1 is less than the total number assigned to
that province on the date of coming into force of this subsection,
there shall be added to the number of members so assigned such
number of members as will result in the province having the same
number of members as were assigned on that date.

(2) The Yukon Territory as bounded and described in the schedule to *Yukon Territory, Northwest*
chapter Y-2 of the Revised Statutes of Canada, 1985, shall be entitled *Territories and Nunavut*
to one member, the Northwest Territories as bounded and described
in section 2 of chapter N-27 of the Revised Statutes of Canada, 1985,
as amended by section 77 of chapter 28 of the Statutes of Canada,
1993, shall be entitled to one member, and Nunavut as bounded and
described in section 3 of chapter 28 of the Statutes of Canada, 1993,
shall be entitled to one member.

51A Notwithstanding anything in this Act a province shall always be entitled *Constitution of House of*
to a number of members in the House of Commons not less than the *Commons*
number of senators representing such province.

52 The Number of Members of the House of Commons may be from Time *Increase of Number of*
to Time increased by the Parliament of Canada, provided the propor- *House of Commons*
tionate Representation of the Provinces prescribed by this Act is not
thereby disturbed.

Money Votes; Royal Assent

Appropriation and Tax Bills 53 Bills for appropriating any Part of the Public Revenue, or for imposing any Tax or Impost, shall originate in the House of Commons.

Recommendation of Money Votes 54 It shall not be lawful for the House of Commons to adopt or pass any Vote, Resolution, Address, or Bill for the Appropriation of any Part of the Public Revenue, or of any Tax or Impost, to any Purpose that has not been first recommended to that House by Message of the Governor General in the Session in which such Vote, Resolution, Address, or Bill is proposed.

Royal Assent to Bills, etc. 55 Where a Bill passed by the Houses of the Parliament is presented to the Governor General for the Queen's Assent, he shall declare, according to his Discretion, but subject to the Provisions of this Act and to Her Majesty's Instructions, either that he assents thereto in the Queen's Name, or that he withholds the Queen's Assent, or that he reserves the Bill for the Signification of the Queen's Pleasure.

Disallowance by Order in Council of Act assented to by Governor General 56 Where the Governor General assents to a Bill in the Queen's Name, he shall by the first convenient Opportunity send an authentic Copy of the Act to One of Her Majesty's Principal Secretaries of State, and if the Queen in Council within Two Years after Receipt thereof by the Secretary of State thinks fit to disallow the Act, such Disallowance (with a Certificate of the Secretary of State of the Day on which the Act was received by him) being signified by the Governor General, by Speech or Message to each of the Houses of the Parliament or by Proclamation, shall annul the Act from and after the Day of such Signification.

Signification of Queen's Pleasure on Bill reserved 57 A Bill reserved for the Signification of the Queen's Pleasure shall not have any Force unless and until, within Two Years from the Day on which it was presented to the Governor General for the Queen's Assent, the Governor General signifies, by Speech or Message to each of the Houses of the Parliament or by Proclamation, that it has received the Assent of the Queen in Council.

An Entry of every such Speech, Message, or Proclamation shall be made in the Journal of each House, and a Duplicate thereof duly attested shall be delivered to the proper Officer to be kept among the Records of Canada.

V Provincial Constitutions

Executive Power

58 For each Province there shall be an Officer, styled the Lieutenant *Appointment of Lieutenant* Governor, appointed by the Governor General in Council by Instrument *Governors of Provinces* under the Great Seal of Canada.

59 A Lieutenant Governor shall hold Office during the Pleasure of the *Tenure of Office of* Governor General; but any Lieutenant Governor appointed after the *Lieutenant Governor* Commencement of the First Session of the Parliament of Canada shall not be removeable within Five Years from his Appointment, except for Cause assigned, which shall be communicated to him in Writing within One Month after the Order for his Removal is made, and shall be communicated by Message to the Senate and to the House of Commons within One Week thereafter if the Parliament is then sitting, and if not then within One Week after the Commencement of the next Session of the Parliament.

60 The Salaries of the Lieutenant Governors shall be fixed and provided by *Salaries of Lieutenant* the Parliament of Canada. *Governors*

61 Every Lieutenant Governor shall, before assuming the Duties of his *Oaths, etc., of Lieutenant* Office, make and subscribe before the Governor General or some Person *Governor* authorized by him Oaths of Allegiance and Office similar to those taken by the Governor General.

62 The Provisions of this Act referring to the Lieutenant Governor ex- *Application of Provisions* tend and apply to the Lieutenant Governor for the Time being of each *referring to Lieutenant* Province, or other the Chief Executive Officer or Administrator for the *Governor* Time being carrying on the Government of the Province, by whatever Title he is designated.

63 The Executive Council of Ontario and of Québec shall be composed of *Appointment of Executive* such Persons as the Lieutenant Governor from Time to Time thinks fit, *Officers for Ontario and* and in the first instance of the following Officers, namely,—the Attorney *Québec* General, the Secretary and Registrar of the Province, the Treasurer of the Province, the Commissioner of Crown Lands, and the Commissioner of Agriculture and Public Works, with in Québec the Speaker of the Legislative Council and the Solicitor General.

Executive Government 64 The Constitution of the Executive Authority in each of the Provinces of
of Nova Scotia and New Nova Scotia and New Brunswick shall, subject to the Provisions of this
Brunswick Act, continue as it exists at the Union until altered under the Authority
of this Act.

Powers to be exercised by 65 All Powers, Authorities, and Functions which under any Act of the
Lieutenant Governor of Parliament of Great Britain, or of the Parliament of the United Kingdom
Ontario or Québec with of Great Britain and Ireland, or of the Legislature of Upper Canada,
Advice, or alone Lower Canada, or Canada, were or are before or at the Union vested
in or exerciseable by the respective Governors or Lieutenant Governors
of those Provinces, with the Advice or with the Advice and Consent
of the respective Executive Councils thereof, or in conjunction with
those Councils, or with any Number of Members thereof, or by those
Governors or Lieutenant Governors individually, shall, as far as the
same are capable of being exercised after the Union in relation to the
Government of Ontario and Québec respectively, be vested in and shall
or may be exercised by the Lieutenant Governor of Ontario and Québec
respectively, with the Advice or with the Advice and Consent of or in
conjunction with the respective Executive Councils, or any Members
thereof, or by the Lieutenant Governor individually, as the Case requires, subject nevertheless (except with respect to such as exist under
Acts of the Parliament of Great Britain, or of the Parliament of the
United Kingdom of Great Britain and Ireland,) to be abolished or altered
by the respective Legislatures of Ontario and Québec.

Application of Provisions 66 The Provisions of this Act referring to the Lieutenant Governor in
referring to Lieutenant Council shall be construed as referring to the Lieutenant Governor of
Governor in Council the Province acting by and with the Advice of the Executive Council
thereof.

Administration in Absence, 67 The Governor General in Council may from Time to Time appoint
etc., of Lieutenant Governor an Administrator to execute the Office and Functions of Lieutenant
Governor during his Absence, Illness, or other Inability.

Seats of Provincial 68 Unless and until the Executive Government of any Province otherwise
Governments directs with respect to that Province, the Seats of Government of the
Provinces shall be as follows, namely,—of Ontario, the City of Toronto;
of Québec, the City of Québec; of Nova Scotia, the City of Halifax; and
of New Brunswick, the City of Fredericton.

Legislative Power

1. Ontario

69 There shall be a Legislature for Ontario consisting of the Lieutenant Governor and of One House, styled the Legislative Assembly of Ontario.

Legislature for Ontario

70 The Legislative Assembly of Ontario shall be composed of Eighty-two Members, to be elected to represent the Eighty-two Electoral Districts set forth in the First Schedule to this Act.

Electoral districts

2. Québec

71 There shall be a Legislature for Québec consisting of the Lieutenant Governor and of Two Houses, styled the Legislative Council of Québec and the Legislative Assembly of Québec.

Legislature for Québec

72 The Legislative Council of Québec shall be composed of Twenty-four Members, to be appointed by the Lieutenant Governor, in the Queen's Name, by Instrument under the Great Seal of Québec, one being appointed to represent each of the Twenty-four Electoral Divisions of Lower Canada in this Act referred to, and each holding Office for the Term of his Life, unless the Legislature of Québec otherwise provides under the Provisions of this Act.

Constitution of Legislative Council

73 The Qualifications of the Legislative Councillors of Québec shall be the same as those of the Senators for Québec.

Qualification of Legislative Councillors

74 The Place of a Legislative Councillor of Québec shall become vacant in the Cases, *mutatis mutandis*, in which the Place of Senator becomes vacant.

Resignation, Disqualification, etc.

75 When a Vacancy happens in the Legislative Council of Québec by Resignation, Death, or otherwise, the Lieutenant Governor, in the Queen's Name, by Instrument under the Great Seal of Québec, shall appoint a fit and qualified Person to fill the Vacancy.

Vacancies

Questions as to Vacancies,
etc.

76 If any Question arises respecting the Qualification of a Legislative Councillor of Québec, or a Vacancy in the Legislative Council of Québec, the same shall be heard and determined by the Legislative Council.

Speaker of Legislative
Council

77 The Lieutenant Governor may from Time to Time, by Instrument under the Great Seal of Québec, appoint a Member of the Legislative Council of Québec to be Speaker thereof, and may remove him and appoint another in his Stead.

Quorum of Legislative
Council

78 Until the Legislature of Québec otherwise provides, the Presence of at least Ten Members of the Legislative Council, including the Speaker, shall be necessary to constitute a Meeting for the Exercise of its Powers.

Voting in Legislative
Council

79 Questions arising in the Legislative Council of Québec shall be decided by a Majority of Voices, and the Speaker shall in all Cases have a Vote, and when the Voices are equal the Decision shall be deemed to be in the Negative.

Constitution of Legislative
Assembly of Québec

80 The Legislative Assembly of Québec shall be composed of Sixty-five Members, to be elected to represent the Sixty-five Electoral Divisions or Districts of Lower Canada in this Act referred to, subject to Alteration thereof by the Legislature of Québec: Provided that it shall not be lawful to present to the Lieutenant Governor of Québec for Assent any Bill for altering the Limits of any of the Electoral Divisions or Districts mentioned in the Second Schedule to this Act, unless the Second and Third Readings of such Bill have been passed in the Legislative Assembly with the Concurrence of the Majority of the Members representing all those Electoral Divisions or Districts, and the Assent shall not be given to such Bill unless an Address has been presented by the Legislative Assembly to the Lieutenant Governor stating that it has been so passed.

3. Ontario And Québec

[Repealed]

81 Repealed.

82 The Lieutenant Governor of Ontario and of Québec shall from Time to Time, in the Queen's Name, by Instrument under the Great Seal of the Province, summon and call together the Legislative Assembly of the Province.

Summoning of Legislative Assemblies

83 Until the Legislature of Ontario or of Québec otherwise provides, a Person accepting or holding in Ontario or in Québec any Office, Commission, or Employment, permanent or temporary, at the Nomination of the Lieutenant Governor, to which an annual Salary, or any Fee, Allowance, Emolument, or Profit of any Kind or Amount whatever from the Province is attached, shall not be eligible as a Member of the Legislative Assembly of the respective Province, nor shall he sit or vote as such; but nothing in this Section shall make ineligible any Person being a Member of the Executive Council of the respective Province, or holding any of the following Offices, that is to say, the Offices of Attorney General, Secretary and Registrar of the Province, Treasurer of the Province, Commissioner of Crown Lands, and Commissioner of Agriculture and Public Works, and in Québec Solicitor General, or shall disqualify him to sit or vote in the House for which he is elected, provided he is elected while holding such Office.

Restriction on election of Holders of offices

84 Until the legislatures of Ontario and Québec respectively otherwise provide, all Laws which at the Union are in force in those Provinces respectively, relative to the following Matters, or any of them, namely,— the Qualifications and Disqualifications of Persons to be elected or to sit or vote as Members of the Assembly of Canada, the Qualifications or Disqualifications of Voters, the Oaths to be taken by Voters, the Returning Officers, their Powers and Duties, the Proceedings at Elections, the Periods during which such Elections may be contin- ued, and the Trial of controverted Elections and the Proceedings in- cident thereto, the vacating of the Seats of Members and the issuing and execution of new Writs in case of Seats vacated otherwise than by Dissolution,—shall respectively apply to Elections of Members to serve in the respective Legislative Assemblies of Ontario and Québec.

Continuance of existing Election Laws

Provided that, until the Legislature of Ontario otherwise provides, at any Election for a Member of the Legislative Assembly of Ontario for the District of Algoma, in addition to Persons qualified by the Law of the Province of Canada to vote, every Male British Subject, aged Twenty-one Years or upwards, being a Householder, shall have a Vote.

227

Duration of Legislative 85 Every Legislative Assembly of Ontario and every Legislative Assembly
Assemblies of Québec shall continue for Four Years from the Day of the Return of the Writs for choosing the same (subject nevertheless to either the Legislative Assembly of Ontario or the Legislative Assembly of Québec being sooner dissolved by the Lieutenant Governor of the Province), and no longer.

Yearly Session of Legislature 86 There shall be a Session of the Legislature of Ontario and of that of Québec once at least in every Year, so that Twelve Months shall not intervene between the last Sitting of the Legislature in each Province in one Session and its first Sitting in the next Session.

Speaker, Quorum, etc. 87 The following Provisions of this Act respecting the House of Commons of Canada shall extend and apply to the Legislative Assemblies of Ontario and Québec, that is to say,—the Provisions relating to the Election of a Speaker originally and on Vacancies, the Duties of the Speaker, the Absence of the Speaker, the Quorum, and the Mode of voting, as if those Provisions were here re-enacted and made applicable in Terms to each such Legislative Assembly.

4. Nova Scotia And New Brunswick

Constitutions of Legislatures 88 The Constitution of the Legislature of each of the Provinces of Nova
of Nova Scotia and New Scotia and New Brunswick shall, subject to the Provisions of this Act,
Brunswick continue as it exists at the Union until altered under the Authority of this Act.

5. Ontario, Québec, And Nova Scotia

[Repealed] 89 Repealed.

6. The Four Provinces

Application to Legislatures 90 The following Provisions of this Act respecting the Parliament of Canada,
of Provisions respecting namely,—the Provisions relating to Appropriation and Tax Bills, the
Money Votes, etc. Recommendation of Money Votes, the Assent to Bills, the Disallowance of Acts, and the Signification of Pleasure on Bills reserved,—shall extend and apply to the Legislatures of the several Provinces as if those Provisions were here re-enacted and made applicable in Terms to the

respective Provinces and the Legislatures thereof, with the Substitution of the Lieutenant Governor of the Province for the Governor General, of the Governor General for the Queen and for a Secretary of State, of One Year for Two Years, and of the Province for Canada.

VI Distribution of Legislative Powers

Powers of The Parliament

91 It shall be lawful for the Queen, by and with the Advice and Consent of the Senate and House of Commons, to make Laws for the Peace, Order, and good Government of Canada, in relation to all Matters not coming within the Classes of Subjects by this Act assigned exclusively to the Legislatures of the Provinces; and for greater Certainty, but not so as to restrict the Generality of the foregoing Terms of this Section, it is hereby declared that (notwithstanding anything in this Act) the exclusive Legislative Authority of the Parliament of Canada extends to all Matters coming within the Classes of Subjects next hereinafter enumerated; that is to say,— *Legislative Authority of Parliament of Canada*

1. Repealed.
1A. The Public Debt and Property.
2. The Regulation of Trade and Commerce.
2A. Unemployment insurance.
3. The raising of Money by any Mode or System of Taxation.
4. The borrowing of Money on the Public Credit.
5. Postal Service.
6. The Census and Statistics.
7. Militia, Military and Naval Service, and Defence.
8. The fixing of and providing for the Salaries and Allowances of Civil and other Officers of the Government of Canada.
9. Beacons, Buoys, Lighthouses, and Sable Island.
10. Navigation and Shipping.
11. Quarantine and the Establishment and Maintenance of Marine Hospitals
12. Sea Coast and Inland Fisheries.
13. Ferries between a Province and any British or Foreign Country or between Two Provinces.
14. Currency and Coinage.
15. Banking, Incorporation of Banks, and the Issue of Paper Money.
16. Savings Banks.

17. Weights and Measures.

18. Bills of Exchange and Promissory Notes.

19. Interest.

20. Legal Tender.

21. Bankruptcy and Insolvency.

22. Patents of Invention and Discovery.

23. Copyrights.

24. Indians, and Lands reserved for the Indians.

25. Naturalization and Aliens.

26. Marriage and Divorce.

27. The Criminal Law, except the Constitution of Courts of Criminal Jurisdiction, but including the Procedure in Criminal Matters.

28. The Establishment, Maintenance, and Management of Penitentiaries.

29. Such Classes of Subjects as are expressly excepted in the Enumeration of the Classes of Subjects by this Act assigned exclusively to the Legislatures of the Provinces.

And any Matter coming within any of the Classes of Subjects enumerated in this Section shall not be deemed to come within the Class of Matters of a local or private Nature comprised in the Enumeration of the Classes of Subjects by this Act assigned exclusively to the Legislatures of the Provinces.

Exclusive Powers of Provincial Legislatures

Subjects of exclusive Provincial Legislation

92 In each Province the Legislature may exclusively make Laws in relation to Matters coming within the Classes of Subjects next hereinafter enumerated; that is to say,—

1. Repealed.

2. Direct Taxation within the Province in order to the raising of a Revenue for Provincial Purposes.

3. The borrowing of Money on the sole Credit of the Province.

4. The Establishment and Tenure of Provincial Offices and the Appointment and Payment of Provincial Officers.

5. The Management and Sale of the Public Lands belonging to the Province and of the Timber and Wood thereon.

6. The Establishment, Maintenance, and Management of Public and Reformatory Prisons in and for the Province.

7. The Establishment, Maintenance, and Management of Hospitals, Asylums, Charities, and Eleemosynary Institutions in and for the Province, other than Marine Hospitals.

8. Municipal Institutions in the Province.

9. Shop, Saloon, Tavern, Auctioneer, and other Licences in order to the raising of a Revenue for Provincial, Local, or Municipal Purposes.

10. Local Works and Undertakings other than such as are of the following Classes:

    (a) Lines of Steam or other Ships, Railways, Canals, Telegraphs, and other Works and Undertakings connecting the Province with any other or others of the Provinces, or extending beyond the Limits of the Province:

    (b) Lines of Steam Ships between the Province and any British or Foreign Country:

    (c) Such Works as, although wholly situate within the Province, are before or after their Execution declared by the Parliament of Canada to be for the general Advantage of Canada or for the Advantage of Two or more of the Provinces.

11. The Incorporation of Companies with Provincial Objects.

12. The Solemnization of Marriage in the Province.

13. Property and Civil Rights in the Province.

14. The Administration of Justice in the Province, including the Constitution, Maintenance, and Organization of Provincial Courts, both of Civil and of Criminal Jurisdiction, and including Procedure in Civil Matters in those Courts.

15. The Imposition of Punishment by Fine, Penalty, or Imprisonment for enforcing any Law of the Province made in relation to any Matter coming within any of the Classes of Subjects enumerated in this Section.

16. Generally all Matters of a merely local or private Nature in the Province.

Non-Renewable Natural Resources,
Forestry Resources and Electrical Energy

Laws respecting non- 92A (1) In each province, the legislature may exclusively make laws in rela-
renewable natural resources, tion to
forestry resources and   *(a)* exploration for non-renewable natural resources in the province;
electrical energy   *(b)* development, conservation and management of non-renewable
natural resources and forestry resources in the province, including
laws in relation to the rate of primary production therefrom; and
    (c) development, conservation and management of sites and facilities in
the province for the generation and production of electrical energy.

Export from provinces of (2) In each province, the legislature may make laws in relation to the
resources export from the province to another part of Canada of the primary
production from non-renewable natural resources and forestry resources in the province and the production from facilities in the
province for the generation of electrical energy, but such laws may
not authorize or provide for discrimination in prices or in supplies
exported to another part of Canada.

Authority of Parliament (3) Nothing in subsection (2) derogates from the authority of Parliament
to enact laws in relation to the matters referred to in that subsection
and, where such a law of Parliament and a law of a province conflict,
the law of Parliament prevails to the extent of the conflict.

Taxation of resources (4) In each province, the legislature may make laws in relation to the
raising of money by any mode or system of taxation in respect of
    (a) non-renewable natural resources and forestry resources in the prov-
ince and the primary production therefrom, and
    (b) sites and facilities in the province for the generation of electrical
energy and the production therefrom,
whether or not such production is exported in whole or in part
from the province, but such laws may not authorize or provide for
taxation that differentiates between production exported to another
part of Canada and production not exported from the province.

"Primary production" (5) The expression "primary production" has the meaning assigned by
the Sixth Schedule.

(6) Nothing in subsections (1) to (5) derogates from any powers or rights *Existing powers or rights* that a legislature or government of a province had immediately before the coming into force of this section.

Education

93 In and for each Province the Legislature may exclusively make Laws *Legislation respecting* in relation to Education, subject and according to the following *Education* Provisions: —

(1) Nothing in any such Law shall prejudicially affect any Right or Privilege with respect to Denominational Schools which any Class of Persons have by Law in the Province at the Union:

(2) All the Powers, Privileges, and Duties at the Union by Law conferred and imposed in Upper Canada on the Separate Schools and School Trustees of the Queen's Roman Catholic Subjects shall be and the same are hereby extended to the Dissentient Schools of the Queen's Protestant and Roman Catholic Subjects in Québec:

(3) Where in any Province a System of Separate or Dissentient Schools exists by Law at the Union or is thereafter established by the Legislature of the Province, an Appeal shall lie to the Governor General in Council from any Act or Decision of any Provincial Authority affecting any Right or Privilege of the Protestant or Roman Catholic Minority of the Queen's Subjects in relation to Education:

(4) In case any such Provincial Law as from Time to Time seems to the Governor General in Council requisite for the due Execution of the Provisions of this Section is not made, or in case any Decision of the Governor General in Council on any Appeal under this Section is not duly executed by the proper Provincial Authority in that Behalf, then and in every such Case, and as far only as the Circumstances of each Case require, the Parliament of Canada may make remedial Laws for the due Execution of the Provisions of this Section and of any Decision of the Governor General in Council under this Section.

93A Paragraphs (1) to (4) of section 93 do not apply to Québec. *Québec*

Uniformity of Laws in Ontario, Nova Scotia, and New Brunswick

Legislation for Uniformity of Laws in Three Provinces

94 Notwithstanding anything in this Act, the Parliament of Canada may make Provision for the Uniformity of all or any of the Laws relative to Property and Civil Rights in Ontario, Nova Scotia, and New Brunswick, and of the Procedure of all or any of the Courts in those Three Provinces, and from and after the passing of any Act in that Behalf the Power of the Parliament of Canada to make Laws in relation to any Matter comprised in any such Act shall, notwithstanding anything in this Act, be unrestricted; but any Act of the Parliament of Canada making Provision for such Uniformity shall not have effect in any Province unless and until it is adopted and enacted as Law by the Legislature thereof.

Old Age Pensions

Legislation respecting old age pensions and supplementary benefits

94A The Parliament of Canada may make laws in relation to old age pensions and supplementary benefits, including survivors' and disability benefits irrespective of age, but no such law shall affect the operation of any law present or future of a provincial legislature in relation to any such matter.

Agriculture And Immigration

Concurrent Powers of Legislation respecting Agriculture, etc.

95 In each Province the Legislature may make Laws in relation to Agriculture in the Province, and to Immigration into the Province; and it is hereby declared that the Parliament of Canada may from Time to Time make Laws in relation to Agriculture in all or any of the Provinces, and to Immigration into all or any of the Provinces; and any Law of the Legislature of a Province relative to Agriculture or to Immigration shall have effect in and for the Province as long and as far only as it is not repugnant to any Act of the Parliament of Canada.

VII Judicature

96 The Governor General shall appoint the Judges of the Superior, District, and County Courts in each Province, except those of the Courts of Probate in Nova Scotia and New Brunswick. *Appointment of Judges*

97 Until the Laws relative to Property and Civil Rights in Ontario, Nova Scotia, and New Brunswick, and the Procedure of the Courts in those Provinces, are made uniform, the Judges of the Courts of those Provinces appointed by the Governor General shall be selected from the respective Bars of those Provinces. *Selection of Judges in Ontario, etc.*

98 The Judges of the Courts of Québec shall be selected from the Bar of that Province. *Selection of Judges in Québec*

99 (1) Subject to subsection two of this section, the Judges of the Superior Courts shall hold office during good behaviour, but shall be removable by the Governor General on Address of the Senate and House of Commons. *Tenure of office of Judges*

(2) A Judge of a Superior Court, whether appointed before or after the coming into force of this section, shall cease to hold office upon attaining the age of seventy-five years, or upon the coming into force of this section if at that time he has already attained that age. *Termination at age 75*

100 The Salaries, Allowances, and Pensions of the Judges of the Superior, District, and County Courts (except the Courts of Probate in Nova Scotia and New Brunswick), and of the Admiralty Courts in Cases where the Judges thereof are for the Time being paid by Salary, shall be fixed and provided by the Parliament of Canada. *Salaries, etc., of Judges*

101 The Parliament of Canada may, notwithstanding anything in this Act, from Time to Time provide for the Constitution, Maintenance, and Organization of a General Court of Appeal for Canada, and for the Establishment of any additional Courts for the better Administration of the Laws of Canada. *General Court of Appeal, etc.*

VIII Revenues; Debts; Assets; Taxation

Creation of Consolidated Revenue Fund
102 All Duties and Revenues over which the respective Legislatures of Canada, Nova Scotia, and New Brunswick before and at the Union had and have Power of Appropriation, except such Portions thereof as are by this Act reserved to the respective Legislatures of the Provinces, or are raised by them in accordance with the special Powers conferred on them by this Act, shall form One Consolidated Revenue Fund, to be appropriated for the Public Service of Canada in the Manner and subject to the Charges in this Act provided.

Expenses of Collection, etc.
103 The Consolidated Revenue Fund of Canada shall be permanently charged with the Costs, Charges, and Expenses incident to the Collection, Management, and Receipt thereof, and the same shall form the First Charge thereon, subject to be reviewed and audited in such Manner as shall be ordered by the Governor General in Council until the Parliament otherwise provides.

Interest of Provincial Public Debts
104 The annual Interest of the Public Debts of the several Provinces of Canada, Nova Scotia, and New Brunswick at the Union shall form the Second Charge on the Consolidated Revenue Fund of Canada.

Salary of Governor General
105 Unless altered by the Parliament of Canada, the Salary of the Governor General shall be Ten thousand Pounds Sterling Money of the United Kingdom of Great Britain and Ireland, payable out of the Consolidated Revenue Fund of Canada, and the same shall form the Third Charge thereon.

Appropriation from Time to Time
106 Subject to the several Payments by this Act charged on the Consolidated Revenue Fund of Canada, the same shall be appropriated by the Parliament of Canada for the Public Service.

Transfer of Stocks, etc.
107 All Stocks, Cash, Banker's Balances, and Securities for Money belonging to each Province at the Time of the Union, except as in this Act mentioned, shall be the Property of Canada, and shall be taken in Reduction of the Amount of the respective Debts of the Provinces at the Union.

Transfer of Property in Schedule
108 The Public Works and Property of each Province, enumerated in the Third Schedule to this Act, shall be the Property of Canada.

109 All Lands, Mines, Minerals, and Royalties belonging to the several *Property in Lands,*
Provinces of Canada, Nova Scotia, and New Brunswick at the Union, *Mines, etc.*
and all Sums then due or payable for such Lands, Mines, Minerals, or
Royalties, shall belong to the several Provinces of Ontario, Québec,
Nova Scotia, and New Brunswick in which the same are situate or arise,
subject to any Trusts existing in respect thereof, and to any Interest other
than that of the Province in the same.

110 All Assets connected with such Portions of the Public Debt of each *Assets connected with*
Province as are assumed by that Province shall belong to that *Provincial Debts*
Province.

111. Canada shall be liable for the Debts and Liabilities of each Province *Canada to be liable for*
existing at the Union. *Provincial Debts*

112 Ontario and Québec conjointly shall be liable to Canada for the Amount *Debts of Ontario and*
(if any) by which the Debt of the Province of Canada exceeds at the Union *Québec*
Sixty-two million five hundred thousand Dollars, and shall be charged
with Interest at the Rate of Five per Centum per Annum thereon.

113 The Assets enumerated in the Fourth Schedule to this Act belonging at *Assets of Ontario and*
the Union to the Province of Canada shall be the Property of Ontario *Québec*
and Québec conjointly.

114 Nova Scotia shall be liable to Canada for the Amount (if any) by which *Debt of Nova Scotia*
its Public Debt exceeds at the Union Eight million Dollars, and shall be
charged with Interest at the Rate of Five per Centum per Annum thereon.

115 New Brunswick shall be liable to Canada for the Amount (if any) by *Debt of New Brunswick*
which its Public Debt exceeds at the Union Seven million Dollars,
and shall be charged with Interest at the Rate of Five per Centum per
Annum thereon.

116 In case the Public Debts of Nova Scotia and New Brunswick do not *Payment of interest to Nova*
at the Union amount to Eight million and Seven million Dollars re- *Scotia and New Brunswick*
spectively, they shall respectively receive by half-yearly Payments in
advance from the Government of Canada Interest at Five per Centum
per Annum on the Difference between the actual Amounts of their
respective Debts and such stipulated Amounts.

Provincial Public Property 117 The several Provinces shall retain all their respective Public Property not otherwise disposed of in this Act, subject to the Right of Canada to assume any Lands or Public Property required for Fortifications or for the Defence of the Country.

[Repealed] 118 Repealed.

Further Grant to New Brunswick 119 New Brunswick shall receive by half-yearly Payments in advance from Canada for the Period of Ten Years from the Union an additional Allowance of Sixty-three thousand Dollars per Annum; but as long as the Public Debt of that Province remains under Seven million Dollars, a Deduction equal to the Interest at Five per Centum per Annum on such Deficiency shall be made from that Allowance of Sixty-three thousand Dollars.

Form of Payments 120 All Payments to be made under this Act, or in discharge of Liabilities created under any Act of the Provinces of Canada, Nova Scotia, and New Brunswick respectively, and assumed by Canada, shall, until the Parliament of Canada otherwise directs, be made in such Form and Manner as may from Time to Time be ordered by the Governor General in Council.

Canadian Manufactures, etc. 121 All Articles of the Growth, Produce, or Manufacture of any one of the Provinces shall, from and after the Union, be admitted free into each of the other Provinces.

Continuance of Customs and Excise Laws 122 The Customs and Excise Laws of each Province shall, subject to the Provisions of this Act, continue in force until altered by the Parliament of Canada.

Exportation and Importation as between Two Provinces 123 Where Customs Duties are, at the Union, leviable on any Goods, Wares, or Merchandises in any Two Provinces, those Goods, Wares, and Merchandises may, from and after the Union, be imported from one of those Provinces into the other of them on Proof of Payment of the Customs Duty leviable thereon in the Province of Exportation, and on Payment of such further Amount (if any) of Customs Duty as is leviable thereon in the Province of Importation.

124 Nothing in this Act shall affect the Right of New Brunswick to levy the *Lumber Dues in New* Lumber Dues provided in Chapter Fifteen of Title Three of the Revised *Brunswick* Statutes of New Brunswick, or in any Act amending that Act before or after the Union, and not increasing the Amount of such Dues; but the Lumber of any of the Provinces other than New Brunswick shall not be subject to such Dues.

125 No Lands or Property belonging to Canada or any Province shall be *Exemption of Public Lands,* liable to Taxation. *etc.*

126 Such Portions of the Duties and Revenues over which the respective *Provincial Consolidated* Legislatures of Canada, Nova Scotia, and New Brunswick had before *Revenue Fund* the Union Power of Appropriation as are by this Act reserved to the respective Governments or Legislatures of the Provinces, and all Duties and Revenues raised by them in accordance with the special Powers conferred upon them by this Act, shall in each Province form One Consolidated Revenue Fund to be appropriated for the Public Service of the Province.

IX Miscellaneous Provisions

General

127 Repealed. *[Repealed]*

128 Every Member of the Senate or House of Commons of Canada shall *Oath of Allegiance, etc.* before taking his Seat therein take and subscribe before the Governor General or some Person authorized by him, and every Member of a Legislative Council or Legislative Assembly of any Province shall before taking his Seat therein take and subscribe before the Lieutenant Governor of the Province or some Person authorized by him, the Oath of Allegiance contained in the Fifth Schedule to this Act; and every Member of the Senate of Canada and every Member of the Legislative Council of Québec shall also, before taking his Seat therein, take and subscribe before the Governor General, or some Person authorized by him, the Declaration of Qualification contained in the same Schedule.

129 Except as otherwise provided by this Act, all Laws in force in Canada, *Continuance of existing* Nova Scotia, or New Brunswick at the Union, and all Courts of Civil *Laws, Courts, Officers, etc.*

and Criminal Jurisdiction, and all legal Commissions, Powers, and Authorities, and all Officers, Judicial, Administrative, and Ministerial, existing therein at the Union, shall continue in Ontario, Québec, Nova Scotia, and New Brunswick respectively, as if the Union had not been made; subject nevertheless (except with respect to such as are enacted by or exist under Acts of the Parliament of Great Britain or of the Parliament of the United Kingdom of Great Britain and Ireland), to be repealed, abolished, or altered by the Parliament of Canada, or by the Legislature of the respective Province, according to the Authority of the Parliament or of that Legislature under this Act.

Transfer of Officers to Canada 130 Until the Parliament of Canada otherwise provides, all Officers of the several Provinces having Duties to discharge in relation to Matters other than those coming within the Classes of Subjects by this Act assigned exclusively to the Legislatures of the Provinces shall be Officers of Canada, and shall continue to discharge the Duties of their respective Offices under the same Liabilities, Responsibilities, and Penalties as if the Union had not been made.

Appointment of new Officers 131 Until the Parliament of Canada otherwise provides, the Governor General in Council may from Time to Time appoint such Officers as the Governor General in Council deems necessary or proper for the effectual Execution of this Act.

Treaty Obligations 132 The Parliament and Government of Canada shall have all Powers necessary or proper for performing the Obligations of Canada or of any Province thereof, as Part of the British Empire, toward Foreign Countries, arising under Treaties between the Empire and such Foreign Countries.

Use of English and French Languages 133 Either the English or the French Language may be used by any Person in the Debates of the Houses of the Parliament of Canada and of the Houses of the Legislature of Québec; and both those Languages shall be used in the respective Records and Journals of those Houses; and either of those Languages may be used by any Person or in any Pleading or Process in or issuing from any Court of Canada established under this Act, and in or from all or any of the Courts of Québec.

The Acts of the Parliament of Canada and of the Legislature of Québec shall be printed and published in both those Languages.

Ontario and Québec

134 Until the Legislature of Ontario or of Québec otherwise provides, the *Appointment of Executive* Lieutenant Governors of Ontario and Québec may each appoint under *Officers for Ontario and* the Great Seal of the Province the following Officers, to hold Office *Québec* during Pleasure, that is to say,—the Attorney General, the Secretary and Registrar of the Province, the Treasurer of the Province, the Commissioner of Crown Lands, and the Commissioner of Agriculture and Public Works, and in the Case of Québec the Solicitor General, and may, by Order of the Lieutenant Governor in Council, from Time to Time prescribe the Duties of those Officers, and of the several Departments over which they shall preside or to which they shall belong, and of the Officers and Clerks thereof, and may also appoint other and additional Officers to hold Office during Pleasure, and may from Time to Time prescribe the Duties of those Officers, and of the several Departments over which they shall preside or to which they shall belong, and of the Officers and Clerks thereof.

135 Until the Legislature of Ontario or Québec otherwise provides, all *Powers, Duties, etc. of* Rights, Powers, Duties, Functions, Responsibilities, or Authorities at *Executive Officers* the passing of this Act vested in or imposed on the Attorney General, Solicitor General, Secretary and Registrar of the Province of Canada, Minister of Finance, Commissioner of Crown Lands, Commissioner of Public Works, and Minister of Agriculture and Receiver General, by any Law, Statute, or Ordinance of Upper Canada, Lower Canada, or Canada, and not repugnant to this Act, shall be vested in or imposed on any Officer to be appointed by the Lieutenant Governor for the Discharge of the same or any of them; and the Commissioner of Agriculture and Public Works shall perform the Duties and Functions of the Office of Minister of Agriculture at the passing of this Act imposed by the Law of the Province of Canada, as well as those of the Commissioner of Public Works.

136 Until altered by the Lieutenant Governor in Council, the Great Seals *Great Seals* of Ontario and Québec respectively shall be the same, or of the same Design, as those used in the Provinces of Upper Canada and Lower Canada respectively before their Union as the Province of Canada.

Construction of temporary Acts   137   The words "and from thence to the End of the then next ensuing Session of the Legislature," or Words to the same Effect, used in any temporary Act of the Province of Canada not expired before the Union, shall be construed to extend and apply to the next Session of the Parliament of Canada if the Subject Matter of the Act is within the Powers of the same as defined by this Act, or to the next Sessions of the Legislatures of Ontario and Québec respectively if the Subject Matter of the Act is within the Powers of the same as defined by this Act.

As to Errors in Names   138   From and after the Union the Use of the Words "Upper Canada" instead of "Ontario," or "Lower Canada" instead of "Québec," in any Deed, Writ, Process, Pleading, Document, Matter, or Thing shall not invalidate the same.

As to issue of Proclamations before Union, to commence after Union   139   Any Proclamation under the Great Seal of the Province of Canada issued before the Union to take effect at a Time which is subsequent to the Union, whether relating to that Province, or to Upper Canada, or to Lower Canada, and the several Matters and Things therein proclaimed, shall be and continue of like Force and Effect as if the Union had not been made.

As to issue of Proclamations after Union   140   Any Proclamation which is authorized by any Act of the Legislature of the Province of Canada to be issued under the Great Seal of the Province of Canada, whether relating to that Province, or to Upper Canada, or to Lower Canada, and which is not issued before the Union, may be issued by the Lieutenant Governor of Ontario or of Québec, as its Subject Matter requires, under the Great Seal thereof; and from and after the Issue of such Proclamation the same and the several Matters and Things therein proclaimed shall be and continue of the like Force and Effect in Ontario or Québec as if the Union had not been made.

Penitentiary   141   The Penitentiary of the Province of Canada shall, until the Parliament of Canada otherwise provides, be and continue the Penitentiary of Ontario and of Québec.

Arbitration respecting Debts, etc.   142   The Division and Adjustment of the Debts, Credits, Liabilities, Properties, and Assets of Upper Canada and Lower Canada shall be referred to the Arbitrament of Three Arbitrators, One chosen by the Government of Ontario, One by the Government of Québec, and One by the Government of Canada; and the Selection of the Arbitrators shall not be made until the Parliament of Canada and the Legislatures of Ontario and Québec have met; and the Arbitrator chosen by the Government of Canada shall not be a Resident either in Ontario or in Québec.

143 The Governor General in Council may from Time to Time order *Division of Records* that such and so many of the Records, Books, and Documents of the Province of Canada as he thinks fit shall be appropriated and delivered either to Ontario or to Québec, and the same shall thenceforth be the Property of that Province; and any Copy thereof or Extract therefrom, duly certified by the Officer having charge of the Original thereof, shall be admitted as Evidence.

144 The Lieutenant Governor of Québec may from Time to Time, by *Constitution of Townships* Proclamation under the Great Seal of the Province, to take effect from a *in Québec* Day to be appointed therein, constitute Townships in those Parts of the Province of Québec in which Townships are not then already consti-tuted, and fix the Metes and Bounds thereof.

X Intercolonial Railway

145 Repealed. *[Repealed]*

XI Admission of Other Colonies

146 It shall be lawful for the Queen, by and with the Advice of Her *Power to admit* Majesty's Most Honourable Privy Council, on Addresses from the *Newfoundland, etc., into* Houses of the Parliament of Canada, and from the Houses of the re- *the Union* spective Legislatures of the Colonies or Provinces of Newfoundland, Prince Edward Island, and British Columbia, to admit those Colonies or Provinces, or any of them, into the Union, and on Address from the Houses of the Parliament of Canada to admit Rupert's Land and the North-western Territory, or either of them, into the Union, on such Terms and Conditions in each Case as are in the Addresses expressed and as the Queen thinks fit to approve, subject to the Provisions of this Act; and the Provisions of any Order in Council in that Behalf shall have effect as if they had been enacted by the Parliament of the United Kingdom of Great Britain and Ireland.

243

As to Representation of 147 In case of the Admission of Newfoundland and Prince Edward Island, or
Newfoundland and Prince either of them, each shall be entitled to a Representation in the Senate
Edward Island in Senate of Canada of Four Members, and (notwithstanding anything in this
Act) in case of the Admission of Newfoundland the normal Number
of Senators shall be Seventy-six and their maximum Number shall be
Eighty-two; but Prince Edward Island when admitted shall be deemed
to be comprised in the third of the Three Divisions into which Canada
is, in relation to the Constitution of the Senate, divided by this Act,
and accordingly, after the Admission of Prince Edward Island, whether
Newfoundland is admitted or not, the Representation of Nova Scotia
and New Brunswick in the Senate shall, as Vacancies occur, be reduced
from Twelve to Ten Members respectively, and the Representation of
each of those Provinces shall not be increased at any Time beyond Ten,
except under the Provisions of this Act for the Appointment of Three or
Six additional Senators under the Direction of the Queen.

Constitution Act, 1982

Schedule B
Constitution Act 1982

Part I
Canadian Charter of Rights and Freedoms

Whereas Canada is founded upon principles that recognize the supremacy of God and the rule of law:

Guarantee of Rights and Freedoms

1 The *Canadian Charter of Rights and Freedoms* guarantees the rights and freedoms set out in it subject only to such reasonable limits prescribed by law as can be demonstrably justified in a free and democratic society.

Rights and freedoms in Canada

Fundamental Freedoms

2 Everyone has the following fundamental freedoms:

Fundamental freedoms

   (*a*) freedom of conscience and religion;

   (*b*) freedom of thought, belief, opinion and expression, including freedom of the press and other media of communication;

   (*c*) freedom of peaceful assembly; and

   (*d*) freedom of association.

Democratic Rights

3 Every citizen of Canada has the right to vote in an election of members of the House of Commons or of a legislative assembly and to be qualified for membership therein.

Democratic rights of citizens

4 (1) No House of Commons and no legislative assembly shall continue for longer than five years from the date fixed for the return of the writs of a general election of its members.

Maximum duration of legislative bodies

Continuation in special circumstances

(2) In time of real or apprehended war, invasion or insurrection, a House of Commons may be continued by Parliament and a legislative assembly may be continued by the legislature beyond five years if such continuation is not opposed by the votes of more than one-third of the members of the House of Commons or the legislative assembly, as the case may be.

Annual sitting of legislative bodies

5 There shall be a sitting of Parliament and of each legislature at least once every twelve months.

Mobility Rights

Mobility of citizens

6 (1) Every citizen of Canada has the right to enter, remain in and leave Canada.

Rights to move and gain livelihood

(2) Every citizen of Canada and every person who has the status of a permanent resident of Canada has the right

(a) to move to and take up residence in any province; and

(b) to pursue the gaining of a livelihood in any province.

Limitation

(3) The rights specified in subsection (2) are subject to

(a) any laws or practices of general application in force in a province other than those that discriminate among persons primarily on the basis of province of present or previous residence; and

(b) any laws providing for reasonable residency requirements as a qualification for the receipt of publicly provided social services.

Affirmative action programs

(4) Subsections (2) and (3) do not preclude any law, program or activity that has as its object the amelioration in a province of conditions of individuals in that province who are socially or economically disadvantaged if the rate of employment in that province is below the rate of employment in Canada.

Legal Rights

Life, liberty and security of person

7 Everyone has the right to life, liberty and security of the person and the right not to be deprived thereof except in accordance with the principles of fundamental justice.

8 Everyone has the right to be secure against unreasonable search or *Search or seizure* seizure.

9 Everyone has the right not to be arbitrarily detained or imprisoned. *Detention or imprisonment*

10 Everyone has the right on arrest or detention *Arrest or detention*
   (*a*) to be informed promptly of the reasons therefor;
   (*b*) to retain and instruct counsel without delay and to be informed of that right; and
   (*c*) to have the validity of the detention determined by way of *habeas corpus* and to be released if the detention is not lawful.

11 Any person charged with an offence has the right *Proceedings in criminal and*
   (*a*) to be informed without unreasonable delay of the specific offence; *penal matters*
   (*b*) to be tried within a reasonable time;
   (*c*) not to be compelled to be a witness in proceedings against that person in respect of the offence;
   (*d*) to be presumed innocent until proven guilty according to law in a fair and public hearing by an independent and impartial tribunal;
   (*e*) not to be denied reasonable bail without just cause;
   (*f*) except in the case of an offence under military law tried before a military tribunal, to the benefit of trial by jury where the maximum punishment for the offence is imprisonment for five years or a more severe punishment;
   (*g*) not to be found guilty on account of any act or omission unless, at the time of the act or omission, it constituted an offence under Canadian or international law or was criminal according to the general principles of law recognized by the community of nations;
   (*h*) if finally acquitted of the offence, not to be tried for it again and, if finally found guilty and punished for the offence, not to be tried or punished for it again; and
   (*i*) if found guilty of the offence and if the punishment for the offence has been varied between the time of commission and the time of sentencing, to the benefit of the lesser punishment.

12 Everyone has the right not to be subjected to any cruel and unusual *Treatment or punishment* treatment or punishment.

Self-crimination 13 A witness who testifies in any proceedings has the right not to have any incriminating evidence so given used to incriminate that witness in any other proceedings, except in a prosecution for perjury or for the giving of contradictory evidence.

Interpreter 14 A party or witness in any proceedings who does not understand or speak the language in which the proceedings are conducted or who is deaf has the right to the assistance of an interpreter.

Equality Rights

Equality before and under law and equal protection and benefit of law 15 (1) Every individual is equal before and under the law and has the right to the equal protection and equal benefit of the law without discrimination and, in particular, without discrimination based on race, national or ethnic origin, colour, religion, sex, age or mental or physical disability.

Affirmative action programs (2) Subsection (1) does not preclude any law, program or activity that has as its object the amelioration of conditions of disadvantaged individuals or groups including those that are disadvantaged because of race, national or ethnic origin, colour, religion, sex, age or mental or physical disability.

Official Languages of Canada

Official languages of Canada 16 (1) English and French are the official languages of Canada and have equality of status and equal rights and privileges as to their use in all institutions of the Parliament and government of Canada.

Official languages of New Brunswick (2) English and French are the official languages of New Brunswick and have equality of status and equal rights and privileges as to their use in all institutions of the legislature and government of New Brunswick.

Advancement of status and use (3) Nothing in this Charter limits the authority of Parliament or a legislature to advance the equality of status or use of English and French.

16.1 (1) The English linguistic community and the French linguistic com- *English and French* munity in New Brunswick have equality of status and equal rights *linguistic communities in* and privileges, including the right to distinct educational institu- *New Brunswick* tions and such distinct cultural institutions as are necessary for the preservation and promotion of those communities.

(2) The role of the legislature and government of New Brunswick to *Role of the legislature* preserve and promote the status, rights and privileges referred to in *and government of New* subsection (1) is affirmed. *Brunswick*

17 (1) Everyone has the right to use English or French in any debates and *Proceedings of Parliament* other proceedings of Parliament.

(2) Everyone has the right to use English or French in any debates and *Proceedings of New* other proceedings of the legislature of New Brunswick. *Brunswick legislature*

18 (1) The statutes, records and journals of Parliament shall be printed *Parliamentary statutes and* and published in English and French and both language versions are *records* equally authoritative.

(2) The statutes, records and journals of the legislature of New *New Brunswick statutes* Brunswick shall be printed and published in English and French *and records* and both language versions are equally authoritative.

19 (1) Either English or French may be used by any person in, or in *Proceedings in courts* any pleading in or process issuing from, any court established by *established by Parliament* Parliament.

(2) Either English or French may be used by any person in, or in any *Proceedings in New* pleading in or process issuing from, any court of New Brunswick. *Brunswick courts*

20 (1) Any member of the public in Canada has the right to communicate *Communications by public* with, and to receive available services from, any head or central of- *with federal institutions* fice of an institution of the Parliament or government of Canada in English or French, and has the same right with respect to any other office of any such institution where

(a) there is a significant demand for communications with and services from that office in such language; or *(b)* due to the nature of the office, it is reasonable that communications with and services from that office be available in both English and French.

Communications by public with New Brunswick institutions

(2) Any member of the public in New Brunswick has the right to communicate with, and to receive available services from, any office of an institution of the legislature or government of New Brunswick in English or French.

Continuation of existing constitutional provisions

21 Nothing in sections 16 to 20 abrogates or derogates from any right, privilege or obligation with respect to the English and French languages, or either of them, that exists or is continued by virtue of any other provision of the Constitution of Canada.

Rights and privileges preserved

22 Nothing in sections 16 to 20 abrogates or derogates from any legal or customary right or privilege acquired or enjoyed either before or after the coming into force of this Charter with respect to any language that is not English or French.

Minority Language Educational Rights

Language of instruction

23 (1) Citizens of Canada

(a) whose first language learned and still understood is that of the English or French linguistic minority population of the province in which they reside, or

(b) who have received their primary school instruction in Canada in English or French and reside in a province where the language in which they received that instruction is the language of the English or French linguistic minority population of the province,

have the right to have their children receive primary and secondary school instruction in that language in that province.

Continuity of language instruction

(2) Citizens of Canada of whom any child has received or is receiving primary or secondary school instruction in English or French in Canada, have the right to have all their children receive primary and secondary school instruction in the same language.

Application where numbers warrant

(3) The right of citizens of Canada under subsections (1) and (2) to have their children receive primary and secondary school instruction in

the language of the English or French linguistic minority population of a province

(a) applies wherever in the province the number of children of citizens who have such a right is sufficient to warrant the provision to them out of public funds of minority language instruction; and

(b) includes, where the number of those children so warrants, the right to have them receive that instruction in minority language educational facilities provided out of public funds

Enforcement

24 (1) Anyone whose rights or freedoms, as guaranteed by this Charter, have been infringed or denied may apply to a court of competent jurisdiction to obtain such remedy as the court considers appropriate and just in the circumstances.

Enforcement of guaranteed rights and freedoms

(2) Where, in proceedings under subsection (1), a court concludes that evidence was obtained in a manner that infringed or denied any rights or freedoms guaranteed by this Charter, the evidence shall be excluded if it is established that, having regard to all the circumstances, the admission of it in the proceedings would bring the administration of justice into disrepute.

Exclusion of evidence bringing administration of justice into disrepute

General

25 The guarantee in this Charter of certain rights and freedoms shall not be construed so as to abrogate or derogate from any aboriginal, treaty or other rights or freedoms that pertain to the aboriginal peoples of Canada including

Aboriginal rights and freedoms not affected by Charter

(a) any rights or freedoms that have been recognized by the Royal Proclamation of October 7, 1763; and

(b) any rights or freedoms that now exist by way of land claims agreements or may be so acquired.

26 The guarantee in this Charter of certain rights and freedoms shall not be construed as denying the existence of any other rights or freedoms that exist in Canada.

Other rights and freedoms not affected by Charter

Multicultural heritage   27 This Charter shall be interpreted in a manner consistent with the preservation and enhancement of the multicultural heritage of Canadians.

Rights guaranteed equally to both sexes   28 Notwithstanding anything in this Charter, the rights and freedoms referred to in it are guaranteed equally to male and female persons.

Rights respecting certain schools preserved   29 Nothing in this Charter abrogates or derogates from any rights or privileges guaranteed by or under the Constitution of Canada in respect of denominational, separate or dissentient schools.

Application to territories and territorial authorities   30 A reference in this Charter to a Province or to the legislative assembly or legislature of a province shall be deemed to include a reference to the Yukon Territory and the Northwest Territories, or to the appropriate legislative authority thereof, as the case may be.

Legislative powers not extended   31 Nothing in this Charter extends the legislative powers of any body or authority.

Application of Charter

Application of Charter   32 (1) This Charter applies

(a) to the Parliament and government of Canada in respect of all matters within the authority of Parliament including all matters relating to the Yukon Territory and Northwest Territories; and

(b) to the legislature and government of each province in respect of all matters within the authority of the legislature of each province.

Exception   (2) Notwithstanding subsection (1), section 15 shall not have effect until three years after this section comes into force.

Exception where express declaration   33 (1) Parliament or the legislature of a province may expressly declare in an Act of Parliament or of the legislature, as the case may be, that the Act or a provision thereof shall operate notwithstanding a provision included in section 2 or sections 7 to 15 of this Charter.

Operation of exception   (2) An Act or a provision of an Act in respect of which a declaration made under this section is in effect shall have such operation as it would have but for the provision of this Charter referred to in the declaration.

(3) A declaration made under subsection (1) shall cease to have effect *Five year limitation*
five years after it comes into force or on such earlier date as may be
specified in the declaration.

(4) Parliament or the legislature of a province may re-enact a declara- *Re-enactment*
tion made under subsection (1).

(5) Subsection (3) applies in respect of a re-enactment made under sub- *Five year limitation*
section (4).

Citation

34 This Part may be cited as the *Canadian Charter of Rights and Freedoms.* *Citation*

Part II
Rights Of The Aboriginal Peoples Of Canada

35 (1) The existing aboriginal and treaty rights of the aboriginal peoples *Recognition of existing*
of Canada are hereby recognized and affirmed. *aboriginal and treaty rights*

(2) In this Act, "aboriginal peoples of Canada" includes the Indian, *Definition of "aboriginal*
Inuit and Métis peoples of Canada. *peoples of Canada"*

(3) For greater certainty, in subsection (1) "treaty rights" includes *Land claims agreements*
rights that now exist by way of land claims agreements or may be so
acquired.

(4) Notwithstanding any other provision of this Act, the aboriginal and *Aboriginal and treaty rights*
treaty rights referred to in subsection (1) are guaranteed equally to *are guaranteed equally to*
male and female persons. *both sexes*

35.1 The government of Canada and the provincial governments are com- *Commitment to*
mitted to the principle that, before any amendment is made to Class 24 *participation in*
of section 91 of the *"Constitution Act, 1867"*, to section 25 of this Act or *constitutional conference*
to this Part,

(*a*) a constitutional conference that includes in its agenda an item relating to the proposed amendment, composed of the Prime Minister of Canada and the first ministers of the provinces, will be convened by the Prime Minister of Canada; and

(*b*) the Prime Minister of Canada will invite representatives of the aboriginal peoples of Canada to participate in the discussions on that item.

Part III
Equalization And Regional Disparities

Commitment to promote equal opportunities

36 (1) Without altering the legislative authority of Parliament or of the provincial legislatures, or the rights of any of them with respect to the exercise of their legislative authority, Parliament and the legislatures, together with the government of Canada and the provincial governments, are committed to

(*a*) promoting equal opportunities for the well-being of Canadians;

(*b*) furthering economic development to reduce disparity in opportunities; and

(*c*) providing essential public services of reasonable quality to all Canadians.

Commitment respecting public services

(2) Parliament and the government of Canada are committed to the principle of making equalization payments to ensure that provincial governments have sufficient revenues to provide reasonably comparable levels of public services at reasonably comparable levels of taxation.

Part IV
Constitutional Conference

[Repealed]   37 Repealed.

Part IV.I
Constitutional Conferences

[Repealed]   37.1 Repealed.

Part V
Procedure For Amending Constitution Of Canada

38 (1) An amendment to the Constitution of Canada may be made by proc-   *General procedure for*
lamation issued by the Governor General under the Great Seal of Canada   *amending Constitution of*
where so authorized by   *Canada*

    (*a*) resolutions of the Senate and House of Commons; and

    (*b*) resolutions of the legislative assemblies of at least two-thirds of the
provinces that have, in the aggregate, according to the then latest
general census, at least fifty per cent of the population of all the
provinces.

  (2) An amendment made under subsection (1) that derogates from the   *Majority of members*
legislative powers, the proprietary rights or any other rights or privileges of the legislature or government of a province shall require a
resolution supported by a majority of the members of each of the
Senate, the House of Commons and the legislative assemblies required under subsection (1).

  (3) An amendment referred to in subsection (2) shall not have effect in   *Expression of dissent*
a province the legislative assembly of which has expressed its dissent
thereto by resolution supported by a majority of its members prior
to the issue of the proclamation to which the amendment relates unless that legislative assembly, subsequently, by resolution supported
by a majority of its members, revokes its dissent and authorizes the
amendment.

  (4) A resolution of dissent made for the purposes of subsection (3) may   *Revocation of dissent*
be revoked at any time before or after the issue of the proclamation
to which it relates.

39 (1) A proclamation shall not be issued under subsection 38(1) before the   *Restriction on proclamation*
expiration of one year from the adoption of the resolution initiating
the amendment procedure thereunder, unless the legislative assembly of each province has previously adopted a resolution of assent
or dissent.

Idem   (2) A proclamation shall not be issued under subsection 38(1) after the expiration of three years from the adoption of the resolution initiating the amendment procedure thereunder.

Compensation   40 Where an amendment is made under subsection 38(1) that transfers provincial legislative powers relating to education or other cultural matters from provincial legislatures to Parliament, Canada shall provide reasonable compensation to any province to which the amendment does not apply.

Amendment by unanimous consent   41 An amendment to the Constitution of Canada in relation to the following matters may be made by proclamation issued by the Governor General under the Great Seal of Canada only where authorized by resolutions of the Senate and House of Commons and of the legislative assembly of each province:

(a) the office of the Queen, the Governor General and the Lieutenant Governor of a province;

(b) the right of a province to a number of members in the House of Commons not less than the number of Senators by which the province is entitled to be represented at the time this Part comes into force;

(c) subject to section 43, the use of the English or the French language;

(d) the composition of the Supreme Court of Canada; and

(e) an amendment to this Part.

Amendment by general procedure   42 (1) An amendment to the Constitution of Canada in relation to the following matters may be made only in accordance with subsection 38(1):

(a) the principle of proportionate representation of the provinces in the House of Commons prescribed by the Constitution of Canada;

(b) the powers of the Senate and the method of selecting Senators;

(c) the number of members by which a province is entitled to be represented in the Senate and the residence qualifications of Senators;

(d) subject to paragraph 41(d), the Supreme Court of Canada;

(e) the extension of existing provinces into the territories; and

(f) notwithstanding any other law or practice, the establishment of new provinces.

(2) Subsections 38(2) to (4) do not apply in respect of amendments in relation to matters referred to in subsection (1). *Exception*

43 An amendment to the Constitution of Canada in relation to any provision that applies to one or more, but not all, provinces, including *Amendment of provisions relating to some but not all provinces*

(a) any alteration to boundaries between provinces, and

(b) any amendment to any provision that relates to the use of the English or the French language within a province,

may be made by proclamation issued by the Governor General under the Great Seal of Canada only where so authorized by resolutions of the Senate and House of Commons and of the legislative assembly of each province to which the amendment applies.

44 Subject to sections 41 and 42, Parliament may exclusively make laws amending the Constitution of Canada in relation to the executive government of Canada or the Senate and House of Commons. *Amendments by Parliament*

45 Subject to section 41, the legislature of each province may exclusively make laws amending the constitution of the province. *Amendments by provincial legislatures*

46 (1) The procedures for amendment under sections 38, 41, 42 and 43 may be initiated either by the Senate or the House of Commons or by the legislative assembly of a province. *Initiation of amendment procedures*

(2) A resolution of assent made for the purposes of this Part may be revoked at any time before the issue of a proclamation authorized by it. *Revocation of authorization*

47 (1) An amendment to the Constitution of Canada made by proclamation under section 38, 41, 42 or 43 may be made without a resolution of the Senate authorizing the issue of the proclamation if, within one hundred and eighty days after the adoption by the House of Commons of a resolution authorizing its issue, the Senate has not adopted such a resolution and if, at any time after the expiration of that period, the House of Commons again adopts the resolution. *Amendments without Senate resolution*

(2) Any period when Parliament is prorogued or dissolved shall not be counted in computing the one hundred and eighty day period referred to in subsection (1). *Computation of period*

Advice to issue proclamation 48 The Queen's Privy Council for Canada shall advise the Governor General to issue a proclamation under this Part forthwith on the adoption of the resolutions required for an amendment made by proclamation under this Part.

Constitutional conference 49 A constitutional conference composed of the Prime Minister of Canada and the first ministers of the provinces shall be convened by the Prime Minister of Canada within fifteen years after this Part comes into force to review the provisions of this Part.

Part VI
Amendment To The Constitution Act, 1867

50 (1) (The amendment is set out in the Consolidation of the *Constitution Act*, 1867, as Section 92A thereof.)

51. (2) (The amendment is set out in the Consolidation of the *Constitution Act*, 1867, as the sixth schedule thereof.)

Part VII
General

Primacy of Constitution of Canada 52. (1) The Constitution of Canada is the supreme law of Canada, and any law that is inconsistent with the provisions of the Constitution is, to the extent of the inconsistency, of no force or effect.

Constitution of Canada (2) The Constitution of Canada includes

(a) the *Canada Act 1982*, including this Act;

(b) the Acts and orders referred to in the schedule; and

(c) any amendment to any Act or order referred to in paragraph (a) or (b).

Amendments to Constitution of Canada (3) Amendments to the Constitution of Canada shall be made only in accordance with the authority contained in the Constitution of Canada.

Repeals and new names　53 (1)　The enactments referred to in Column I of the schedule are hereby repealed or amended to the extent indicated in Column II thereof and, unless repealed, shall continue as law in Canada under the names set out in Column III thereof.

(2)　Every enactment, except the *Canada Act 1982*, that refers to an enact- *Consequential amendments* ment referred to in the schedule by the name in Column I thereof is hereby amended by substituting for that name the corresponding name in Column III thereof, and any British North America Act not referred to in the schedule may be cited as the *Constitution Act* followed by the year and number, if any, of its enactment.

54　Part IV is repealed on the day that is one year after this Part comes into *Repeal and consequential* force and this section may be repealed and this Act renumbered, conse- *amendments* quentially upon the repeal of Part IV and this section, by proclamation issued by the Governor General under the Great Seal of Canada.

54.1　*[Repealed]*

55　A French version of the portions of the Constitution of Canada referred *French version of* to in the schedule shall be prepared by the Minister of Justice of Canada *Constitution of Canada* as expeditiously as possible and, when any portion thereof sufficient to warrant action being taken has been so prepared, it shall be put forward for enactment by proclamation issued by the Governor General under the Great Seal of Canada pursuant to the procedure then applicable to an amendment of the same provisions of the Constitution of Canada.

56　Where any portion of the Constitution of Canada has been or is enacted *English and French versions* in English and French or where a French version of any portion of the *of certain constitutional texts* Constitution is enacted pursuant to section 55, the English and French versions of that portion of the Constitution are equally authoritative.

57　The English and French versions of this Act are equally authoritative. *English and French versions of this Act*

58　Subject to section 59, this Act shall come into force on a day to be fixed *Commencement* by proclamation issued by the Queen or the Governor General under the Great Seal of Canada.

259

59 (1) Paragraph 23(1)(*a*) shall come into force in respect of Québec on a day to be fixed by proclamation issued by the Queen or the Governor General under the Great Seal of Canada.

Commencement of paragraph 23(1)(a) in respect of Québec

Authorization of Québec

(2) A proclamation under subsection (1) shall be issued only where authorized by the legislative assembly or government of Québec.

Repeal of this section

(3) This section may be repealed on the day paragraph 23(1)(*a*) comes into force in respect of Québec and this Act amended and renumbered, consequentially upon the repeal of this section, by proclamation issued by the Queen or the Governor General under the Great Seal of Canada.

Short title and citations

60 This Act may be cited as the *Constitution Act, 1982*, and the Constitution Acts 1867 to 1975 (No. 2) and this Act may be cited together as the *Constitution Acts, 1867 to 1982*.

References

61 A reference to the "*Constitution Acts, 1867 to 1982*" shall be deemed to include a reference to the "*Constitution Amendment Proclamation, 1983*".

Index

A

Abella, Rosalie, 153
Aboriginal peoples, 26–27, 31, 83, 142
abortion, 85, 91–92, 141
absolute monarchy, 38
accountability, 42, 56
    cabinet, 40–42, 118, 129, 160
    judges, 153
    Members of Parliament (MPs), 160
Accountability Act, 198
administrative law, 137–38
administrative tribunals, 138
advertising, 179
advertising, third-party, 174
affirmative action, 200
Alberta, 24, 74–75, 82, 143
    Aberhart government, 82
    representation in House of Commons, 120
    "senators-in-waiting," 133
amending formulas, 15, 60
    Canadian Constitution, 25, 27–29
    Meech Lake Accord (proposed), 31
    United States Constitution, 25
American regime. *See* United States
appeal, right of, 140–41
appeal courts, 2, 141, 145–46, 148–49
arbitration, 136
aristocracy, 4
Aristotle, 5
    Politics, 4
asymmetrical federalism, 73–74
Atlantic Canada. *See also* Maritimes
    Supreme Court judges, 150
Atlantic Smoke Shops v. Conlon, 66n1
Attorney-General of Alberta, 143
Auditor General, 122, 124
Australia, 11, 59
    law requiring citizens to vote, 207
authority
    in a democracy, 202
    in federal regimes, 59
    in unitary systems, 59
Axworthy, Tom, 128

B

backbenchers, 126–29
Baier, Gerald, 73–74
bandwagon effect, 206
Bennett, R. B., 140
Berger, Thomas, 142

bicameralism, 71–72

Big M Drug Mart v. The Queen, 139, 143

bilingualism, 26, 83–84, 182

Bill 101, 88

Bill 178, 92

Bill of Rights (Canadian), 83–84

bills

    government, 123

    private members', 123, 127–28

Bleu politicians, 181

Bloc Québécois, 46, 49, 102, 169, 181, 183–84,
        186–88

Boothe, Katherine, 73–74

Britain, 59

    Bill of Rights (1689), 18–19

    colonial constitutions, 38–39

    Constitution, 17–18, 22–23, 58, 117

    constitutional monarchy, 98

    judiciary, 140

    Parliament, 7, 25, 117

    Parliament Act (1911), 18

    Reform Act (1832), 18–19

    rights and freedoms, 81–82

    unitary regime, 14

    utilitarian approach to liberty, 9

British Columbia, 24, 60–61, 74–75, 185

    electoral reform and, 172

    representation in House of Commons, 120

    Supreme Court, 142

British common law, 137

British Commonwealth, 54

British North America, 60–62

British North America Act (BNA Act), 22n3

brokerage parties, 185–88

Brooks, Stephen, 142–43

Bush, George W., 52

by-elections, 173

Byng, Julian Hedworth George Byng, Viscount,
        102

C

CA 1867, 22, 29, 62, 68, 78, 100, 107

    amending provisions, 25

    on electoral districts, 164

    federal pre-eminence under, 24, 63

    on judiciary, 135–37, 140, 144, 148–49, 152

    preamble, 23, 37, 58, 98–99, 116, 140, 163

    on Senate, 129–30

    statute of British Parliament, 25

    taxation under, 64, 66

CA 1982, 22, 24, 31–32, 78, 80, 84, 88, 107, 119

    Aboriginal peoples, 26

    amending formula, 25, 27–29, 60

    Charter (*See* Charter of Rights and Freedoms)

    equalization payments, 26, 68

    on judiciary, 142, 154

    on right to vote, 159

    on Senate, 133

    on timing of elections, 172

cabinet, 40, 98, 103–6

    accountability, 41–42, 118, 129, 160

    appointment of ministers, 40

    collective responsibility, 105

    executive power, 104

    legislative power, 104

    membership, 52, 106

    ministerial responsibility, 112–14

    representation for women and visible
        minorities, 106, 162

    representative (regional) of the country, 106

    transfer of parliamentary power to, 118

cabinet committee system, 106–7, 110

cabinet government, 42–43, 129

Cadman, Chuck, 118n1

Campbell, Colin, 132

Campbell, Gordon, 106n6

Campbell, Kim, 44–45, 199

Canada Act, 1982, 26–27

Canada Action Party, 185–86

"Canada Clause," 31

Canada Customs, 112

Canada Elections Act, 173

Canada Health Act, 75

Canada Health Transfer (CHT), 68

Canada Social Transfer (CST), 68

Canada Unity Fund, 122

Canada's health care system. *See* health care

Canada/United States institutional differences,
        50–57

Canadian Alliance Party, 182

Canadian Bar Association, 151

Canadian Broadcasting Corporation (CBC), 204

Canadian Charter of Rights and Freedoms. *See* Charter of Rights and Freedoms

Canadian Constitution. See *CA 1867; CA 1982;* Constitution of Canada

Canadian Judicial Council, 142

Canadian Labour Congress (CLC), 183

Canadian Pacific Railway, 181

candidates (electoral), 173–74
limits on spending, 174

capital punishment, 85, 92, 182

Cartier, George-Étienne, 181

caucus (parliamentary caucus), 47, 126, 161

central agencies, 112

centralization, 65

centralized federal unions, 63, 65, 69

centre/periphery division, 61

Chaoulli, Jacques, 154

Charest, Jean, 144

Charlottetown Accord, 31, 74, 151–52, 162
"Canada Clause," 31
referendum, 32, 70

Charron, Louise, 153

Charter of Rights and Freedoms, xi, 9, 11, 26, 30, 56, 77–93, 139–40, 153–54
entrenchment, 78, 83–85, 155
judicial independence under, 143–44
notwithstanding clause, 87–88
opposition to, 84–87
political impact, 91–93
Section 1 "loophole," 89–91

"Charter of the Global Greens," 184

Chief Clerk of the Privy Council, 109

Chief Electoral Officer, 173

China, 185

Chong, Michael, 110

Chrétien, Jean, 45, 51, 110–11, 115
cabinet size, 104
reforms to political party financing, 191

Chrétien government, 32, 122
legislation on gun control, 196

Chrétien Liberals, 182

Christian Heritage Party, 185–86

civic education, ix, xii, 16, 194, 207–9

civic participation, 178

civil servants, 109, 114

civil service, 98, 112–15. *See also* Public Service Commission

Clarity Act, 32

Clark, Joe, 41, 48

Clarkson, Adrienne, 100

classical federalism, 64–65

classical liberalism, 181

Clerk of the House, 122

Clinton, Bill, 55

closure, 126

coalition (proposed 2008), 46, 49, 102, 192

coalition governments, 169

collective responsibility, 40, 105

colonial constitutions (British), 38

Combines Investigation Act, 78–80

common law, 16, 137, 148

Communist Party, 185

concurring opinion (Supreme Court), 151

conditional grants, 67

Confederation, 39, 61, 181. See also *CA 1867*

confidence of the House, 45, 111, 129, 160, 172–73
appointment of prime minister and, 101–2
democratic legitimacy and, 51–53
minority governments and, 47–49
non-confidence, 102, 128
prime minister's obligation if confidence lost, 41, 44
proposed rule changes, 128–29

conformism, 203, 205

Conservative Party (1867–1896), 64

Conservative Party of Canada, 88, 120, 153, 166–67, 186
classical liberalism, 181
financing, 192
ideology, 182

constituencies, 163, 189

Constitution Act, 1867. See *CA 1867*

Constitution Act, 1982. See *CA 1982*

Constitution of Canada, 11, 22–30. See also *CA 1867; CA 1982*
fusion of powers, xii
judicial review of (*See* judicial review of the constitution)
patriation of the Constitution, 25–27

Constitution of the United States, 7, 19–21, 39
amending formula, 25
federalism, 58–59, 62, 69
separation of powers under, 50

constitutional conventions, 16–18, 26, 32, 43, 82, 98, 100, 107, 130
constitutional forms, 16–22
constitutional laws, 16, 19–20, 22, 30
constitutional monarchy, 98
constitutional reform, 70
constitutionalism, 11, 208
constitutions
    amending formula, 15
    definition, 13
    division of powers, 14–15
Controlled Drugs and Substances Act (CDSA), 86
convention of ministerial responsibility, 112–13
conventions for the formation of a government, 43–44
Cooperative Commonwealth Federation (CCF), 183, 187
cooperative federalism, 65
corporate and union donations to political parties, 191–92, 198
Council of the Federation, 72
Court Party, 154–55
courts, 145–50. *See also* judiciary
    Canada's integrated judicial system, 148
    dual system (United States), 146–47
    federalism and, 146–47
    hierarchy, 146–47
    inferior courts, 146, 148–49
    Provincial Courts, 148–49
    Section 92 courts, 149
    Section 96 courts, 149
    Section 101 Courts, 149
    superior courts, 146, 148–49
    Supreme Court (*See* Supreme Court of Canada)
Créditistes, 186
Criminal Code of Canada, 137
criminal law, 62, 137, 149
Crown, 38, 43, 63, 97–99. *See also* Governor General; Queen
    advice of ministers, 40
    appointment of a prime minister, 44
    delegation of executive power, 41
    ultimate responsibility for choosing government, 44
Crown in Canada, The (MacKinnon), 103

D

decentralization, 182–83. *See also* centre/periphery division
    pressure for, 73–75
decentralized federalism, 63, 69, 147
delegates, MPs as, 160–61
democracy, 4, 39, 85, 93, 178, 205
    American style, 7
    Aristotle's view of, 5
    authority in a, 202
    in Canadian regime, 7–8
    direct democracies, 6
    indirect, 6–7, 41
    parliamentary (*See* parliamentary democracy)
    participatory, 184
    requirement for well-informed political participation, 194
democratic accountability, 42, 56
democratic citizenship, 207
"democratic deficit," 128, 153
democratic legitimacy, 51–53, 132, 173. *See also* confidence of the House
"democratic mandate," 161
democratic socialism, 187
deputy minister, 114–15
deputy prime minister, 109
Deschenes, Jules, 144
Dicey, A.V., 85n6
    Introduction to the Study of Law of the Constitution, 16n1
Dickson, Brian, 91
Diefenbaker, John, 45, 47, 83
Dion, Stéphane, 40, 46, 102, 200
direct democracies, 6
direct taxation, 63–64, 66
disallowance, 63–64
dissenting opinion (Supreme Court), 151
dissolution of Parliament, 102, 109, 119, 172
"distinct society," 31
diversity, 184. *See also* multiculturalism
division of powers (in federal systems), 14–15, 20, 24, 27, 62, 69
doctrine of political neutrality, 141–42
doctrine of states' rights, 61
Dominion government, 60
Dominion of Canada, 23, 58

Duceppe, Gilles, 46, 188

Duplessis government, 82

Durham, John George Lambton, Earl of, 39

E

ecological wisdom, 184

Edmonton Journal, 79

education, 67–68

    political education, 207–8

    post-secondary education, 68

elected judiciary, 153

election results, 175

    broadcasting, 174

election spending, 174

elections, 159–75, 178

    (1921), 187

    (1935), 187

    (1940), 166

    (1957), 45

    (1958), 166

    (1963), 47

    (1972), 45

    (1980), 41, 167

    (1984), 166, 208

    (1988), 174

    (1993), 45, 131, 182, 187

    (1997), 51, 187

    (2000), 51, 187, 190

    (2004), 182, 184, 208

    (2006), 48, 161, 208

    (2008), 48, 51, 166, 185, 207–8

    (2011), 41, 104, 133, 167–69, 174, 181, 183–85,
        208

electoral districts, 164, 173

electoral systems, 101, 162–72, 184

    Mixed Member Proportional (MMP) system,
        170

    multi-member STV system, 172

    party list system, 168, 170, 199

    proportional representation (PR), 168–71, 199

    single transferable vote (STV), 171–72

    single-member plurality (SMP) (*See* single-
        member plurality (SMP) electoral
        system)

Elizabeth II, Queen, 98–99

emergency federalism, 65

Emerson, David, 161

entrenchment, 16, 20, 26, 77, 83–84, 151, 155

enumerators, 173

equality, 5–8, 11, 208

    of condition or of opportunity, 181

    fundamental principle of democracy, 5

    before the law, 140, 144

equalization payments, 68

    controversies, 69

    entrenchment in constitution, 26, 68

estimates (of public expenditure), 124

Ethics Commissioner, 122

Ethics Committee, 127

euthanasia, 85, 153

Exchequer Court, 149

executive accountability to the House of
        Commons, 40. *See also* collective
        responsibility; responsible government

executive federalism, 65

executive power, 13–14, 135

    delegated by Crown, 41, 98–100

    democratic control, 40

    prime minister and cabinet, 98, 103–4 (*See also*
        prime ministerial government)

extra-parliamentary wing (of political parties),
        190–91

F

Fair Representation Act, 120

Family Compact, 39

Fathers of Confederation

    choice of federal union, 58, 62–63, 69, 72

    view of judiciary, 135, 147, 149–50

    views on democracy, 6–7, 129

Federal Accountability Act, 115

Federal Court of Canada, 149

federal debt and deficit, 74

federal spending power, 67–68

federal subsidies, 66. *See also* equalization payments

federalism, x, 11, 58–75, 146, 208

    asymmetrical federalism, 73–74

    authority in, 59

    Canada compared with United States, 61,
        69–72

    classical, 64–65

    cooperative, 65

decentralization, 73–75

development in Canada, 63–65 (*See also* Fathers of Confederation)

disallowance, 63–64

emergency, 65

federal pre-eminence, 62

finance and federal-provincial relations, 65–69

objections to, 61

quasi-federalism, 63–64

reservation, 63–64

unitary compared with federal systems, 59

federal-provincial division of powers, 30, 72, 152

under *CA 1867*, 24–25, 62–63

residual power, 62

federal-provincial relations, 59–60, 65–69

female. *See* women

First Ministers' Conference, 72

first reading (bills), 123

first-past-the-post, 163

fiscal capacity, 68–69

fiscal federalism, 66

"Fixed Dates for Election?" (Forsey), 51n3

fixed election date, 51–52, 172–73

floor-crossing, 161

Forsey, Eugene, 49

"Fixed Dates for Election?," 51n3

France, 9, 14, 59

Franklin, Benjamin, 21

Fraser, John, 113

Fraser, Sheila, 122

free market economy, 181–83

free speech, 208

free trade, 174, 182–83

Free Trade Agreement with United States, 131

free votes, 128

freedom of assembly, 83

freedom of association, 185, 198

freedom of expression, 8, 174

freedom of religion, 82–84, 139

freedom of speech, 82–84, 198

freedom of the press, 8, 206, 208

freedom of thought, 185

French/English divisions, 60–61

French and English languages, use of, 24. *See also* bilingualism

French Canadians, 60–61, 182. *See also* Québec

in cabinet, 106

Liberal Party, 64, 182

fusion of powers, xii, 43, 55

G

Gang of Eight, 26–27

Geithner, Timothy, 52

general elections, 173

Germany, 14, 59, 184

Gomery Commission, 114

Goods and Services Tax (GST), 55, 131

government bills, 123

Governor General, 46, 50, 52, 99–100, 172, 192. *See also* Crown

advised by prime minister, 100–101, 103

appointment of prime minister, 101, 108

British nobles as, 99

Canadian citizens as, 100

ceremonial functions, 103

guardian of responsible government, 53, 101–2

head of state, 101, 103

official head of armed forces, 103

reserve powers, 101–3

sounding board for prime minister, 101

Throne Speech, 119

Great Depression, 65

Green Party, 167, 181, 184–86, 199

gun control, 182–83, 196

H

Hansard, 122, 124

harm principle, 9

Harper, Elijah, 31

Harper, Stephen, 33, 47–49, 102–3, 182

Accountability Act, 198

appointment of Supreme Court judges, 153

cabinet, 41, 107

claim that Canadians had elected him prime minister, 46

denounced proposed coalition as "coup d'état," 46

fixed election date legislation, 172

JACs under, 151–52

no deputy prime minister, 109

political party financing, 174, 191–92

prime ministerial government, 110–11

Senate reform, 133–34
timing of elections, 51–52
head of government, 53. *See also* prime minister
head of state, 53. *See also* Governor General
health care, 63, 65, 67–68, 70, 75
    Chaoulli case, 154
    Medicare system, 138, 183
    universal medical insurance, 55
"Her Majesty's Loyal Opposition." *See* Official
    Opposition
Hnatyshyn, Ramon, 44, 100
House of Commons, 43, 72, 99, 118
    business, 123–25
    committees, 127
    distribution of seats in (fig.), 164
    membership and officers, 120–22
    plan of House (fig.), 121
    reform proposals, 128–29
    representation by population, 130
    Rules of Procedure, 125–26
    Speaker, 121
    Standing Orders, 125
    votes of (non-)confidence (*See* confidence of
        the House)
House of Representatives, 71
HST, 66
Hudson's Bay Company, 60
human rights, 8–9, 78, 81–82. *See also* rights and
    freedoms
human rights codes, 78n1
Hunter, Lawson, 79
Hunter v. Southam, 78–80

I
ideological parties, 186–88
ideology, 179
    Bloc Québécois, 183
    centralization *vs.* decentralization, 63–65,
        69–71, 73–75
    classical liberalism, 181
    Conservative Party, 181–82
    Cooperative Commonwealth Federation
        (CCF), 183, 187
    Green Party, 184
    Liberal Party, 182–83
    New Democratic Party (NDP), 183

preservation *vs.* change, 180
socio-economic matters, 181
impartiality, 121, 138, 140, 142
"inalienable" rights, 8
income taxes, 66–67
independent MP, 177
India, 59
indirect democracy, 6–7, 41
indirect taxation, 66
individualism, 178
inferior courts, 146, 148–49
informed consent, 202
Insite safe injection facility, 86–87
institutional differences
    Canada and the United States, 50–57
Intercolonial Railway, 24
interest aggregation, 178–79
interest groups, 155, 195–98, 203
    lobbying, 196–97
    problems, 197–98
    role in a liberal democracy, 197
Intergovernmental Affairs, 110
Internet, 195
Introduction to the Study of Law of the Constitution
    (Dicey), 16n1
Ireland, 59
Israel, 11

J
Japan, 11, 59
Japanese Canadians during World War II, 82, 85
Jean, Michaëlle, 100
Jefferson, Thomas, 21
judges, 141
    appointment, 109, 149–54
    fixed salaries, 144, 149
    middle- or upper-middle-class backgrounds,
        142
    political accountability, 153
    political neutrality, 141–42
    power (*See under* judiciary)
    royal commissions, 138–39
    security of tenure, 144
"The Judges Affair," 144
judicial activism, 155
Judicial Advisory Committees (JACs), 151–52, 155

judicial commissions of inquiry, 138

Judicial Committee of the Privy Council (JCPC), 23, 150

judicial restraint, 155

judicial review of the constitution, 30, 63–64, 83, 87, 136, 139–40

judiciary, 25, 84–85, 135–56. *See also* courts; judges

    adversarial character of, 141, 145

    equality before the law, 140, 144–45

    expanded role of, 136

    impartiality, 140–43

    judicial independence, 140, 143–44

    political impact, 140

    politics of appointments, 151–54

    power, 14, 135, 137, 139

    private party disputes, 136–37

    public law cases, 137–38

    reform movement, 151–52

    social policy and, 154–55

jurisdiction. *See* provincial jurisdiction

K

Kennedy, John F., 52

King, Mackenzie, 102, 191

kingship, 4

Kissinger, Henry, 52

L

Latin America, 54

Laurier, Wilfrid, 64, 182

Layton, Jack, 46

leadership conventions, xi, 178, 189

leadership selection

    all-member vote, 189

Leblanc, Roméo, 100

legal aid programs, 145

Léger, Jules, 100

legislative power, 13–14, 38–39, 42, 98–99, 104, 135

Lévesque, René, 88

    An Option for Québec, 71n5

liberal democracy, 8, 10–11, 77–78, 85, 185, 193–94

    party politics and, 178

Liberal Party, 45, 47, 49, 64, 102, 122, 167, 181–83, 186–88, 208

    financing, 191–92

    ideology, 182–83

Liberal Party (New Brunswick), 165

Liberal-Conservatives (pre-Confederation), 181

liberalism, 8

Liberal-NDP coalition (proposed), 46, 49, 102, 192

Libertarian Party, 185

liberty, 5, 8–11, 52, 54–56, 82, 181, 208

lieutenant-governors, 63

line departments, 112

linguistic minorities, 11

lobbying, 132, 196–98

Locke, John, 21, 38–39, 54, 136

    social contract, 19–20

The Lord's Day Act, 139

Lower Canada (Québec), 38, 181

Lyon, Stirling, 84–85, 87

M

M. v. H., 92

Macdonald, John A., 62, 64, 106, 181, 191

MacKinnon, Frank, *Crown in Canada, The*, 103

Madison, James, 21, 198

majority government, 47, 49, 55, 104, 166, 169, 172

majority opinion (Supreme Court), 151

majority rule, 77–78

mandate, 54, 160–61

Manitoba, 24

Manning, Preston, 182

marijuana, 85

Maritime Bank case (1892), 65

Maritime colonies, 61, 130

Maritimes, 183. *See also* Atlantic Canada

Martin, Paul, 93, 109, 111, 128, 153

Marxist-Leninist Party of Canada, 185–86

Massey, Vincent, 100

Mazankowski, Don, 109

McKenna, Frank, 165

McLellan, Anne, 109

McNamara, Robert, 52

McTeague, Dan, 127

media, 203–5

    coverage of political parties, 179

    ownership, 204–5

mediation, 136

medicare system, 138, 183

Meech Lake Accord, 31–32, 74, 92, 151–52, 183

Meighen, Arthur, 48, 102

Members of Parliament (MPs), 40, 120

    accountability, 160

    backbenchers, 126–29

    floor-crossing, 161

    government members and opposition, 120–21

    as representatives, 160–61

microcosm theory of representation, 162

Mill, John Stuart, 9

ministerial responsibility, 112–14

ministers. *See* cabinet

minority government, 47–49, 169, 186, 188

minority rights, 10, 78, 85

Mixed Member Proportional (MMP) system, 170

mob rule, 5, 7. *See also* tyranny of the majority

mobility rights, 84

monarchy, 4, 7. *See also* Crown; Queen

Montesquieu, Charles de Secondat, 38–39, 54

Morgentaler, Henry, 91–92

Mulroney, Brian, 18, 31–32, 44, 88

    appointment of senators, 131

    cabinet size, 104

    PMO under, 109

multiculturalism, 84, 182. *See also* diversity

multi-member electoral districts, 171, 199

multi-member STV system, 172

multi-party systems, 185

multiplicity of interests, 198

municipal government, 59–60

Munro, John, 144

N

Narcotic Control Act, 90–91

National Action Committee on the Status of
    Women (NAC), 200

National Citizens Coalition, 174

National Energy Policy, 119

national government in Canada, 59–64. *See also*
    federalism

"national policy," 181

natural laws, 136

natural rights, 8

natural rights school of liberalism, 9

negotiation, 136

New Brunswick, 24, 60, 136

    elections (1987), 165

    equalization payments, 68

    proportional representation and, 171

    representation in House of Commons, 165

"New Deal" legislation, 140

New Democratic Party (NDP), 47, 49, 102, 167,
    181, 186–88

    democratic socialism, 183

    financing, 192

    formation, 183

    influence on national policy, 183

    Senate abolition, 132

New Zealand, 184

Newfoundland, 60

Newfoundland and Labrador, 69

Nixon, Richard, 52

non-confidence. *See* confidence of the House

non-renewable resources, 27

non-violence, 184

notwithstanding clause, 87–88

Nova Scotia, 38–39, 60, 136, 138

O

Oakes, David Edwin, 90, 98

Oakes test, 91

Obama, Barack, 52, 55

official bilingualism, 182

Official Opposition, 56, 118, 120–21, 181, 183–84,
    188

oligarchy, 4

"one-line votes," 129

"one-person, one vote," 164

Ontario, 29, 64, 136, 167

    equalization payments, 68

    MMP proposals, 171

    Supreme Court judges, 150

Ontario election (1985), 46

Operations Committee, 107, 109

"opinion makers," 201

An Option for Québec (Lévesque), 71n5

organic statutes, 16, 18, 24, 83, 151

P

Palin, Sarah, xi

Parliament, 38, 72, 98–99, 116–34
  dissolution of, 102, 109, 119, 172
  golden age, 117
  House of Commons (*See* House of Commons)
  opposition (*See* Official Opposition)
  prorogation of, 102–3, 119
  Question Period, 124
  role, 117–19
  Senate (*See* Senate [Canada])
Parliament Act (1911), 18
Parliamentary Calendar, 119
parliamentary committees, 115
parliamentary crisis of 2008. *See* political crisis of
  2008
parliamentary democracy, 6–7, 11, 117
parliamentary government, 42, 129, 192
parliamentary secretaries, 104
parliamentary sovereignty, 84
parliamentary supremacy, 85n6, 87–88
parliamentary wing (of political parties), 190–91
Parti Québécois, 33, 88
participation. *See* political participation
participatory democracy, 184
party discipline, 53–54, 56, 117–18, 127, 177, 192
party government, 192
party leaders, 111, 189
  all-member vote, 189
  leadership conventions, xi, 178, 189
  power, 189, 193
party list system, 168, 170, 199
party members, MPs as, 160–61
party politics, 178, 193
party representation, 160
party systems, 177, 185
  Canada, 42, 154, 176–77, 185–88
  multi-party systems, 185
  United States, 154
party unity, 111
patriation of the Constitution, 25–26
pay equity legislation, 200
"peace, order, and good government" clause, 30,
  62, 64
Pearson, Lester, 47–48, 106
plurality, 163
political crisis of 2008, xii, 46, 49, 102, 192
political divisions or cleavages

centre and periphery, 61 (*See also*
  decentralization)
  French and English, 61 (*See also* Québec
  nationalism)
political education, 207–8. *See also* civic education
political instability, 169
political participation, 185, 194–95, 208–9
political parties, 101, 117–18, 154, 176–93, 202–3
  brokerage parties, 185–87
  Canada's major parties, 181–85
  Canadian party system, 42, 154, 176–77,
    185–88
  commercial advertising, 179
  designed for winning elections, 191
  educational function, 179
  as electoral machines, 189
  electoral success and, 179–80, 201
  extra-parliamentary wing, 190–91
  federal and provincial party relationship, 190
  financing, 174, 178, 191–92
  five functions of, 178–79
  formulation of public policy, 179
  ideological parties, 186, 188
  organization, 188–91
  parliamentary wing, 190–91
  pragmatism, 180
  protest parties, 186
  recruitment, 178
  single-issue parties, 184, 186
political regimes. *See* regime
polity, 5
polls, 173. *See also* public opinion polls
post-secondary education, 68
Powell, Colin, 52
precedents, 137
preservation *vs.* change, 180
president (United States), 50, 56
  direct mandate from the people, 54
prime minister, 40, 43, 45, 97–98, 107–9
  accountability, 129, 160
  appointment by Governor General, 101
  appointment of cabinet ministers, 44, 52, 162
  appointment of judges, 150
  appointment of senators, 130
  authority to organize cabinet committee
    system, 106

chair of Priorities and Planning Committee, 107

control of legislative activity, 56

democratic legitimacy, 47, 51, 53–54

dependent on confidence in House of Commons, 111

head of government, 53

must resign if government has lost confidence of the House of Commons, 44

popularity with voters, 111

powers based on constitutional convention, 107

right to advise Governor General, 100–101, 104, 108–9, 119, 172

spokesperson for cabinet, 108

spokesperson for the government, 110

timing of elections, 50–52, 172

prime ministerial government, xi, 110–11

Prime Minister's Office (PMO), 109

Prince Edward Island, 24, 60, 106, 171

equalization payments, 68

representation in House of Commons, 120, 165

Prince Edward Island Terms of Union Act, 1871, 24

Priorities and Planning Committee, 107

private law, 136–37

private members' bills, 123, 127–28

private sphere, 8, 10

Privy Council Office (PCO), 109

proclamation of bills, 123

Progressive Conservative Party (PC), 44, 47, 174, 182, 187, 208

Progressive Party, 182, 187

property rights, 129, 132, 136

proportional representation (PR), 168–71, 199

prorogation of Parliament, 102–3, 119

protest parties, 186–87

Province of Canada, 60. *See also* Lower Canada (Québec); Upper Canada (Ontario)

Provincial Courts, 148–49

provincial governments, 14, 27, 59–60, 62, 136, 148

dependence on federal subsidies, 66

input into appointment of Supreme Court judges, 151–52

provincial judges, 151

provincial jurisdiction, 24, 31, 63–65, 67, 73–74, 136

provincial law society, 151

provincial rights, 64, 182

Public Accounts Committee, 115, 124, 127

public expenditure

scrutiny in House of Commons, 124

public law, 136–38

public opinion, 55, 131, 193, 201–3

conformism, 203, 205

interest groups and, 197

mass media and, 203

public opinion polls, 204

bandwagon effect, 206

effect on elections, 206

mass marketing tool, 205

media attention, 206

public regulation or ownership of natural resources and key industries, 181

Public Service Commission (PSC), 112. *See also* civil servants

public sphere, 10

publicly funded per-vote subsidies, 174, 192

publicly owned media, 204

Putnam, Robert, 207

Q

quasi-federal systems, 63–64

Québec, 26, 29, 60, 64, 67, 74–75, 82, 136

asymmetrical federalism, 73–74

ban on private health insurance, 154

Bill 101, 88

Bill 178, 88

civil code, 137, 148, 150

"distinct society," 31

interest in proportional representation, 171

on patriation of the constitution, 26, 31, 88

referendum on Québec sovereignty (1995), 32, 70, 74

separatism, 70

sovereignty or "renewed federalism," 70

support for Liberal Party, 167

Supreme Court judges, 150

veto, 31, 142

Québec Conference (1864), 62

Québec nationalism, 64, 70, 73, 110

Québec v. Ford, 92

Queen, 98–99. *See also* Crown; Governor General

head of state, 53
Queen v. Drybones, 83
Queen v. Morgentaler, 91–92
Queen v. Oakes, 89
Queen's Privy Council for Canada, 104
Question Period, 124–25

R

R. v. Sharpe, 91
racial and religious tolerance, 206
racial equality, 83
racism, 138
Radical Marijuana Party, 185–86
reading in (to law), 81
rebellions (Upper and Lower Canada), 39
redistribution of wealth, 181
reference procedure, 139–40
Reference re Secession of Québec, 32
Reform Act (1832), 18–19
Reform Party, 111, 182, 186–87
regime, 3–5, 11, 49
    Aristotle's typology, 4–5
    Canada *vs.* United States, x–xii, 7–8
regional disparities, 64, 68, 70, 73
regional minorities, 11
regional protest parties, 169, 184, 186–87
Registered Education Saving Plans, 127
Registrar of Lobbyists, 198
representation, 160–62
    Canadian model, 160–62
    as mandate, 160–61
    microcosm theory, 162
    by population, 130
    as trustees, 160–61
representative democracy, 6–7, 159
republican regimes, 7
reservation, 63–64
residual power, 15
resolutions, adoption of, 124
responsible government, x–xii, 11, 22, 37–57, 105,
        114, 117, 159, 186–87
    accountability, 56–57
    as "cabinet government," 7, 42–43
    collective responsibility, 40, 105
    compared to separation of powers, 53–57
    conventions of, 23, 40–41

federalism and, 71–72
fixed election dates and, 51, 172
forming a government, 43–47
Governor General as guardian of, 53, 101–2
institutional implications, 49–54
logic of, 160
ministerial responsibility, 112–13, 115
responsibility of executive to legislature, 40
Restrictive Trade Practices Commission, 79
Returning Officer, 173–75
ridings, 163
right not to be subjected to cruel or unusual
        punishments, 84, 86
right to enjoyment of property, 83
right to retain legal counsel upon arrest, 83
right to vote, 84
rights and freedoms, 20, 22, 81–82, 142, 208. *See
        also* Charter of Rights and Freedoms;
        human rights
    Aboriginal people, 83, 142
    charters or bills of rights, 15
    "inalienable" rights, 8
    natural rights, 8–9
rights of French Canadians, 182
Roseman, Frank, 79
Rothstein, Marshall, 153
"Rouge" politicians of Québec, 182
royal assent, 17, 98–99, 123
Royal Canadian Mounted Police (RCMP), 138
royal commissions, 136, 138
rule of law, 10, 144, 208
Rupert's Land, 24
Russell, Peter, 86, 138, 141, 148
Russia, 14

S

sales taxes, 66
same-sex marriage, 88, 93, 182–83
Saskatchewan, 24
Sauvé, Jeanne, 100
Schachter v. Canada, 81
Schreyer, Ed, 100
scrutineers, 175
search and seizure laws, 79
second reading (bills), 123
Section 92 courts, 149

Section 96 courts, 149
Section 101 Courts, 149
Section 52 remedy (of *CA 1982*), 80–81
Senate (Canada), 4, 18, 31, 33, 99, 129–31
    appointment to, 109, 130
    constitutional conventions, 130
    Free Trade Agreement bill, 131
    link to business elite, 132
    regional equality, 72, 130
    sober second thought, 129
    usefulness, 132–33
Senate (United States), 71
Senate reform, 33, 131–34
    abolition option, 132
    elected Senate, 132–33
    limitation of term, 133
    "senators-in-waiting," 133–34
Senate Reform Act, 133
separation of powers, x–xii, 38–39, 50, 52, 186
    compared to responsible government, 54–57
Sergeant-at-Arms, 122
Sgro, Judy, 113
Singh v. Minister of Employment and Immigrations, 92
single transferable vote (STV), 171–72
single-issue parties, 170, 184, 186
single-member plurality (SMP) electoral system,
    163, 165–67, 172
    artificial majority government, 166–67, 169, 186
    disadvantages Green Party, 185
    disadvantages third parties, 206
    encouraging regionalism, 186
    favouring leading national parties, 165–67, 186
    favouring regional parties, 166–67, 169
    handicaps smaller national parties, 167, 186
    premium on victory, 187
single-party systems, 185
slavery, 61
social and economic inequalities, 6
social capital, 207
social contract, 19–20
Social Credit Party, 47
social justice, 184
social media, 195
social services, 68. *See also* welfare
Social Union Framework (1999), 74
Speaker (of House of Commons), 121

special interests. *See* interest groups
spending limits of candidates, 174
sponsorship scandal, 114, 122, 138, 184
St. Laurent, Louis, 45
standing committees (House of Commons), 127–28
Standing Orders, 125
stare decisis, 137
state intervention in the economy, 181, 183
statute, 123
statutory law, 16
Stornoway, 120
Sunday shopping, 85, 153
superior courts, 146, 148–49
Supreme Court (United States), 83, 146, 150, 153
Supreme Court Act, 150
Supreme Court of Canada, 26, 79, 81, 83, 85–86,
    89, 93, 139, 144, 149–51, 154, 174. *See*
    also judges; judiciary
    composition of, 150
    microcosm theory of representation, 162
    politics of appointments, 151–54
    reform movement, 152
    reviewing nominations to, 153
Supreme Court of Canada Act, 24
    organic statute, 151
Supreme Court of Canada decisions
    abortion (*Morgentaler*), 91–92
    Chaoulli decision, 154–55
    death penalty *(United States v. Burns)*, 92
    French-language signs (Ford), 92
    French-only signs, 88
    Insite decision, 86–87
    Oakes, 90–91
    in *R. v Sharpe*, 91
    Reference re Secession of Québec, 32
    refugee claims (Singh), 92
    same-sex couples (*M. v. H.*), 92
    Valente v. The Queen, 143–44
sustainability, 184
Suzuki, David, 184
Sweden, 11, 59
Switzerland, 59

T
taxation, 63–64, 66–67
television age, 110

territories, 60n1
    representation in the House, 120
third reading (bills), 123
third-party advertising, 174
Thomson and Southam newspaper chains, 79
"three-line votes," 128
Throne Speech, 119
timing of elections, 50–52, 172
Tocqueville, Alexis de, 178, 203, 205
token women, 200
Treasury Board, 107, 112
Trudeau, Pierre, 10, 26, 45, 83–84, 87, 106, 144
    PMO under, 109
    representation in his cabinet, 167
    vision of bilingual Canada, 83–84
Trudeau government, 119
Truman, Harry S, 56
trustee theory of representation, 160–61
"two-line votes," 129
tyranny, 4, 38
tyranny of the majority, ix, 5

U
unconditional grants, 68
Underhill, Frank, 177
Unemployment Insurance Act, 81
unitary systems, 14, 59, 61
United Nations, 92
United States v. Burns, 92
"Unity Reserve," 115
universal medical insurance, 55
Upper Canada (Ontario), 38–39, 181
Upper Canadian "Reformers," 182
United States, 14
    bicameralism, 71
    Bill of Rights, 83
    cabinet appointments, 53
    Civil War, 61
    Congress, 71
    dual court system, 146–47
    Founding Fathers, 21, 38, 57, 71–72

House of Representatives, 71
    imperial design, 60, 64
    model of federal regime, 146
    natural rights school of liberalism, 9
    party system, 154
    presidential race (2008), xi
    separation of powers, 38, 50, 53–55
    timing of elections (fixed terms), 50
utilitarianism, 8–9

V
Valente v. The Queen, 143–44
Vanier, Georges, 100
veto, 29, 31, 142
Victoria proposal (1971), 84
visible minorities in cabinet, 106
voting in Canada, 172–75, 207
Vriend v. Alberta, 81

W
welfare, 68
welfare state, 183
Western alienation, 70, 74
Western Canada, 167
    Senate reform, 133
    Supreme Court judges, 150
Western Canadians, 31
western expansion, 181
White, Theodore, 197
Williams, Danny, 69
Wilson, Michael, 113
"winner-take-all," 165
women, 169
    cabinet representation, 106
    elected to Parliament, 199
    leaders of political parties, 199
    in politics, 198–201
women's groups, 31
working class, 183